KNOWLEDGE TO POLICY

KNOWLEDGE TO POLICY
MAKING THE MOST OF DEVELOPMENT RESEARCH

FRED CARDEN

International Development Research Centre
Ottawa • Cairo • Dakar • Montevideo • Nairobi • New Delhi • Singapore

 **SAGE** www.sagepublications.com
Los Angeles • London • New Delhi • Singapore • Washington DC

Jointly published in 2009 by

 SAGE Publications India Pvt Ltd
B1/I-1 Mohan Cooperative Industrial Area
Mathura Road, New Delhi 110 044, India
www.sagepub.in

SAGE Publications Inc
2455 Teller Road
Thousand Oaks, California 91320, USA

SAGE Publications Ltd
1 Oliver's Yard, 55 City Road
London EC1Y 1SP, United Kingdom

SAGE Publications Asia-Pacific Pte Ltd
33 Pekin Street
#02-01 Far East Square
Singapore 048763

International Development Research Centre
P.O. Box 8500
Ottawa, ON, Canada KIG 3H9

info@idrc.ca
www.idrc.ca

ISBN (e-book): 987-1-55250-417-8

Second Printing 2009

Published by Vivek Mehra for SAGE Publications India Pvt Ltd, Phototypeset in 10/12 pt Palatino by Star Compugraphics Private Limited, New Delhi and printed at Chaman Enterprises, New Delhi.

Library of Congress Cataloging-in-Publication Data

Carden, F. (Fred)
    Knowledge to policy: making the most of development research/Fred Carden.
        p. cm.
    Includes bibliographical references and index.
    1. Economic development—Research—Evaluation.   2. Economic policy—Evaluation.
    I. Title.

HD77.C37   338.9—dc22   2009   2009007156

ISBN: 978-81-7829-930-3 (PB)

The SAGE Team: Rekha Natarajan, Meena Chakravorty, Rajib Chatterjee and
                            Trinankur Banerjee

Contents

SECTION III: TECHNICAL NOTES

List of Tables and Boxes

Foreword

For almost 200 years investigators have been amassing systematic information in an effort to influence public policy. One of the early efforts was a study by Guerry in 1833 that attempted to show that education did not reduce crime (Cullen 1975: 139). Other statisticians analyzed different data with different methods to disprove such a contention. Another early effort was a French study in 1844 that measured the value of a canal project by calculating the maximum tolls that users would pay (Toulemonde and Rochaix 1994). The idea that good data should influence policy has a long pedigree. Social scientists have been hopeful that once accurate research tools and statistics are available, policymakers will pay attention to them and do something different from what they were apt to do in the absence of such knowledge.

In recent times, the production of what used to be called 'applied research' and what is now commonly known as policy research became a big enterprise in the United States and elsewhere. Government began funding studies to find out what the conditions were like on the ground and how well current policy interventions succeeded in remedying social ills. Investigators in the field of natural and biological sciences continued to seek knowledge that would lead to social and economic innovations and improvements in the lot of humankind. In addition a large number of social scientists became engaged in the effort to study economic and social processes, and especially to evaluate the effects of policy interventions.

What became obvious fairly rapidly was that natural and biological research was likely to be put to use fairly readily when it made a profit for its implementers. New household products and new pharmaceuticals based on new research were often put into production. Another type of research that was likely to be adopted was that needed by the government for national defence or other well accepted and uncontested public functions. Economic research, too, was often influential for purposes like tracking economic conditions, such as the cost of living, unemployment, money supply, and making forecasts. But the kinds of research apt to be done by social scientists, including the new speciality of programme evaluation, were not likely to have direct and immediate effects on public policy. Equally in the doldrums were those studies that pointed to agricultural, biological, or technological changes that were in contention in the society.

Nevertheless, for a long time it was assumed that knowledge is power. Good research would lead to better policy. The accepted theory was that valid knowledge would drive out error and imprint itself on public policies across domains. No one in the policy world, it was thought, would want to pursue a course that ran counter to the best knowledge that the sciences produce. However, by the 1970s even the less perceptive observers had to admit that research findings did not always prevail. Neglecting research findings was a common recreation in arenas of action.

What was going wrong? Was it a matter of communication? Did not policymakers hear about the new research findings? Was it a matter of denseness? Did not policymakers understand the import of the research? Could it be that old bugaboo of politics? Were preoccupations with partisan issues and personal ambitions sidetracking the knowledge that research produced? Was it a matter of values? Did policymakers slough off findings that were inconsistent with their beliefs and ideologies? Maybe it was simply a matter of time. Researchers were expecting quick adoption of findings into policy when it might take years for research to have an effect. Many other hypotheses were offered to account for the spotty record of research influence.

In the mid-1970s, social scientists began doing empirical investigations of the extent to which policymakers and government officials were 'using' the findings of research. One of the early findings was that 'use' was a slippery concept. Policymakers would rarely sit around waiting for the chunk of evidence that would settle an issue. Much more often they had a lot of experience of their own on the issue. They had other sources of information and advice. They had concerns that research did not address—issues such as the preferences of constituents or of campaign donors. Research was only one input into the complexities of policy making.

Nor was research often the dominant influence. Decision makers worked in organizations that had their own traditional modes of work and rules of the game. In an organization there were political interests at play, ideological convictions, countervailing information from other sources, concerns about the ability of staff to implement new activities however promising, considerations of cost, political reception of budgetary requests, jockeying for advantage in the bureaucracy, and the accumulated weight of tradition. It seemed that an expectation of policy responsive to research findings was in many cases unrealistic.

But the new set of empirical studies that began to analyze what was going on showed that the situation was not as bleak as some had thought it was. Research findings were not always lightly tossed aside. They might not have immediate and direct influence on decisions, but over a period of time they did seem to have consequences. Policymakers said that they valued research. They wanted to know what good studies said. Research, it seemed, was a source of news. It provided new concepts and ideas. It offered a new angle of vision on old dilemmas. The release of a research report was an occasion for collective discussion and perhaps re-thinking. It gave decision makers an opportunity to reconsider what they were doing and not doing. For those in authoritative positions, research had manifold values.

The field of international development is a vital arena in which these kinds of elements play out. International development has been the site of a number of important investigations (Yin et al. 1988; Reimers and McGinn 1988; Court et al. 2005; Stone and Maxwell 2005; Livny et al. 2006). Two features tend to distinguish international development from other sites where empirical investigations of the effects of research have been conducted. One is that the key decision makers in developing societies often lack well developed institutions to seek out and absorb research findings, review them critically, and consider their implications for local issues. There is no straightforward and clear-cut place in the government structure to undertake such functions. Furthermore, the individuals who staff the top positions in government may not have had much individual experience with home-grown research and evaluation designed to fit their purposes. Second and collaterally, most of what decision makers in these countries know about research has usually come from international agencies such as the World Bank, and the Bank usually has its own agenda to pursue. The agenda is meant for the benefit of the developing world, but it is not built from their own experience. The consequent stance of domestic decision makers has often been initial resistance to the research message and/or a buckling under the demands of the international agency irrespective of the cogency of the findings. The World Bank not only comes bearing findings; it is also the source of important funding.

In newer investigations of the influence of research and evaluation, further insights begin to emerge. Some conditions seem to predispose policymakers to take research findings seriously. Analysis of these conditions suggests that there is something in the larger surround that makes a difference. It is not only the competence and interest of the specific decision makers who handle an issue that matters, or even the conditions in the organization in which they work. Features of the larger environment—such as the number of points of access through which research findings can flow, the openness of the system to the entry of new ideas, the democratic nature of decision making—seem to make a system more or less responsive. It is these kinds of characteristics that cross-national comparisons begin to highlight.

The current study from IDRC (International Development Research Centre) adds a great deal to our understanding of what happens. In this book, Fred Carden discusses a range of issues that determine how much effect research studies have on the bureaus, legislatures, and administration of governments in developing countries. One of the great advantages of this study is that it builds on earlier research and does not start from the supposition that research will shift a decision from A to B by the power of its data and analysis. It looks for subtler effects, it takes a longer time horizon, and it is alert to the many unexpected ways in which research findings seep into public debates. It also realizes that one good channel of communication is people—the movement of people from one place to another. A researcher becomes the head of a government bureau and brings his research knowledge with him. The head of a government agency serves on the advisory committee to a research study and absorbs the findings *in situ*, putting them to use back at the agency when a relevant situation arises.

A study like this opens many avenues for further research. If this study is replicated, it would provide the opportunity to answer many more questions. In a sense, each situation is *sui generis*, and generalizing is a tempting but risky business. But with more data on more places, from IDRC and other agencies, we are likely to know even more than we do now. One possibility, a bit blue-sky at present, is to be able to compare different fields of government activity. As international development research encompasses the full range of technological, biological, and social research, empirical investigations about the fate of the research might be able to go on and compare outcomes across domains. Does agriculture have a better chance of putting research findings to use than education or health services? Does research that deals with issues in which participants have unequal status, like labour and management, have a harder time making its way into policy than research where participants share similar status? What is it about the structure of telecommunications or social services or other areas of government activity that make them more or less receptive to research inputs? Although these are extraordinarily complex issues, and furthermore, things have the untidy habit of changing over time, it would be wonderful to make progress in addressing them.

As research moves to identify the social environment and institutional structures that underlie successful development and the on-the-ground activities and leadership strategies that move development along, the policymakers should take advantage of the emerging knowledge. There is no sense in doing useful research if policy ignores it. A movement has been building to encourage decision makers at all levels to attend to the findings of research. The first advocates were researchers who were promoting the use of their work. More recently some political officials have joined the movement. The health field has been particularly active in encouraging the use of research findings in policy making. Health policy sees the model of biological and clinical research and its adoption by health professionals, and health services policy is a natural analogue. The push to give research a central role in policy was probably given its greatest impetus by Tony Blair's government and its promotion of 'evidence-based policy'.

The message of evidence-based policy was: Decision makers at every level should attend to the findings that emerge from research, data series, evaluation, and analysis. They should discard hoary old shibboleths when evidence demonstrates that they are misguided. They should undertake the kinds of activities that, according to research, yield positive outcomes. They need to pay attention to the evidence that researchers produce in order to improve the calibre of the policies they enact. Those are the taken-for-granted assumptions.

As we have already noted, such assumptions are overly optimistic, particularly in developing countries without a tradition of analyzing the consequences of research. But if one could not expect policymakers to base policy on evidence, one could at least take account of the facts in the situation. Some of the original proponents of evidence-based policy backed off to 'evidence-influenced policy', and later to acknowledge the value of the even less ambitious 'evidence-informed policy'. To many people, research seems an eminently worthy endeavour. It brings the fresh wind of reality into the councils of policy. It shows new relationships and concepts at work. But there is virtue in setting expectations at a reasonable level.

The study described in this book is one of the most recent studies to look four-square at the effects of research in international development. Fred Carden has undertaken an investigation to examine the consequences of 23 research projects funded by the IDRC. As with all IDRC research grants, the research projects were conducted by nationals of the developing nations they were studying. Their subject matter ranged from information technology to health and from international trade to agriculture. Fred's investigation began with 25 studies that IDRC staff identified as having been successful in influencing policy. He and his staff developed a common data collection instrument that field investigators would use to find out about events surrounding each study, and several training sessions were held to be sure that all the field investigators had the same understanding. The use of a common framework enhanced the opportunity to collect comparable information on each case. After intensive fieldwork, 23 cases were completed. It was a heroic job.

The study started from a sophisticated understanding about how research percolates into policy making. The investigators did not expect the research to have direct and immediate effects on policy in the nations studied. Rather they were sensitive to the subtle and diverse ways in which knowledge gleaned from research can seep into the ideas of policymakers over time. They sought the channels of communication and identified the communicators, intended and unintended, who brought the message into arenas of decision. They were alert to the different kinds of effects that can emerge from confrontation with research evidence.

I have to own that I am not a neutral observer of this study or of the manuscript. I was deeply involved, although not until after the initial planning and instrument development had been completed. I attended one of the training discussions with the field investigators, interacted with them over the course of the fieldwork, attended meetings with IDRC staff and board, and I undertook an analysis of the completed data. With two of my advanced doctoral students, Svetlana Karuskina-Drivdale and Shahram Paksima, I spent months analyzing the case reports, writing abstracts of the cases, categorizing processes and events, identifying themes, and writing a report. We could not hope to attain Fred Carden's detailed knowledge of the cases or of IDRC, but Svetlana, Shahram, and I contributed to the enterprise.

Having owned up to my involvement, I still have to say that I think this was a formidable investigation. I have participated in other studies of the consequences of research for policy, and I have not seen one that drew on the expertise of all the parties to the research–policy interaction with the same depth and rigour. Fred Carden has made a distinguished contribution to the literature on the influence of research on policy. He has combined a sophisticated understanding of the research field and the international development field. What he has to say is well worth hearing.

If I were to pick a bone with him, and this is probably not the task of a foreword, it would be to question his apparent assumptions about the virtues of research. He seems to believe that research is always good and right and that policy that follows its conclusions is always an advance over what came before. Would that it were so. But researchers are fallible too, and for all the golden glow that surrounds words like research, evidence, and learning, we do not always know what the outcomes might have been had policymakers chosen to ignore the research.

Still, we have learned a great deal from this study. It gives us concrete examples of the kinds of direct and indirect effects that research has had in different policy domains. Importantly, it identifies the conditions that have to be in place before research is taken seriously in the policy arena. It outlines circumstances that affect the degree to which research is heeded, a formulation that owes much to Svetlana's analysis. Nor should we ignore the methodological contributions that this investigation makes. Other investigators of this topic would be well advised to examine the methodology carefully and to take advantage of some of the innovations that IDRC introduced into the study.

One of the happy pieces of news that comes trailing along at the fringes of the study is that it is being 'used'. IDRC has been paying careful attention to its findings. The moral of the story is that influence can come to good research done with rigorous design and method, relevant to the interests and concerns of an agency, communicated frequently and with formidable opportunities for feedback from its audiences, and with something important to say. That is a very hopeful message indeed.

Carol H. Weiss
Professor Emerita,
Harvard University

Preface

No single factor more powerfully affects the course of a country's development than the quality of its governance. Where governance is open, accountable and effective, and where public policy promotes innovation and equity in a lively economy, development is more likely to serve the interests of the people. Informing good governance describes this urgent purpose of development research—to discover, assemble, and communicate the knowledge needed for development that is sustainable and democratic.

To improve lives, especially the lives of poor people, development research will almost always have to influence policy in order to influence development. But how? That question and some illuminating answers are the subject of this volume. The exploration recorded here—extraordinary in scope and methodology—has uncovered critical variables in the interaction of development research and policymaking. More than that, it presents evidence-based strategies that researchers and policymakers can deploy to bring timely knowledge to bear on public policy and action.

The research evaluation outlined in these pages has already had effect in our own organization, Canada's IDRC. IDRC's support for research is now more than ever directed to drawing together researchers from developing countries, citizens, and members of the policy community in the design, conduct, and application of research. In development research, getting a new discovery into policy and practice is just as important as the discovery itself. Increasing the productivity of our investments in development research has been one of the immediate rewards of this evaluation project, but not the only one.

The more extensive significance of the findings is simply put. Research, done right, can fortify the elements of democratic governance essential to sustainable development. By strengthening a country's capacities for discovering, sharing, and using knowledge, development research helps governments become more transparent, responsive, and successful.

As many of the cases profiled here suggest, research can contribute to better governance in at least three ways. First, research encourages open inquiry and debate. Second, it empowers people with the knowledge to hold governments accountable. And third, research enlarges the array of policy options and solutions available to the policy process.

Open inquiry and debate—real freedom of thought and expression—are basic to sound democratic governance. Public and tolerant arguments, without fear of reprisal, along with a readiness for change are all marks of a society that encourages innovation. Research also generates the evidence, and the habits of fair-minded analysis, that can help resolve disputes peacefully and accommodate differences.

As a practical matter, open government simply yields better solutions to a society's problems. As a matter of principle, moreover, people have a right to participate in the decisions that will govern their future. But this consent of the governed is only meaningful if it is an informed consent. Research—especially when it involves the participation of people in their own homes and communities—equips citizens with the knowledge to take part in public policy deliberations and to judge the performance of governments. Research, thereby reinforces democratic accountability.

By expanding the choices available to citizens and policymakers, research can reframe old problems and social divisions with new solutions and compromises. Trustworthy evidence can counteract partisan prejudice and dispel suspicion. Moreover, research can inspire the technical, social, and commercial invention that creates new options for development progress. These remarkable effects are not inevitable or effortless as each section of this volume makes plain.

The first section sets out key findings in a format helpful to researchers, policymakers, and the institutions that support research for development. These chapters underline a fundamental point: to influence policy decisions and actions, researchers need to devise and carry out their work according to their country's own political, social, and economic circumstances.

The second section of the volume sketches each of the research cases examined in the evaluation. All of them speak of the defining question: How can researchers maximize the influence of their research on public policy? The particulars of experience emerge in revealing outline, and again the pattern is clear. Research influences policy best when researchers adjust to the prevailing realities of place and time—doing research that explicitly answers specific policy problems, engaging the policy community, and activating political interest in their endeavours.

The third section of the book tells the story of the evaluation itself—its origins, challenges, methodology, and outcomes. Professionals in policy and project evaluation will obviously be attracted to the details. But this is a story for a much broader readership. The issues addressed during the five years of the evaluation cast fresh perspective on the day-to-day decisions that confront policymakers, researchers, and funding agencies in developing countries.

All in all, the evidence and arguments presented in this pioneering work are both valuable and persuasive. The findings and pragmatic recommendations are already fostering development research that is more efficient and productive. And they strengthen the promising proposition that research, well designed and executed, can improve the democratic governance that sustainable development demands.

Maureen O'Neil
President & CEO
Canadian Health Services Research Foundation
Past-President
International Development Research Centre

Acknowledgements

This study was a truly participatory undertaking. The preparation of this final report benefits from interactions with a great number of people. First and foremost, the partners and staff of the IDRC who freely gave their time and skills over the course of the study. It was their interests and needs that drove it. I would particularly like to thank all those—more than 100 people—who participated to comment on and conduct preliminary analysis of cases, at workshops in Johannesburg, Bangkok, Montevideo, Montebello, and Ottawa. The advisory group in Ottawa gave much thought and care in their suggestions and recommendations: Rohinton Medhora, John Hardie (replaced by Lauchlan Munro), Terry Smutylo, Ronnie Vernooy, Linda Waverley, with important external inputs from Diane Stone and Carlos Vergara. The ongoing support of Maureen O'Neil, Past-President of IDRC, gave us much encouragement.

The active involvement of Carol Weiss in the design of the study was invaluable; we benefited enormously from her long experience in policy evaluation. The involvement of her research team—Svetlana Karuskina-Drivdale and Shahram Paksima, in the analysis was central to the structure of the findings. Under Professor Weiss' guidance, these two researchers combed several thousand pages of qualitative data and did so diligently and thoroughly. The insights of this team were invaluable.

Without the evaluators who conducted the case studies, we would not have had the rich data-set we worked with. Their energy and care in ensuring that they followed a common term of reference and their responsiveness to modifications along the way made the cases both rich in data and a wonderful set of stories for the use of research: Bienvenido Argueta, Chris Ackello-Ogutu, David Brooks, Leanne Burton, Sarah Earl, Bryon Gillespie, Fernando Loayza, Luis Macadar, Zenda Ofir, Kirit Parikh, María Pía Riggirozzi, André Saumier, Terry Smutylo, Eman Surani, Iryna Lyzogub, Bob Pomeroy, Khamate Sene, Ramata Thioune, Tracy Tuplin, and Diana Tussie.

Evert Lindquist provided much intellectual encouragement in the design and development of this study and early synthesis work. The framework he developed in collaboration with IDRC sparked many useful avenues of inquiry and debate, and enriched the case studies significantly.

As this study unfolded, similar work began in other agencies. The privilege to work with John Young and his team in the Research and Policy in Development programme at the Overseas Development Institute (ODI) contributed tremendously to our learning and thinking on issues of policy influence. Diane Stone introduced us to the Global Development Network's project on Bridging Research to Policy and she later made substantive contributions to our own discussions.

Through her full-time engagement with this study for two years, Stephanie Nielson was my main partner in this endeavour; her thorough preparation of a literature review and ongoing care in ensuring consistency in the case studies through active work with the case study authors, and patience and forbearance with both me and them, were central to the development of a set of case studies that could be analyzed together. Working with this many people in several phases of the study would not have been possible without her constant collaboration and enthusiasm.

John Hay was an invaluable colleague who helped me put the ideas together in a clear and accessible manner. His constant push for clarity puts the findings of this study into practice. Any errors remain mine.

Completion of the manuscript was made possible through a Fellowship in Sustainability Science at Harvard University's Center for International Development, a fellowship generously supported by the International Development Research Centre and the Sustainability Science Programme at Harvard University. Their support is gratefully acknowledged.

Finally, my colleagues in the Evaluation Unit, many of whom are mentioned elsewhere in these acknowledgements, generously gave me the time and space to carry out this study and supported it in many ways. Without their support this work would not have been possible.

Fred Carden

The Findings

Making Research Count

From African schoolrooms to Southeast Asian fishing villages, from Latin American trade policy to Middle East water management, hard evidence proves the point that development research, done right, can improve public policy and help accelerate development progress. When research is well designed and executed—and skilfully communicated—it can inform policy that is more effective, more efficient, and more equitable. But experience proves another point just as certainly; in all the confusions and frustrations of making policy in developing countries, development research frequently fails to register any apparent influence whatsoever. What explains those successes and the failures? And to put the question more directly, how best can researchers and policymakers bring timely, relevant, and reliable new knowledge to bear on policy decisions in developing countries?

The urgency of that question is plain to see. For researchers—and the organizations that fund researchers—the overarching objective of development research is to improve the lives of people in developing countries. More often than not, public policy is an indispensable instrument for converting new knowledge into better lives and better futures. And the urgency is equally pressing for the policy community. After all, systematic access to evidence-based research advice can dramatically improve the chances of deciding and carrying out policy that achieves intended results and attracts durable public support. Researchers and policymakers do not always speak the same language. But they can find a common cause in the pursuit of development policy that is just and sustainable.

Agreement on such a common cause is not effortless or inevitable, of course. Just and sustainable governance is not a priority for bad governments, and good governments struggle every day to balance diverse and seemingly conflicting policy objectives; at most, research will only count as one among many influences in the policy process. Researchers, for their part, do not all commit themselves to policy relevance; some believe, quite fairly, that research accomplishes more when it is unconstrained by policy goals and free to follow in its own directions. For present purposes, however, let us assume at least a latent willingness among policymakers to hear some potentially helpful research advice—and a willingness among researchers to give it.

To work at making research count is to act on the powerful logic that propels and justifies development research anywhere. This is research that informs stronger policy, that engages citizen participation in accountable government, that releases a country's economic energies and inventions, that fosters the capacity of marginalized people in poor countries to discover new choices for growth and change. This is research for better governance.

Governing in the South is Different and Harder

To maximize the influence of development research on public policy and action, the best first step is to assess how that policy is actually made. Many volumes of public-administration literature have been devoted to that subject—almost all of it focused on policymaking in the industrialized democracies of the North. The underlying themes and ideological preferences shaping this literature have varied, but the key assumptions have remained remarkably uniform. Mainly, these models assume that citizens and groups outside government can and do influence policy decisions; researchers therefore constitute one of the many interest groups competing for a government's attention. The models also assume reasonably stable and predictable institutional arrangements for reaching governmental decisions and carrying them out—legislatures, cabinets, government departments and agencies, and so on. Furthermore they assume an array of lively and critical academic, journalistic, and think-tank communities busily trying to inform and influence government decisions. These conventional policy-process models are typically represented graphically as a set of overlapping or inter-permeable spheres of interest and influence.

Nobody familiar with the difficult uncertainties and scarcities that characterize governance in a developing country gives great weight to these Northern-based schemes, and for good reason. Whatever their strengths are in explaining government in rich countries, they seldom yield a very convincing portrayal of decision making in poor countries. On the contrary, Southern countries generally display a mix of distinguishing features markedly different from those of the North, features that help determine whether and how development research can ever influence policy. In short, affecting policy with good research is challenging anywhere, and especially difficult in developing countries.

Among distinctive features of governance in developing countries, the following commonly stand out.

Democratic institutions and customs are often precarious

Most of the policy-process frameworks shaping Northern analyses presume the operation of democratic institutions, and the popular exercise of the usual democratic rights and freedoms; they presume free speech, and specifically the freedom to speak frankly to the government. Where democratic government is absent, or frail and undependable, these presumptions cannot apply. Violence, corruption, and incapacity within government institutions, all militate against the safe assumptions of democratic policymaking, and against any orderly influence of research on policy.

Policymakers have less autonomy

International financial institutions and major aid donors often deploy considerable influence in Southern countries' policymaking. Politicians and officials in these countries need to anticipate the responses of these external influences as they prepare and adopt public policy. But lack of autonomy can also translate into a strategic escape from responsibility, as authorities blame outsiders for specific government action or inaction. Irresponsibly or not, political leaders with their hands tied may not give consideration to research advice even when it is available.

Staff turnovers, in research organizations and in government, weaken both research and policy influence

Personnel turnover can challenge institutions anywhere, but it tests Southern institutions more severely. Turnover tends to be higher where the work is unrewarding, both financially and professionally. In research organizations, that tends to encourage emigration to better jobs and prospects. In government departments, it can lead to insufficient understanding of the insights that research can bring to policy problems.

Developing countries often lack the intermediary institutions that carry research to policy

Rich countries display an abundance of research institutes, think tanks, university departments, and independent media, all engaged in the noisy explorations and arguments of democratic governance. These are the knowledge brokers often absent in developing countries—the transactors who connect research findings to policy issues and political controversies. Typically the local business sector in developing countries is similarly weak in research capacity, and transnational corporations rarely invest in local developing-country research. As a result, the mechanisms of policy influence are missing.

Implementation challenges are greater

In any country there are gaps between the stated aims of a policy and its outcomes, because design and implementation can never fully anticipate all contingencies. But the gaps open more deeply in developing countries for three reasons. First, policy design capabilities may be weak, and policy designed by international agencies may fail to reflect local conditions and government priorities. Second, good policy can be defeated by inadequate administrative, legal, or management capacity in execution. And third, implementation can be undercut by graft or incompetence unchecked by sufficient monitoring and accountability.

'Personal' relationships can lead to misgovernment

Cronyism undermines good governance anywhere. It is a special threat where democratic institutions, civil service professionalism, and the conventions of countervailing power are all weak. Fostering personal relationships between research and policy communities is good for government—a point that has been addressed in the pages that follow. But rule by insiderism and influence-peddling is a vice in any country, and it diminishes the prospects for research to influence policy. Researchers can compete in a policy contest of ideas, but not when the game is rigged by string pullers and special favours.

Policymakers lack confidence in their own researchers

Policymakers around the world are inclined sometimes to dismiss researchers as naive to worldly realities. That attitude can be amplified in developing countries where policymakers are unfamiliar with current scientific or scholarly approaches, or view universities as troublemaking sites of opposition to government. When policymakers see a need for research, they often turn to expatriates, either because foreigners are considered more reliable or because canvassing foreigners might attract favour from aid donors. But relying on foreign researchers cannot, by itself, add to domestic research capacity.

Researchers in development often lack hard data

Advocates of increasing research for development policy make a mistake when they take for granted the availability of hard data as the foundation for policy advice. In fact, developing countries often suffer a shortage of basic statistical and other data fundamental to drawing reliable conclusions. Without an agreed fact base, policy arguments are more likely to turn on issues of power and prejudice than on evidence. Verifiable evidence is the researcher's stock-in-trade; without it, researchers have little claim to policy influence.

Southern countries too seldom share research among themselves

Research findings and methods usually travel North to South. As a consequence, research experiences in the South are neglected, and valuable opportunities for information exchange among Southern researchers are lost. Northerners lose out as well; consider, for example, what could be learned from the South about development planning for North American aboriginal communities. No poor country can afford this missed potential for research collaboration with others in the South.

Demand for research can be missing

Much of the Northern-based knowledge-to-policy literature assumes an active demand among policymakers for the knowledge that research can supply. To truth to tell, hard-pressed decision makers in governments of developing countries often know little about the help that research can offer them, and are therefore indifferent to the value of building local research capacity in the long run. Research activity is discouraged accordingly, even where the country's objective needs are intense and growing.

Researchers sometimes must construct their own research-to-action machinery

Northern writers on the use of research for policy influence usually presume the existence of functioning policy networks or decision regimes, that is, institutionalized interactions of researchers and policymakers by which policymaker interests are conveyed to the research community, and research findings are relayed back into the policy community. In the first place, no such networks or regimes necessarily exist in a developing country. And in the second place, commissioned research in a poor country might well be directed less to government authorities than to local farmers, say, or miners, or urban market women. This is a bottom-up dynamic of research for change, in which official government policies might operate more as obstacles than as instruments of action. It is a research approach that has proved to be productive in many different settings, but it places added obligations on researchers to imagine and assemble new relationships with the people who can put research discoveries to work in their own lives.

Bringing Research to Policy-making Connections in Difficult Conditions

Fortunately, these undeniably discouraging impediments to research-based policy-making do not all occur at once in every developing country. They ordinarily emerge in different combinations in different countries, and the combinations shift over time.

Better still, circumstances arise even in the most unpromising conditions that can suddenly create new opportunities for researchers to influence policy and achieve real development progress. History points to three critical moments when research can become exceptionally influential.

First, economic crisis, unambiguous policy failure or radical political change can inspire policymakers to seek research advice that they would previously have ignored or dismissed. These abrupt attitudinal swings reward researchers who are already prepared to present specific and practical solutions to policymakers' problems.

Second, societies and political systems undergoing transition have generated new and unexpected opportunities for researchers to influence fresh policy in the making. Settings as different as South Africa and Vietnam have proven hospitable to evidence-based policy guidance in the midst of turbulent change.

Third, the advent of new and pervasive technologies encourages policymakers to explore new questions, and to try new answers. The revolutions in information and communication technologies—from cellular phones to web-based commerce and education—have caused policymakers to search out knowledgeable advice. When a problem or solution is so obviously unprecedented, policymakers can more safely admit ignorance. Again, researchers who already have helpful findings in hand are best placed to answer policymakers' questions with prompt and reliable advice.

The well prepared researcher can, in other words, seize the moment for influence when it occurs. Obstacles and defects in policymaking processes can be overcome when development research is devised and executed well, and communicated to policymakers in a form that contributes to timely and pragmatic decisions.

More than that, effective research can serve to correct the very conditions that block the easy transmission of new knowledge into policy. In Tanzania, community-based research in rural public health helped improve the design and funding of health services. In the Philippines and Bangladesh, systematic analyses of household poverty have improved economic policy processes. In Jordan, neighbourhood studies of wastewater reuse have altered government approaches to conservation of water supplies. Research can make for better governance—and better governance encourages more research.

Box 1.1: Risks and Rewards—The Mozambique Case

It was a high-risk undertaking. But a research project in Mozambique—which led directly to ground-breaking policy for information and communication technologies in development—showed that research can succeed even in the hardest circumstances.

Mozambique in the late 1990s was a poor country in a poor region. Poverty was extensive, research capacity was sparse, and the country still suffered the wounds of a long and horrific warfare.

Even so, there were opportunities. Mozambique had achieved a measure of post-war stability. Its government was committed to national development, and sensed the pressures and potential in the global ICT (Information and Communication Technology) environment. And there was a small community of ICT champions eager to launch research into affordable and accessible ICTs, especially for poor people. Notwithstanding the obvious risks—little was known about ICT possibilities in southern Africa—IDRC was ready to place a bet with funding for research.

The project was divided into three components: creation of a national ICT advisory committee and secretariat; formulation of ICT policy to put before the government; and pilot projects, to test rural telecentres and the uses of ICTs in schools and teacher training. The components worked together. The committee and secretariat provided energetic leadership and coherence, and engaged with top government officials. Policy formulation gave the research focused purpose. Field research discovered what ordinary people would want from telephones and the Internet (and what they would pay for)—and defined the obstacles of cost for connectivity and equipment. Data from pilot-project monitoring had a powerful impact on policymakers.

Why did the Mozambique research succeed? Evaluation turned up answers.

There was a compact circle of policymakers; research managers knew who needed influencing. Senior members of the advisory committee and secretariat were fully networked with political leaders. The government was unusually committed to making effective ICT policy; the Prime Minister and President were personally involved. Mozambican champions were determined. And Mozambique's ICT research was linked, through an IDRC-supported initiative known as Acacia, with similar projects in Senegal, South Africa, and Uganda. Synergies were shared as research proceeded.

The research had verifiable effect. In 2000, Mozambique approved its ICT policy—the first in Africa. And Mozambique established a reputation as a developing-world pioneer in applying ICTs for development.

The interaction of development research and public policy is the subject of this book. Drawing on the observations and conclusions of an extensive evaluation of some 23 case studies (see Table 1.1)—covering more than 60 projects in over 20 countries, and described in Section II—these pages report practical strategies for better research and better policy. This work is therefore addressed both to the research community and the policy community, as well as to national and international organizations that invest in development research.

But first, as a fair warning, it has to be understood that there is no list of 'best practices' when it comes to research influencing public policy. Influence is more process than product, a current of activities and relationships interacting with each other. Influence, moreover, is a means to an end and not an end in itself. The purpose of development research is not to culminate in a briefing book or a cabinet minister's speech; the aim is to improve the lives of poor people in poor countries. This takes time. And it requires the building of relationships

Table 1.1: The Cases at a Glance

Name of Case (start–end dates)	Goal	Research Outputs
1. MIMAP, the Philippines (1990–2002) Micro Impacts of Macro Adjustment Policies	To develop poverty modelling and monitoring capacity to inform poverty alleviation strategies.	Different economic models such as CGE (Computable General Equilibrium); CBMS (Community-based Monitoring System) poverty monitoring system designed; provincial database and poverty monitoring maps of Palawan Province; research reports and focus studies.
2. MIMAP, Bangladesh (1992–2001)	1. To increase the understanding of poverty and to promote dialogue among researchers, politicians, government officials, and NGOs in the search of equitable and effective policies of poverty alleviation. 2. To develop an analytical framework to analyze the key macroeconomic and structural adjustment policies on the poor.	Poverty Monitoring System, first at national level then addition of a local level system; computerized information system for data management; development of a CGE model and training on its use; focus studies on poverty related issues (*inter alia*, role of public expenditure, agriculture and rural poverty, efficiency of rural markets, human resource development and the poor).
3. Vietnam Programme (1993–2001)	To start three different projects. 1. VISED (Vietnam Sustainable Economic Development Programme): Research capacity building to support the national research programme under four themes; environment, economy, and legal and small grants. 2. VEEM (Vietnam Economic and Environment Management Programme): Capacity for knowledge-based policy development in economic integration and NRM (Natural Resource Management). 3. MIMAP: Develop and apply a poverty monitoring system; and develop econometric (CGE) models for analysis at the national level.	Four studies under VISED: 'Foundations for Regional Development', 'Organizations and Management of Export Processing Zones', 'Formulation and organization of shareholding companies' and 'Establishing a system for credit funds'; various small grant research reports, highly varied. VEEM: Five reports in 2001 on trade liberalization and its impacts; and on industrial competitiveness in textiles and garment industry; computerized trade database (one of a kind in Vietnam). MIMAP: CBMS; CGE models; analysis using these models were conducted on distribution and equity impact of fiscal policy and trade reform.

(*Table 1.1 continued*)

(Table 1.1 continued)

Name of Case (start–end dates)	Goal	Research Outputs
4. LATN (1998–2002) Latin American Trade Network	1. To conduct policy-oriented research on emerging issues in international trade relations. 2. To support the process of agenda building and policy formulation in LAC (Latin America and Caribbean) countries in response to emerging trends in the international system. 3. To harness existing research capacity in LAC countries to engage in international trade negotiations and contribute to HRD. 4. To strengthen collaboration among participating institutions with a view to long-term sustainability of the network.	Working papers and policy briefs on: overarching issues such as preconditions for trade coalitions, bargaining and relationships between multilateralism and regional integration initiatives; emerging issue from a LAC perspective, such as international investment, competition policy, financial services, telecoms, IPR (Intellectual Property Rights), dispute settlement, etc.; country case studies to identify optimal or feasible national responses in international trade relations; website, newsletters, conferences; training courses; meetings with officials, and consultancies. Books are planned.
5. G-24 TSS (1988–2003) Group of 24 Technical Support Service	1. To assist developing countries in building their capacity in international monetary negotiations. 2. To strengthen their technical preparedness and their ability to participate in, and contribute to all phases of discussion and negotiation within the framework of the Fund and the World Bank.	Research papers—web and traditional dissemination—in two main areas: Technical economic research; Normative research (that is, on the role and performance of international financial institutions). Phase I: 32 research studies Phase II: 36 research studies Phase III: 27 research studies Phase IV: 15 research studies 11 volume set of International Monetary and Financial Issues for the 1990s, 24 papers in the G-24, Discussion Paper Series.

6. Arsaal, Lebanon (1995–2004)	Phase 1: To evaluate the sustainability of major farming systems, and to examine the viability of establishing a network of users to improve sustainable community development through direct involvement of local beneficiaries in formulating, and implementing resource management strategies. Phase II: To evaluate options developed in Phase I, and to increase focus on gender analysis as key to sustainable resource management.	The Arsaal project led to the creation of the Environment and Sustainable Development Unit in 2001, a new multi-disciplinary group at the American University of Beirut. It lead to (or, resulted in) a land use map of Arsaal, a degradation hazard map and a land capability map. Professional articles or conference presentations from Phase I; 14 MSc theses; several brochures, videos, newspaper articles; tools for rural development in arid areas were developed; and a book entitled *Research for Development in the Dry Arab Region: The Cactus Flower* by Shadi Hamadeh, Mona Haidar, and Rami Zurayk, published by Southbound/IDRC in 2006.
7. Peru–Copper Mining (1991–93)	To assess the impact of mining activities on water resources in southern Peru, and present the results to the International Water Tribunal II, February 1992. Phase I: To explore the social, legal, and ecological aspects of pollution from mining waste discharges. Phase II: To explore the effects of the quantitative distribution of water resources in the region.	A report to the International Water Tribunal II which led to findings against the practices of the mining company. No research output, but SPCC (Southern Peru Copper Corporation mining company) changed its policies and practices and started some environmental projects addressing environmental degradation.
8. ECAPAPA, East Africa (1997–2002) Eastern and Central Africa Programme for Agricultural Policy Analysis	To improve the policy environment for the purpose of enhancing agricultural technology generation and adoption to reduce poverty and environmental degradation. Two sets of three projects: 1. To determine farm household financial profitability of recommended crop varieties under different agro-ecologies; to test the extent to which multi-disciplinary teams work together on socio-economic issues affecting national agricultural research institutes.	Only three projects were completed, so outputs were limited. No dissemination materials of note produced. Final reports are available from three projects, interim reports from the others.

(Table 1.1 continued)

(Table 1.1 continued)

Name of Case (start—end dates)	Goal	Research Outputs
	2. To develop multi-stakeholder approaches for managing conflicts over natural resources in ECA (East and Central Africa); to provide guidance for *in situ* efforts as well as for external support to deal with conflicts in NRM.	
9. Greywater reuse, Jordan (1998–2005)	Involved five projects: 1. To facilitate policy development in support of urban agriculture at municipal and national levels in order to enhance urban food security.	1. Research into policies and practices on greywater reuse. 2. Installation of on-site treatment plants in Ramallah. 3. An evaluation study.
	2. To build capacity in, and conduct applied research in optimizing small-scale trickling filters for treating greywater for reuse in home gardens in peri-urban areas.	4. Increased demand from households for greywater kits; workshops on irrigation requirements; workshops to train plumbers and electricians on management of systems; proposed building code revisions; graduate research on greywater reuse is underway.
	3. To assess technical reliability and safety, sustainability, and potential for scale-up of a permaculture experiment in Tafila. 4. To optimize and validate a system for reusing greywater in home gardens. 5. To increase greywater recovery and increase its handling safety (this last project was not reviewed in this study).	5. Led to a revision of national housing codes and establishing a national committee to create greywater reuse guidelines; replication of the greywater treatment kits in the Middle East and North Africa; ratified Hyderabad Declaration; and a network of policymakers, researchers, private sector, and beneficiaries.

10. EMDU, Ukraine (1994–2002) Environmental Management Development in Ukraine	Phase I: To help establish the capacity of Ukrainian institutions to manage the Dnipro water system and its uses; contribute to the reduction of water pollution in the southern Dnipro; and forge long-term collaborative linkages between Canadian and Ukrainian public and private organizations. Phase II: To strengthen environmental reforms in Ukrainian institutions and industry; heighten environmental awareness among scientists, decision makers, and the general population; to expand the network of public, private, and third sector organizations working on environmental issues; and to foster linkages between standards and programmes.	1. National Environmental Management Information System connected to 19 provincial offices along the Dnipro River. 2. Regional Management Information System. 3. A body of Ukrainian environmental legislation was collated, published, and made available to NGOs, and public and educational institutions. 4. Baseline water quality survey completed. 5. Health risk assessment of drinking water quality. 6. Various surveys and audits on water quality and other water issues. 7. The training of 90 individuals. 8. Changes in factories' emission systems along the Dnipro River. 9. *Preserving the Dnipro River: Harmony, History, and Rehabilitation,* V.V. Shevchuk, G.O. Bilyavsky, V.M. Navrotsky, and O.O. Mazurkevich. Mosaic Press/IDRC (2005).
11. High Altitude Mining, Peru (1990–93)	To gain recognition of the incidence of Chronic Mountain Sickness in high altitude mining, and to influence national policy.	Book was published, and two studies on the subject were recognized.
12. Fisheries Network, South East Asia (1983–96)	1. To improve the capacities to manage the fishery, and to indirectly influence policy and management regimes. 2. To increase supply of social researchers on fisheries and strengthen institutions.	Over 50 research reports were produced over the life of the project; a special publication series was developed.
13. SRISTI, India (1993–present) Society for Research and Initiatives for Sustainable Technologies and Institutions	To protect natural resources by documenting local innovations based on indigenous knowledge, the protection of property rights, and recognition and dissemination of innovations.	1. Creation of databases including over 13,000 documented local innovations disseminated in six local languages. 2. A network of over 1,000 local groups supported by newsletters and other means.

(Table 1.1 continued)

(*Table 1.1 continued*)

Name of Case (start–end dates)	Goal	Research Outputs
		3. Royalty sharing agreements with a private company on three veterinary medicines. 4. Validation of several plant-based medicines.
14. TEHIP, Tanzania (1996–2004) Tanzania Essential Health Interventions Project	To test the feasibility and measure the impact of an evidence-based approach to local health planning in two districts in Tanzania.	1. Developed 10 tools to collect, organize, and present data on mortality and disease. 2. Analyzed data for policy options. 3. Research on governance and organizational design.
15. Acacia, Mozambique (December 1997–December 2003)	1. To support national efforts to strengthen linkages to the global economy. 2. To support rural access to ICTs. 3. To share learning about ICT policies in the region.	Use of pilot projects as a form of action research, short-term studies, and input into draft national policy papers, but not rigorous academic research.
16. Acacia, Uganda (1999-2002)	To demonstrate how access to ICTs helps communities solve their own problems; to build a body of knowledge on improving access by rural people, the poor, and disadvantaged communities; to strengthen rural access to ICTs.	1. Produced pre-inception studies on the relevance of Acacia action research for Uganda. 2. Produced several studies (on capacity, policy, infrastructure, and technology) used by the ICT Policy Task Force; the National Acacia Secretariat played a representative role on the committees that drafted national ICT policy. 3. Surveys and research studies on telecentres as well as issues around rural access, and studies on the development of relevant content. 4. Studies commissioned to provide background information and answers to specific policy questions. In this category are the studies conducted to inform the

		Rural Communications Development Policy process, the telecentre baseline studies and the four studies initially commissioned in 1998 to examine the status of ICTs in Uganda.
17. Acacia, South Africa (1995–2002)	To support communities in the use of ICTs for problem solving and community engagement; to enhance ICT access by rural and disadvantaged communities.	As an action research initiative some of the outputs relate to processes, including representation on policy initiatives such as the Task Team of the Government Communications and Information Service, representation to the e-commerce policy processes.
18. Acacia, Senegal (1997–2002)	To foster a national strategy and coordinated framework for ICTs, through a series of demonstration projects, and through regulation and research projects.	A study of tele-services for the Government of Senegal Representation on bodies developing local and national ICT policies and strategies, and hosting fora on ICT policy and implementation, involving the government, the private sector, and the public. (These are included here as output because of the strong action orientation of Acacia and its intent to leave the major research to a special component of Acacia, the Evaluation and Learning System.)

(Table 1.1 continued)

(*Table 1.1 continued*)

Name of Case (start–end dates)	Goal	Research Outputs
19. ICT Policy, Nepal (1999) Information and Communication Technology Policy	To foster a national ICT policy and strategy by means of a participatory process.	Six background studies: 1. Universal access to information 2. Information and communication technology infrastructure 3. Human resource development 4. Software production and application 5. Electronic commerce (e-commerce) 6. Electronic governance (e-governance)
20. Water Demand Management, Syria (1997–2001)	The formulation of long-term management strategies for the suitable use of brackish water in supplemental irrigation of field crops in the dry areas of Syria.	Six Master's Theses, one PhD dissertation, and one peer-reviewed article (Hagi-Bishow and Bonnell 2000).
21. Water Demand Management, Tunisia (1992–2000)	To design a comprehensive strategy for managing the country's water demands in order to prevent any rationing due to a potential shortage, while delaying the major supply investments under consideration.	1. Five papers on resource allocation and decentralization. 2. Four papers on residential water demand estimation. 3. A mathematical model for determining optimal cropping in dry areas. 4. A model on integrated water-environment management and a paper on the same (based on the willingness to pay).

22. MIMAP, Senegal (2000–2002)

1. To construct a profile of the poverty in Senegal and develop a monitoring system.
2. To develop tools to analyze the impact of macroeconomic policies on income distribution.
3. To specifically study poor people's access to financial services, the gender dimension of poverty, and the relation between education and poverty.
4. To encourage dialogue among development actors working in the fight against poverty (researchers, policymakers, NGOs, and financiers).

The research outputs were largely blended with the overall research outputs of the research centre involved. The core recognized output from the MIMAP team was its leadership in the development of the Poverty Reduction Strategy Paper for Senegal, a paper required by the World Bank as part of programming, not a research output per se. The volume and importance of this work to the national agenda sidetracked the original research agenda.

23. Education Reform, Guatemala (2000–2002)

To influence educational policy in Guatemala by formulating a proposal from an indigenous perspective that could influence the planning and execution of the education budget in the context of the Education Reform and the National Education Plan (2000–2020).

Background research studies that resulted in a Research Report on financing education in Guatemala.

between members of the research and the policy communities—relationships of trust, strengthened by reliable, helpful work on both sides of the research–policy partnership.

The premise here is that development research, where it is well designed, conducted, and communicated, can improve public policy in ways that advance sustainable democratic development. The evidence, and the examples, show how that influence is achieved.

The inquiry begins with a simple, yet necessary question: What is influence? This is the starting point for the next chapter.

Policy Matters

New knowledge achieves influence in a dynamic interaction of research and policy. On one side of that interaction, the policy or the political setting shapes constraints and opportunities for researchers to do their work and to try to influence public policy. On the other side, research activity and discovery can alter the policy environment by creating new choices, framing new policy questions, and introducing new solutions to policy problems. Ultimately, research can affect the way government decisions are made. This is an interaction that benefits researchers and policymakers alike. For researchers, it means doing and disseminating development research that has real effects on public policy and action. For the policy community, it means having a ready supply of evidence-based options for timelier, stronger, and more responsive policy decisions.

At best, research is only one element in the fiercely complicated mix of factors and forces behind any significant governmental policy decision. Policies in most governments, most of the time, are the outcomes of all the bargains and compromises, beliefs and aspirations, and cross-purposes and double meanings of ordinary governmental decision making. This is why it is usually a mistake to adopt a model that imagines policymaking as a rational, orderly, or unitary and linear progression from problem to decision and solution. Close observation of how public policies are actually made and executed leads to a more complicated—but more realistic—picture of outcomes affected by personality, chance, imperfect understanding, and negotiation. To say that research has exerted an influence in a particular case is only to say that the influence of research has counted as one of numerous influences. The thread between cause and effect in a policy decision invariably gets tangled in the coalitions and contradictions of policy processes in any country. This is transparently true of democratic governments, and less transparently, but no less true, of dictatorships and oligarchies.

Furthermore, it is best to acknowledge that research itself is far from monolithic or single-minded. On the contrary, pure and applied research is conducted everywhere with very diverse intentions, motives, and expectations. These differences—along with the surprises that so often divert research into new directions—customarily carry researchers to inconsistent, and even contradictory findings and advice for policy. As a rule, these inconsistencies and contradictions in advice are not well received by policymakers. The dynamism of this research and policy interaction explains why influence is so hard to track and measure.

But what is influence? IDRC's evaluation of development research projects around the world, in very different political contexts, confirmed three overall categories that describe how research can affect policy.

First, research can expand policy capacities. Research can strengthen the institutional framework supporting policymaking by enhancing the policy community's own collective ability to assess and communicate innovative ideas, and by cultivating new talents for analyzing and applying incoming research advice.

Second, research can broaden policy horizons. Policy is often frustrated by a scarcity of choices. Research can improve the intellectual framework surrounding policymaking by introducing new ideas to the policy agenda, by ensuring that information comes to policymakers in a form and language they can quickly grasp and use, and by fostering helpful dialogue between researchers and decision makers. Researchers win the respect and gratitude of policymakers by providing new insight or information that can unlock those zero-sum, 'either-or' policy dichotomies that so often seem to constrict debate and decision.

Box 2.1: Three Kinds of Influence in Vietnam

In Vietnam they called it Doi Moi (rough translation: reconstruction)—an ambitious programme of economic modernization in the direction of competitive markets and freer trade. But it was launched by authorities with little or no knowledge of policymaking in a market economy, and they called on IDRC for assistance. With the explicit objective of influencing policy, IDRC-supported a sequence of research programmes centred on environment and resource management, trade, and poverty reduction.

Influencing policy is not just about altering a particular decision. Maximum influence occurs when research helps the policy community grow its own capabilities to assess evidence and analyze options; or when research enlarges the array of choices for policymakers; or when research improves the procedures of policymaking.

Expanding policy capacities. As Doi Moi began, Vietnam's policy institutions were weak; Vietnamese economists, schooled in Marxism, were largely unfamiliar with Western economic analysis. IDRC's research contribution proved significant, in the judgement of later evaluation. Research programming encouraged inter-institutional networks to disperse new knowledge and skills across Vietnamese organizations. One example was the preparation of a large, computerized trade database. Over the years, Vietnam's policy and research institutions learned the practices and rewards of cooperation.

Broadening policy horizons. If expanding policy capacities means strengthening the institutional framework, broadening policy horizons means rebuilding the intellectual framework. Example: in Vietnam, research in trade policy and competitiveness helped inform a new understanding that existing tariff and export promotion policies were not producing intended results. A key question in these settings is how new knowledge can be diffused into the highest levels of decision making. One explanation from Vietnam: participation of a few intermediaries, with influential relationships in both research and policy communities, facilitates knowledge transfer.

Affecting decision regimes. Attributing influence here is tentative; in the complications of policy arguments and outcomes, it is rarely easy to specify with certainty how research has affected policy processes. In Vietnam, it was especially hard. Still, there are signs that research evidence was considered by policymakers, and that policy decisions reflected those findings. To some degree at least, the practices of fact-based policy analysis and decision seem to have been adopted in the changing procedures of Vietnamese policymaking.

Third, research can affect decision regimes. The quality of a policy can be determined as much by the procedures of deliberation and decision as by its content. Research findings can improve the policy-process framework by helping to open and rationalize the procedures of legislating, administering, and evaluating government policies and programmes. Skills and attitudes characteristic of good research—not least, a spirit of curiosity and fact-based argument—can improve the operations of government.

The crucial point about these three categories of influence is that they go well beyond changing particular policies. The most meaningful and lasting influence is less about specific policy change than about building capacity—among researchers and policy people—to produce and apply knowledge for better development results. This kind of influence can take years, or even decades, to take effect or become apparent. But it is no less important for that.

How do we know if a policy or decision has been influenced by research? It is never easy to tell with certainty. For all the reasons mentioned above, research is invariably only one of the forces affecting policy outcomes; attribution of causes to effects is likely to be conjectural except in rare cases. (This is one realm where it is usually easier to 'prove' the negative as there can be no visible influence by a given body of research on a given policy or action.) Still, as the evidence offered in the following pages will show, it is sometimes possible to trace the effects of research on policy debates and outcomes. Sometimes the evidence is remarkably straightforward: an affirmation from the policy community itself that research findings, that were well communicated, have seemed to open minds—if not change them—in favour of better decisions.

Regimes and Receptivity

Scholars of public administration and policy processes have invented an imposing diversity of types and classifications to describe how government decisions are made and enforced. For the practical purposes of getting research to policy, a three-part analytical scheme that has proved useful to researchers and policymakers is discussed below.

Routine decision regimes focus on matching and adapting existing programmes and policy repertoires to emerging demands. There is scant debate on overall policy design, and none on fundamental underlying principles or objectives.

Incremental decision regimes will debate options and values on selected issues as they emerge onto the policy agenda. But these regimes seldom engage in deeper questioning of choices when they can avoid it. And they evade, whenever possible, comprehensive re-examination of issues spanning the whole policy horizon. They advance carefully, in small steps.

Fundamental decision regimes embrace thorough-going and even radical reconsiderations of policies and strategies, not least when authorities want to give expression to revolutionary political change. South Africa's first freely elected post-apartheid government is a case in point. Such regimes are relatively rare, but they present unique opportunities to researchers ready with timely and convincing advice.

This is not, of course, the only possible categorical scheme available. Another common and similar taxonomy divides government performance according to its overarching style: transactional, transitional, or transformational. In all these schemes, however, the truth to recall is that no government represents any such category in its pure state—or at least, not for long.

Over time, most governments display more than one style as demands, personalities, and priorities arise and recede. Fundamental decision regimes, for instance, are often followed by quieter phases of incrementalist consolidation and implementation. Styles can merge and mutate, occasionally with surprising speed.

What matters, for policy research, is that the dominant style of government—the decision regime features that prevail at the relevant moment—will carry implications for the research to policy dynamic.

Routine decision regimes will be attracted to data, analysis, and prescriptions that reinforce or only slightly modify pre-existing policy preferences and routines. They are usually resistant to research that explicitly challenges their foundational assumptions and beliefs.

Incremental decision regimes will entertain policy propositions that identify alternatives and compromises for solving selected issues already on the policy agenda. They will not usually invite or welcome wholesale rethinking of existing policy or conventional wisdom. They want to address any big ideas in small pieces.

Fundamental decision regimes will be far more open to research and debate that challenges the logic and value assumptions of existing policy—especially if the regime is already committed to overturning existing policy. They are also typically readier to re-examine the whole policy agenda, not merely to repair parts of it.

If these characterizations are realistic, a daunting conclusion necessarily follows. As policy-making in most countries is generally routine or incremental and rarely fundamental, most policy regimes will show an inbuilt bias against adopting innovative research findings. Routinists prefer information that reinforces preformed opinions and expectations; incrementalists only want to know what will get them through another day or controversy. So we should not be shocked when policymakers profess—as they often do—that in the normal course of their duties they do not find 'big question' research all that helpful. Generally, these are not the questions they want answered—or even asked.

Corollaries follow from this conclusion. First, development researchers can usually expect resistance among policymakers to research advice that threatens to undermine long held assumptions. Second, researchers should nonetheless organize and communicate new knowledge so as to influence even routine and incremental decisions, because those are the decisions that policymakers normally prefer to make. And third, researchers should assign themselves the long-term work of building capacity, expanding horizon, and regime improvement. Slowly percolating good and helpful policy approaches through the policy community will test researchers' patience, but it can pay off as minds open and attitudes change.

Context Counts

For the most part, researchers seeking to influence policy can expect to encounter a measure of institutional reluctance among policymakers. Except when they are attempting to manage a political transition or some crisis, especially an economic crisis, government leaderships usually do not spontaneously invite innovative advice from the research community; on the whole, they do not avidly search out fresh problems—or welcome unsettling solutions. To achieve influence, researchers, and their policymaking allies, need to devise strategies suited to the political context in which they work.

Strategy making starts with a closer study of governmental receptivity to proffered research. And here IDRC's 23 case studies of research-for-policy have yielded helpful guidance. The study uncovered five different policy/political contexts—each summoning a specific strategic approach by researchers intending to move knowledge into policy. In summary, governments and policy communities tend to sort themselves into these five recognizable categories of research and policy interaction.

Clear government demand

In this welcoming context, policymakers want knowledge, and are prepared to act on it. Also, policymakers enjoy a capacity to receive and understand research-based policy advice when it is presented, and to apply it practically to the policy problems before them. The policy window is wide open to researchers. To make their most effective contribution, researchers need to build relationships of trust with decision makers, and establish a reputation for providing knowledge that is timely and dependable.

The likelihood of exercising influence in such a context is high. Habits and patterns of communication are in place, policy capacity is sufficient, and policymakers show a healthy appetite for research information and recommendations.

Government interest in research, but leadership absent

The window of influence is only partially open in this context. The salient policy issue is well known to government authorities, and is considered important. But the structures to implement recommendations from research are missing. Policymakers have not yet taken the lead in deciding what to do, and no clear decision making process is evident.

Circumstances like these call for leadership from researchers themselves—beginning with careful attention to communication between research and policy communities. Experience shows that researchers, by actively engaging policymakers, can propel the transmission of relevant research into the policy discourse. But these circumstances also demonstrate that governmental interest by itself does not guarantee that research will actually influence policy decisions or action. To have influence, research needs a plan of implementation, or a champion among policymakers willing to put the research to work.

Government interest in research, but with a capacity shortfall

Again, the window for research influence appears half-open. Leaders in the policy community acknowledge the significance of the issue; they might already have addressed it in preliminary stages. They may also have affirmed the potential value of research. But they have not invested the necessary resources in capacity for adoption or implementation—either because no such resources are available, or because other policy priorities have been judged more pressing, and are fully occupying all available capacity. Links between research and decision processes under these conditions are generally weak. Researchers therefore face a twofold challenge. They have to help build capacity for the conversion of research knowledge into policy and action. And they have to try to move the issue up the ranks of decision-making priorities. Case studies have identified effective strategies to meet both these challenges.

A new or emerging issue activates research, but leaves policymakers uninterested

For researchers, this scenario has proven both familiar and frustrating. Galvanized by an intriguing new question, or by the promising appearance of new answers, researchers achieve significant advances in solving some development problem. Yet policymakers remain either indifferent or averse to the research or its promise. The issue may simply have failed to register with the policy community as a matter worth pursuing. Or it might incite unwelcome controversy, or jeopardize some vested interest. And if potential beneficiaries of the research—people who would be well served by its implementation—never know of its existence, the research itself will probably lack political support.

This turns out to constitute a high-risk policy environment for researchers and their work, and it is a context that recurs throughout the research world. A considerable number of our 23 cases fell into this class of governmental receptivity, particularly in their early phases. In some of these cases, researchers managed to open the policy window, and engage the attention of decision makers; in other cases they failed, and the window slammed shut. Chances of success are improved when researchers and their supporters apply adroit strategies of advocacy, communication, and education—within and beyond the policy community itself.

Government treats research with disinterest, or hostility

Here the window of influence is tightly closed. Policymakers are preoccupied by other priorities, or may even be hostile to the issues, or to the contributions made available from research. (We found no explicit governmental hostility to research in our cases. But the line between deliberate, methodical indifference and overt hostility amounts to a distinction without a difference.) Where policymakers demonstrate no receptivity whatsoever to research, it could be said that the researchers themselves are ahead of their time. Nor should it be wholly surprising if innovative (or lucky) research occasionally surges to a conclusion well before policymakers are ready for its implications. In any event, anyone involved in development research should arm themselves with patience, determination, and a clear-eyed recognition that attracting the interest of policymakers can demand long and systematic persuasion. It is also worth noting that in policy, as in science, things change. Attitudes evolve; preferences shift; needs arise; priorities are realigned; governments acquire new leadership. Windows open.

To summarize, research and policy influence each other in a dynamic interaction. That creates opportunities and constraints for researchers, and for policymakers. The meaning of influence itself is variable and context specific. Besides affecting particular policies, research can expand policy capacities, broaden policy horizons, and alter the nature of policy making regimes. In fact, influence often emerges only after years have passed; the most lasting effects of research may have more to do with improving the quality of governance than evaluating with the outcomes of individual policy arguments or government decisions.

Research influence will be determined only partly by the strength of the research findings, or the power of the researcher's logic. Much will be determined by the character of the decision regime in which the research is conducted and disseminated—whether the policymaking is pre-eminently routine or incremental (which is to say, cautiously conservative), or more radically fundamental in its approaches to conventional wisdom and novel ideas.

And there is finally the issue of receptivity—whether the policy community actively invites research advice, or is indifferent or oblivious, or effectively closed to all research-based interventions in policy discussions.

What experience does demonstrate, however, is that each of these classes of receptivity calls for definable strategies by which researchers and research advocates can maximize their prospects of influencing public policy and development action. Policy influence is undeniably a complicated phenomenon. But all is not chance and circumstance. Researchers can design, conduct, and report their work for best effect on policy and action. That is the subject of the following chapter—an account of what works, and what does not—based on an evaluation of almost two dozen cases in more than 20 developing countries.

What Works, What Doesn't

Development research interacts over time with its policy/political context, and each can affect the other. Nevertheless, researchers and their supporters must work within the context that presents itself. Even if they aim ambitiously to alter the ways public policy is decided and carried out, researchers will represent at most a modest measure of all the forces working on a country's policy process. The nature of the economy and the society, the characteristics of governmental leaders, the pressures and tensions of political continuity and change—all have powerful influences on the conduct and outcomes of policymaking.

All of which is to say that development researchers are likely to maximize their influence on policy by designing and conducting research, and communicating results to the policy community, so as to fit the policy/political context that surrounds them. But there are no simple tactics to accomplish this, no all-purpose directions to influence. Contexts are too complicated for any such easy approaches, and too changeable.

In particular, the policy community's receptivity to research advice frequently changes as the research unfolds. Sometimes policymakers who were once dismissive of research grow more responsive, or leave office. Sometimes the currents of change flow against research, and an early prospect of influence goes unfulfilled. And sometimes research itself affects receptivity, convincing doubting decision makers that research has provided helpful answers after all.

The preceding chapter set out five recognizable categories of research and policy inter-action. The discussion now turns to the evidence of cases, and some of the strategies that have enhanced the influence that research exerts on development policy and action.

Clear Government Demand

The researcher enjoys a unique advantage whenever decision makers express a real and specific interest in receiving research information or guidance. Policymakers in these cases usually sense a particular need for advice, command an ability to apply that advice, and exercise the authority to arrange its implementation. Researchers in these situations are spared the necessity of elaborate advocacy or details of presentation. If decision makers need an expansive policy brief they will ask for it; if they simply want new data they will say so. Policymakers have already concluded that the issue is important, the time for decision is right, and that the advice of the researcher is trustworthy.

Box 3.1: Engaging with Policymakers in Senegal

The chance to influence policy can arise with startling speed when a government recognizes its own urgent need for research-based advice. Prepared and responsive researchers can seize that moment with dramatic effect—as a team of economists discovered in Senegal.

Ranking among the world's poorest countries, Senegal had nonetheless achieved notable economic progress as a result of policy decisions years earlier. Annual GDP growth was averaging 5 per cent, and inflation had subsided significantly. But the numbers of poor people kept rising; a 2001 survey found a rural poverty rate of 80 per cent.

To address these shocking poverty levels, IDRC in 2000 chose Senegal's Centre de Recherche en Économie Appliquée (CREA) to lead a programme known as MIMAP. MIMAP concentrates on a simple question: How do macroeconomic policies affect poor people in their families and communities? Answering that question takes researchers deep into the complexities at the root of persistent poverty.

MIMAP in Senegal (one of a dozen MIMAP projects in Asia and Africa) was scarcely three months old when Senegal's government asked CREA to help develop its Poverty Reduction Strategy Paper (PRSP), required by the International Monetary Fund and the World Bank in countries qualifying for special debt relief. The PRSP specifies how a government plans to deploy newly available funds to reduce poverty; the overlap with CREA's MIMAP research was unmistakable.

And CREA's able economists were ready for the challenge. Some already had a reputation for reliability in the policy community; several had experience in public administration. Coincidence had brought the PRSP project together with MIMAP research. Energetic flexibility enabled researchers to exploit the opportunity.

The collaboration favoured researchers and policymakers. The government successfully produced a PRSP, a strategy designed not by foreigners but by a Senegalese consensus of academic, NGO, commercial and policy communities; this national ownership made implementation easier. At the same time, researchers worked with attentive government support, and won new respect from policymakers.

The case also highlights an observation common in such episodes: Research can have its strongest influence when it responds to the economic pressures and deadlines confronted by policymakers. All else equal, economic need draws policymakers most powerfully towards the advice of researchers.

Trust—this is the most critical strategic asset of the researcher where government demand for research knowledge is strong. The very existence of that demand nearly always signals that researchers have built enduring relationships in the policy community. By the time senior decision makers call on researchers for advice, those researchers have usually established their own reputation for reliability; they are known to policymakers as people who can bring results of high quality research to the policy table in a timely and comprehensible fashion. This strategic investment in building trust among policymakers typically contributes to creating the demand for research that leads to influence.

Curiously, political demand for research can arise in two apparently opposed conditions; when the research issue is old and familiar, and when the questions are new and not yet understood.

Familiar and recurring issues tend to be institutionalized in the government; the course to implementation is clear, the implementing departments or agencies have been designated, and the high policy decisions to proceed have often been taken. The question now is mostly about how to act, not whether to act.

Case in point: when the government of Senegal decided to produce a comprehensive PRSP, it turned to a Senegalese economic research organization for help. This was a crucial move; drafting the PRSP was an urgent requirement for winning debt relief through multilateral development banks. And as it happened, the research group, supported by IDRC, had already embarked on a wide-scale analysis of poverty in Senegal, and was well placed to integrate its own research into the PRSP policy process. Better still, the research team had earned a reputation for quality, enhanced by the team leader's own relationship with the government officials. The work of preparing the PRSP document reinforced both the reputation and the relationship. Trust developed and influence followed.

On the other hand, the sudden hurdle of an unfamiliar and even alarming policy challenge can generate demand for research advice just as powerfully. The riddles of regulating and fostering ICTs have inspired governments almost everywhere to seek advice on how to realize the benefits of these new systems. In places as dissimilar as Nepal and Mozambique, government authorities have acknowledged how little they understood about the implications of ICTs for development, and called on researchers for guidance. In Nepal and across Africa, the novelty of ICTs induced a close and enduring collaboration between researchers and governments.

Government Interest in Research, but Leadership Absent

Here we are dealing with an issue well known, at least superficially, to decision makers in government, who recognize that it carries public policy implications. But when there is no clear decision process in play, and the government does not take the lead in determining what to do, there is a need and an opportunity for members of the research project to take a leadership role. The research team faces two primary strategic considerations: communicating with decision makers, and strengthening the institutional structures available to implement the recommendations or implications flowing from its research. Communication can inform and encourage decision and action. At the same time, if there is no system in place to implement the proposed recommendations, the research findings may never be acted upon.

The case of the Tanzania Essential Health Interventions Project (TEHIP) is instructive. TEHIP researchers, in tight collaboration with local health workers and rural villagers, were assessing the real health service needs of people in their own households. The challenge now was to design and execute a programme by institutionalizing TEHIP approaches within the central Ministry of Health. A lack of coordination among the various players in the health sector led to a slowdown of the project after its pilot phase. Practical progress began to emerge only after months of preparatory work involving researchers, international donors, and government authorities.

In the Philippines, an extensive survey of poverty had been undertaken as part of a multi-national research project known as MIMAP. As an early outcome, the need to increase and institutionalize poverty monitoring in order to address the poverty gap was articulated by MIMAP researchers. Their work resonated with the policymakers. But again, as with TEHIP, the challenge was to advance beyond local-level action, and to establish a poverty monitoring system nationwide. It grew obvious that government leadership and implementation both had to correspond to the realities of governmental decentralization in the Philippines (a factor that will be addressed directly in Chapter 4).

MIMAP-Bangladesh, on the other hand, provides an example of successful institutionalization of research activities within national government institutions. The project staff worked from the very beginning to train officials in the Bureau of Statistics and in the National Planning Commission to use MIMAP analysis tools, thus vesting the project's policy implementation with officials themselves. And the timing was fortuitous: the staff at one of these government bodies in Bangladesh was also involved in designing a national economic development plan, as well as the country's PRSP, and they drew on the MIMAP research in formulating these documents. Research had influence by careful attention to communicating with government officials, and by working to insert the research itself into the policy process.

These and other cases confirm that government interest in research is not in itself a guarantee of research influence. Where official interest is evident but implementation leadership is absent, the research team may need to cultivate leadership by cooperating with relevant decision makers, for example, providing training along with timely and relevant policy information.

Government Interest in Research, but with a Capacity Shortfall

Sometimes there is no dispute that a particular research subject is also an important policy matter. Government officials might even accept the wisdom of early decision and implementation in principle. In practice, however, action is forestalled by a lack of capacity, or because it has been trumped by other policy priorities. In this context, research participants should first of all be concerned with enhancing governmental research capacities and with promoting the issue up the priority list confronting the policymakers. It is generally premature to contemplate implementing research while the policy environment still displays an acute lack of capacity, or while the issue itself has not registered as an urgent priority within the policy community.

These conditions can be overcome, as demonstrated in our cases by the Environmental Management Development in Ukraine (EMDU) programme. The Dnipro River is widely recognized as critical to economic development in Ukraine. It has been described as the lifeblood of the country. Everyone also recognized that the Dnipro's severe pollution was a menacing problem. Local researchers had carried out research on water quality for years before the IDRC funded project was initiated. Even so, the research was chronically underfunded, and research technologies had fallen badly out of date. The new IDRC project moved to correct these deficiencies. It strongly advocated the use of advanced, low-cost water testing technologies, and laid out plans for bringing data and evidence to policy formulation on water management. Also, the project team worked with government officials on the use of evidence in decision making, inspiring a change of attitudes as well as managerial technique.

But building capacity was only part of the story. Significantly, researchers also worked on creating popular support for the project among the general public—support that tended to attract and hold policymakers' attention to the research. The synergies in the research project's strategy were obvious. The introduction of low-cost technologies, and more productive decision-making processes encouraged adoption and implementation, while public advocacy and education infused political energy into Dnipro pollution monitoring as a worthy political priority. Researchers can simultaneously remedy a capacity shortfall in government (making action easier), while promoting the political salience of an issue (making action more compelling).

A New or Emerging Issue Activates Research, but Leaves Policymakers Uninterested

This context is defined by a near complete indifference among the country's policymakers to an issue of new or rising importance to researchers. The issue simply fails to mobilize official scrutiny or political interest—and attracts little or no public attention. While individuals in the government might know of the issue or some of its significance, the subject may be contentious, or lack sponsoring support from a key political constituency.

Researchers seeking to influence policy in such circumstances need to pursue a three-part strategy. First, assemble and consolidate a strong research agenda by producing evidence-based policy advice worth heeding. Second, implement a coherent plan of advocacy that brings the research and its value to decision makers within the policy community. And third, energize popular interest in the issue, and in the policy approaches being proposed. All three parts of the strategy work together. Generating timely and policy relevant research advice, packaged in a form digestible by policymakers, is the essential first step to winning their notice. Effective advocacy serves to close the loop between information and decision. And public dissemination—especially among constituencies with direct interests in the issue, and who may exercise their own influence on policymakers—helps transform official indifference into attentive deliberation and action.

This last point is critical. Where government officials and political elites show no interest in a question that has activated researchers, the solution very often is to share research discoveries and policy prescriptions with a diverse public with a stake in the policy outcome. Ideally, communities are engaged in the research itself, almost from the start; as a result, community members understand the implications of the research, and stand ready to apply their own efforts in favour of government action.

As in other contexts, researchers struggling against the indifference of policymakers might need to contribute directly to capacity building to facilitate analysis and implementation. But the institutional issues here are usually less important than just getting the issue on the table. The potential for failure is high in this environment, but the risk is worth taking. Success can be achieved.

Much can be learned along those lines from what could be called the instructive failure of hard-pressed researchers in Guatemala. The overall objective in that project, supported by IDRC and a Mayan organization, was to support reforms in education financing with respect to indigenous peoples, especially girls. But at the time it was not the government's priority to focus on ethnic and gender differences in educational spending; the country was undergoing political and economic turmoil, recovering from a lengthy and divisive civil conflict, and government leaders were concentrating more on creating unity than on recognizing diversity and special needs. This was an essential condition for the research team to acknowledge. Without addressing this central political fact, the message from researchers seemed bound to fail; however strong their advocacy, however careful their timing, however meticulous they were in reaching the right policy people. The case is telling because it reveals the implacability of governmental indifference even to constructive advice and the cost of misreading the political surroundings when devising and conducting policy research.

Happier experiences emerge from more successful research enterprises. In India, the Society for Research and Initiatives for Sustainable Technologies and Institutions (SRISTI) has documented and circulated more than 10,000 grass-roots innovations and traditional practices in the Indian agricultural sector. But SRISTI has also created awareness among policymakers and institutionalized its activities through government structures. It accumulated convincing evidence, tailored its appeal to specific decision makers, and proactively created networking opportunities for government officials and project staff. Public authorities, once indifferent, became allies and advocates of SRISTI's work.

Similarly, researchers in coastal Peru (working in support of a local NGO, with IDRC funding), helped to create pressure on government authorities and private industries to initiate a large-scale environmental clean-up of damage caused by copper mine tailings. The NGO carried out research on the problems, built relationships with officials and members of the community, and generated wide publicity for their problems. They were also able to draw the interest of an international tribunal in the matter, resulting in a report condemning both the company responsible and the lax government enforcement of environmental laws. The lesson learnt again is: in the face of governmental indifference, strong research needs to be supplemented by concentrated advocacy in the policy community along with a lively mobilization of local and national public opinion.

Government Treats Research with Disinterest, or Hostility

Policymakers in this environment are actively resistant to hearing research advice, and may actually be hostile to the issue itself. Either research has reached policymakers long before they are ready to listen, or the politics of the moment militate against whatever research might have to offer. A research team in these conditions must exercise a robust sense of purpose and a clear recognition from the start that the project carries a low probability of policy influence. Still, sometimes the best to be hoped is that with time and fortitude researchers can outlast the political resistance and ultimately receive a friendlier hearing.

Peru again provides a good example—this time in a research project exploring the health effects of high altitude mining. There is a commonly held view that while high altitude living can be physically demanding, people adapt over time and that the adverse effects of any occupation are relatively the same at high and low altitudes. Contradicting this comforting belief, researchers here found that small-scale, artisanal mining high in Andean Peru harmed the health of miners and their families much more than at low altitudes. Peru's Ministry of

Health, like the mining industry, was unreceptive to these results. Furthermore, many in the mining communities shared the traditional belief about adaptation to high altitudes, so there was little opportunity, at least in the short-term, to rally public activism in support of a health protecting policy change. Any chance of early policy influence was subsequently hampered as Peru, with other South American countries, underwent major economic policy changes, including labour market liberalization, and the privatization of state-owned companies, all of which have tended to weaken the miners' union that was active on the issue.

Summary

Whether a development research project influences public policy depends decisively, but not only, on the context of its time and place. Influence is easiest to achieve where policymakers' receptivity to research is high and where their capacity to apply research is adequate. Where receptivity is minimal and adaptive capacity is weak, influence is much harder to achieve.

What the cases tell us, however, is more complicated than that and more hopeful. Indeed, two striking conclusions emerge from these case studies. The first conclusion is that research can make a difference in policy even where receptivity in the beginning appears unpromising. Researchers can maximize their influence in almost any circumstance by conducting their work, and communicating their results to decision makers and the public, according to a coherent and context-appropriate strategy. The second inescapable conclusion is that things change, both in research and in policymaking. Research projects can, and should, adapt to their changing surroundings. The policy context, meanwhile, often changes while the research is under way. In some cases, research itself seems to have changed policymakers' minds, thereby opening the policy community to the value of research, building trust between researchers and policymakers, and enhancing receptivity. Using the categories defined in this chapter, Table 3.1 presents the cases according to their contextual fit. It illustrates, in the first column, the conditions at the beginning of the intervention and in the second column the changes that occurred over the life of each case as the context evolved, whether through their influence or through other influences.

Notably, among the research projects studied here, few that started in a context of low or no receptivity ended in that same context. Most, like SRISTI in India and the copper mining case in coastal Peru, eventually spoke to the policy community in contexts of improved receptivity; a couple, like the high altitude mining project in Peru, did not.

Given these variabilities, receptivity categories cannot by themselves entirely explain the degree of influence that research ultimately exerts; there is no perfect linear relationship between receptivity and influence. To understand the research to policy dynamic more fully, and more usefully, it is worth exploring some other key factors at play, both in the context of policy, and in the conduct and communication of research. This is the objective in Chapter 4.

Table 3.1: Analysis of 23 Case Studies by Context and over Time

Context	Beginning of Project	End of Project
1. Clear government demand	MIMAP[1]-Senegal Nepal ICTs[2] Economic Reform-Vietnam Acacia[3]-South Africa Acacia-Mozambique Acacia-Uganda Acacia-Senegal	MIMAP-Senegal Nepal ICTs Economic Reform-Vietnam Acacia-South Africa Acacia-Mozambique Acacia-Uganda Acacia Senegal AFSSRN[4] SRISTI[5]
2. Government interest in research, but leadership absent	TEHIP,[6] Tanzania MIMAP-Bangladesh MIMAP-Philippines LATN[7] G-24[8]	TEHIP, Tanzania MIMAP-Bangladesh MIMAP-Philippines LATN G-24 (24 countries) Copper mining, Peru Greywater reuse, Jordan
3. Government interest in research, but with a capacity shortfall	Environmental management, Ukraine	Environmental management, Ukraine Arsaal, Lebanon?[9] (local)
4. A new or emerging issue activates research, but leaves policy-makers uninterested	High-altitude mining, Peru Copper mining, Peru ECAPAPA[10] Arsaal, Lebanon AFSSRN SRISTI Greywater reuse, Jordan Financing Education Reform Water Demand Management, Tunisia	
5. Government treats research with disinterest, or hostility	Brackish water irrigation, Syria	Brackish water irrigation, Syria Arsaal, Lebanon (national) Financing Education Reform Water Demand Management, Tunisia ECAPAPA High-altitude mining, Peru

Notes:
1. MIMAP: Micro Impacts of Macroeconomic and Adjustment Policies
2. ICT: Information and Communication Technology
3. Acacia: A series of Information and Communication Technology for Development programmes
4. AFSSRN: Asian Fisheries Social Science Research Network
5. SRISTI: Society for Research and Initiatives for Sustainable Technologies and Institutions
6. TEHIP: Tanzania Essential Health Interventions Project
7. LATN: Latin American Trade Network
8. G-24: The Group of 24 developing countries designated by the larger Group of 77 developing countries to represent them on international financial reform issues
9. Arsaal: Project for sustainable improvement of marginal land in Arsaal, Lebanon
10. ECAPAPA: Eastern and Central Africa Programme for Agricultural Policy Analysis

Managing Research, Exploiting Contingencies

4

Development research is customarily carried out in conditions of hardship, scarcity, and sometimes personal danger. The logic of that reality is embedded in the purpose of the research itself; research undertaken to improve the economic, social, and political conditions prevailing in developing countries. Yet even in these inhospitable circumstances, it is possible to produce research that influences policy and action. If the design, conduct, and communication of research all meet the demands of the policy/political context, it can genuinely improve lives and livelihoods while promoting sustainable and democratic development.

The dynamic interaction of development research with its policy/political context was described in Chapter 3, and various strategic approaches to research were suggested. What follows here is practical detail, an array of experience-tested recommendations for producing research that can have effect.

Any such recommendations must begin with the re-emphasis of a simple-sounding observation: managing research in a developing country is usually hard. Assembling needed facilities and equipment in the midst of shortages; overcoming funding uncertainties and disappointments; recruiting, training, and retaining talented staff—all these and innumerable other difficulties inevitably confront the development research manager.

Retaining skilled and energetic research staff proves to be a remarkably common challenge. In more than a few of the IDRC supported projects, self-confidence, ambition, and marketable skills acquired in those same projects, led to considerable staff turnover. No magic solutions present themselves; the usual preventives against excessive turnover include careful recruitment followed by the standard incentives and rewards for continued productive contributions to the research enterprise. But one other finding gives added encouragement. Even in projects with high turnover, SRISTI and the Jordan greywater projects among them, continuity at leadership levels enabled successful policy influence despite staff changes at other levels. Much can be accomplished when research team management remains intact.

Along with assiduous internal management of the research itself, three critical operational recommendations emerge from the cases. First, establish the project's explicit intent to influence policy and action. Second, create and sustain strong networks for research collaboration and policy advocacy. And third, devise and execute a coherent programme of communication and

Box 4.1: Saving Water and Improving Policy in Jordan

Throughout the Middle East and North Africa, as in many other regions, freshwater scarcities threaten the security of urban and rural poor people. The crisis is felt severely in Jordan, where rapid urbanization exposes millions to water shortages and uncertain food supplies. An important part of the remedy will be more productive urban agriculture, using more recycled greywater. This objective inspired a remarkable set of Jordanian research projects.

Greywater—left over from showers, baths and sinks—constitutes an under-used but potentially significant water resource. It can prove particularly valuable for irrigating city gardens, a crucial source of food and income for developing country families. In Jordan, a series of IDRC-supported projects—each building on the others—demonstrated the value of greywater, and led to policy changes aimed at fostering wider greywater use.

The first study focused on data gathering in Amman. Among other things, it found that one in six households worked at urban agriculture, that 40 per cent were using untreated greywater, and that urban farming was entirely unregulated.

A second project, with Palestinians in the West Bank, tested an improved design for a small, cheap greywater filter made from recycled plastic bottles. This project also addressed cultural and religious concerns about the use of wastewater, engaging local sheiks to advise the community on the advantages of using greywater.

In a third project, CARE Australia helped explore methods of soil and water conservation in southern Jordan. An IDRC funded evaluation showed how the project raised family incomes and encouraged community cooperation and conservation.

A fourth project, conducted in Tafila, served to increase greywater recovery while making it easier and safer to handle. It stimulated the production of environment-friendly soaps. It demonstrated the promise of more efficient irrigation and greywater tolerant crops. And it promoted policy changes to advance wider public acceptance of greywater recycling.

The projects together achieved influence partly because authorities recognized Jordan's water crisis and welcomed research-based solutions. But the projects displayed other key attributes. Among them: strong networking and communications among researchers, policymakers, donors, NGOs and householders; the credibility of participants; and strategic leadership applying lessons learned in sequential projects. All these qualities contributed to research that influenced local action and national policy.

dissemination, systematically introducing research into the policy process. Let us consider each of these recommendations in turn.

Establishing Intent to Influence

Generally speaking, a development research project is more likely to influence policy and action if the intent to influence is expressly included among its original objectives. Intent here is not merely a state of mind, although a shared sense of mission can animate a lengthy project and give it direction. More than that, intent is method. Intent informs the early research questions. It helps decide the pace and conduct of investigation or experiment. Crucially, it frames the content and vocabulary chosen for reporting research results to the policy community and to the public. And as important as any other consideration, intent to influence imparts purpose to the work of cultivating lasting relationships between researchers and policymakers.

Much of this might strike some as self-evident. As a category of applied research, development research seems intrinsically undertaken to affect public policy and somehow inspire action by governments or others. It may be so. But frequently a disconnection occurs between the way researchers think about research and how they think about policy. Too often, influence is a late-stage add-on to the research project. For best effect, it should form part of the research design from the start.

By way of example, LATN—the Latin American Trade Network was created in 1998 as a regional research apparatus expressly mandated to help Latin American countries respond to global economic issues and engage in trade negotiations. Intent to influence defined its mission from the beginning and thereby gave direction to its operations over the years. Its continuing, pragmatic focus has been to deliver policy relevant research that meets the needs of the region's decision makers.

LATN's successes bear out the experience of others in another respect as well. Influence runs far deeper than just affecting a particular policy or programme. It has the long run effects of expanding policymaking capacities in government; broadening policy horizons with new questions and new answers; and improving policy regimes by strengthening the procedures of deliberation, decision, and policy execution. Establishing intent to influence as an explicit part of the research strategy requires an investment in these long-lasting interactions of research with policy.

One further point about influence is that declaring intent is always better late than never. In Southeast Asia, IDRC undertook a long-term commitment of support to the Asian Fisheries Social Science Research Network (AFSSRN). Confronting combined threats of overfishing and environmental degradation, AFSSRN's early mission was to reinforce the region's capacity to explore, especially the economic and social dimensions of coastal fisheries. It took several years before the network concentrated its focus more sharply on generating explicit policy advice, years in which AFSSRN researchers developed their collective skills and reputation. As their own research capacities grew, they applied their proven competence with new and explicit intent to influence policy. In turn, public policy and local practice have been improved.

Creating Networks for Research and Policy

AFSSRN, LATN, and many other collaborations have proven the diverse and sometimes surprising rewards of organizing research in networks of shared purpose. Networks can redress the afflictions common to research throughout the developing world—not just the usual shortages of money and facilities, but the isolation and distance often felt by poor country researchers alone in their work. The benevolent multiplier effects of networks can be dramatic in their pooling of resources, experiences, and discoveries. In a research universe too readily dominated by North to South flows of knowledge and influence, networks empower Southerners to create and share their own knowledge and influence in cooperation between researchers and policymakers.

The most effective networks are the ones that map out their own strategies for influence early on. They make policy influence an explicit part of their programme. They try to ensure that all stakeholders actively engage in the network's activities. They consult widely with policymakers and others in setting the evolving research agenda. They carefully heed the changing needs of policymakers. And they invest in the undeniably long work of cooperatively pursuing a common cause.

LATN, the network of Latin American trade policy researchers, has displayed many of these qualities: an early and express policy orientation, wide-ranging enlistment and engagement of researcher participants, and patient persistence in building research to policy relationships. LATN, like the social scientists in AFSSRN, also showed another significant, though unexpected, trait of successful networks—a fluid mobility of personnel between the research and the policy communities. In Latin America, Asia, and Africa, a number of accomplished researchers have migrated into the policymaking community, while seasoned government officials have enjoyed sojourns into research and analysis. Naturally enough, these career convergences greatly enhance working relationships between researchers and policymakers; more than occasionally the researcher and the policymaker is one and the same person. Network collaborations multiply the opportunities for these interactions transnationally.

Communicating with Policymakers and the Public

One might as well be frank about this. Researchers in the main are uncomfortable communicating with officials and politicians in the policy community. Scientists and scholars recoil at the mention of cultivating extended relationships in the turbulence, confusions, and reversals of governmental bureaucracy and politics. And they despair at the prospect of simplifying and compressing the complexities of their own research to catch the distracted attention of decision makers.

The misgivings are normal and misplaced. Development research is more than discovering fresh answers to clever questions. Development researchers are increasingly expected to formulate, assemble, and articulate the meaning and policy implications of their work to the policy community and to the public. As one exasperated researcher lamented at a conference on these matters, researchers now are supposed to 'be like Erin Brokovich [or at least like Julia Roberts]. . . . You have to have the legs, the looks, . . . you have to do the research . . . dissemination work, strategy work, publication work. . . . Come on, I'm a researcher.'

Legs, no; strategy, yes. Repeating for emphasis: Influence demands communication. And communication is best understood as a long-term process of building trust and confidence between researchers and policymakers, punctuated by just-in-time deliveries of information or advice that helps decision makers decide. All of this takes patience and organized effort.

Imagine a development research project planned to last five years. The communication strategy should start in Year One. First steps might include informal conversations or half-hour introductory briefings with mid-level government officials. (Middle ranks can be more stable than politically exposed higher echelons in government bureaucracies; your contacts now are more likely to be still in government five years from now.) Early communications should probably also include interested constituencies outside the national government, in business associations, farm and labour organizations, professional societies, and the like. Depending on the research subject, policy people in other levels of government should be engaged, whether in provincial legislatures or city councils.

Some of the most influential communications can occur with ordinary women and men in their own homes and communities. To enquire about health or education or affordable Internet access, ask the experts—the families living inside these questions. These are the people whose cooperation or resistance might well determine the effectiveness of a later policy; mutual education between researchers and communities can foster understanding of the impending policy decision and support for its implementation.

As the research proceeds and results start to accumulate, communication with policymakers can become more specific and timelier. By now vocabulary and format assume importance. Usually, policymakers will show little curiosity about the original research questions and still less about theory and methodologies that properly concern research professionals. Instead, policymakers will be grateful for clearly and concisely stated answers to the questions that concern them in their own work.

Timing is everything or almost everything. Policymakers will spend endless months ignoring researchers utterly and then insist on instant answers. Researchers intending to influence policy will spend those months readying their case, never certain when opportunity will knock. As Louis Pasteur famously said of research and chance, 'fortune favours the prepared mind'.

Policymakers inhabit a community of confounding dilemmas. They seldom thank researchers for complicating a policy problem with more mysteries and contradictions. What policymakers most often want is unambiguous, quickly understood information that contributes to a decision. This does not mean researchers should overstate their confidence in a policy solution, however, it does mean researchers should straightforwardly say what they know, and explain if asked, what they do not know. Researchers can make room in their advice for insight and informed intuition, but they must also make it clear where the facts give way to probability and prediction. Rarely will a researcher produce the complete solution to the problem of the day. And sometimes policymakers are helped simply by a reassurance that they are not alone—that nobody else knows what they do not know. This kind of timely, concise, candid communication builds trust and influence.

Exploiting Contingencies

Project management, explicit intent, building networks, communication—these fall within the power of researchers and their colleagues to arrange. Other factors—attributes mainly of the policy/political setting—lie outside the direct control of research managers. Call them system contingencies, the institutional or political variables to which, in any context, researchers should fine-tune their strategies for bringing knowledge to policy. Five of these system contingencies deserve special mention.

Stability of decision-making institutions

Achieving policy influence for development research usually means two things: making personal connections with policymakers, and entrenching the research itself in the institutional memory of the policy community. Where policymakers come and go rapidly and unpredictably, and where institutional memory fails, influence is impaired. These are not uncommon contingencies in developing countries.

In IDRC's Guatemalan education case, research influence was impeded when far-reaching structural changes moved decision-making powers away from the executive and into the legislative branch of government. Unprepared for these institutional instabilities, researchers found themselves unable to lobby legislators effectively; influence suffered as a result. In the high altitude mining project in Peru, budget cuts led to the elimination of a government institution dealing with occupational health issues, removing what could have been a valuable institutional ally in converting research into policy reform. The research produced findings, but the absence of a receptive government agency combined with an unhelpful turn in overall government policy direction, blocked implementation of those findings in policy or action.

The river pollution project in Ukraine was similarly challenged by institutional instability. But in this case, researchers largely overcame the challenges by addressing their research-based messages to a wider public through television programmes, for example. They moreover identified a particularly stable government structure, the presidency, for special attention. Mobilizing public opinion and focusing on the most stable decision-making institutions of government, can give some protection against the hazards and harms of institutional instability.

Another strategy, as noted earlier, is to work with the middle levels of the government bureaucracy where institutional memory is often strongest and staff turnover less damaging. Members of the LATN trade policy network successfully used this approach. Still another strategy is to search out more stable decision-making bodies in subnational governing structures, a point to be addressed below. A village council, a state government, or a district school board sometimes makes the best partner for putting research into practice.

Capacity of policymakers to apply research

In many developing countries, weak government capacity is practically a definition of the national development problem. Without capacity to create conditions in which economic and social change can flourish, it often seems that little else can happen to advance development progress. Weak capacity to absorb and implement research is a common and chronic contingency faced by researchers.

But researchers have remedies. In the LATN case, government officials at first were unfamiliar with some basic concepts of trade negotiations. LATN researchers in response devoted more of their time than planned to educate public officials. Likewise, when the Group of 24 developing country governments set up a Technical Support Service to conduct research on urgent global economic questions, it did not necessarily mean G-24 ministers and officials were equipped to act on the research results. In fact, researchers found ministers initially sceptical of the econometrics generated by the research and wary of adopting any measure that might displease the World Bank or the International Monetary Fund. In such contingencies, research teams should plan and invest in the time needed to build policymaking capacity through training and advocacy. It is unwise to presume that busy officials and ministers will immediately understand the assumptions or language or statistics of research conclusions.

More often than not, the time will come in bringing research to policy when the attentive researcher becomes teacher to a policymaker pupil.

Decentralization, or tight central control?

Whether a country's policymaking is institutionally decentralized or not, on the evidence, seems to have little bearing on whether research influences policy. What matters much more is aligning any project's plan for influence with the real world structures of political decision-making. This starts with a reading of the country's constitution; if health policy is made by provincial or regional authorities, they are the natural audience for health research findings. But contingencies of decentralization rarely end with the black letter law of a constitution. To maximize the influence of research, researchers need to understand informal and unwritten policymaking practice, and sort out the distributions of power that policymakers are trying to achieve.

When MIMAP researchers in the Philippines assembled their poverty monitoring systems, their plan was successfully instituted in the province of Palawan, where they began. Later it was implemented across a second province, Bulacan. As poverty monitoring and alleviation were decentralized responsibilities in the Philippines, it required considerable effort and time to achieve nationwide adoption of MIMAP policy approaches.

In Tanzania's TEHIP project, the central government was interested in promoting decentralized decision-making by health workers at the district and local levels. The pilot project—assessing health needs by talking to people in their households—helped to guide the decentralization programme from one district to another.

As in TEHIP, many of IDRC's ICT projects have also reflected a central government's own objective of decentralizing regulation and facilitation of information and communication technologies. In city markets and village schoolrooms, in farmers' fields and in fishing boats, appropriate and decentralized approaches have democratized ICT innovation and transformed livelihoods. But researchers have had to understand the decentralizing forces and purposes at work.

Tight centralized control over national policymaking can work for or against research influence, depending on the research. Political centralization tends to encourage the national level policy effects of research when the research contributes to national interests as perceived by the central authorities. In Vietnam, economic research was avidly consumed by the government as it strove to introduce market-based economic reforms. The subject of the research and the thrust of its results, was already of interest to the (centralized) policy community. As a contrary case, in Syria—where policymaking was resolutely centralized—research on irrigation was never utilized, in large part because irrigation itself was not a priority of the government.

In sum, research projects carry a better probability of exercising influence when the intended level of influence corresponds to the country's decision-making structures. If the project aims to have a national effect in a system where those decisions are made locally, initial outcomes are likely to disappoint. What is the solution? When designing a development research project, it is best to explore structures and processes of policymaking in the relevant subject matter, chart degrees and directions of centralization–decentralization, and align project execution and reporting to fit those policymaking realities.

Special opportunities of countries in transition

As suggested in earlier chapters, countries undergoing political, economic, and social transition can open unique opportunities for research to influence public policy and action. Policymakers in these conditions are alive to unorthodox thought and innovation; young institutions in formative phases are flexible and public opinion often welcomes anti-conventional propositions. Systems in transition alter not only the contents of policies but the procedures of governance. Research can influence both the policy and the rules for debating and determining the policy.

Researchers supported by IDRC have exerted their influence in exactly these contingencies, from Ukraine to South Africa, to Vietnam. In Ukraine, research informed new procedures for transparent and accountable environmental management in the context of changing governance. Research in South Africa prepared the ground for post-apartheid social and economic change and supported the country's first majority government. In Vietnam, research informed and reinforced economic reform. Transitions are not gentle settings for research; upheavals and setbacks are endemic. But patient and opportunistic research can have sudden and enduring influence on the course of events.

Economic crisis and pressures on government

Economic crisis or intensifying economic pressures on policymakers often represent a promising contingency for researchers looking to influence policy. In most of the cases where governmental receptivity to research was highest, government leaders were responding to some economic imperative. MIMAP projects appeared to succeed because governments were under pressure from international lenders to produce a PRSP. Vietnamese officials and politicians needed to attract foreign donors, and satisfy potential partners in trade agreements by introducing credible policy reforms. Many governments have invited research guidance for regulating and encouraging ICTs for development. The evidence altogether supports the simple dictum that research influence is strongest when it plainly answers the country's economic needs as felt by its government. (This rule applies even where the research itself is not chiefly about economics. Research into health services can capture official attention, for instance, where it promises more efficient allocations within straitened health care budgets.) Where economic need is not a pressing priority, researchers will probably have to undertake a more elaborate programme of education and persuasion among decision makers and the public at large.

These five system contingencies in some sense complete the array of receptivity contexts set out in Chapters 2 and 3. The lesson of experience is that in any general context the particular system contingencies of policy and politics will colour the prospects and strategies for achieving policy influence.

Over time, however, receptivity and system contingencies move, merge, and evolve, partly as a result of research discovery and advocacy. For the research community, making the most of these transformations will call for both agility and tenacity. This is the subject of the chapter to follow.

Research and the Politics of Policy

5

As our cases illustrate, policy processes are seldom straightforward. The structures, procedures, and personalities engaged in political decision and governmental action all define the setting in which research can influence policy. Moreover, settings change. The twofold implication for research strategy is inescapable. First, getting research into policy means directing research knowledge specifically to those in the policy process who are best placed to adopt and apply that knowledge. Second, influencing policy will call for agile adaptation by researchers when the policy setting changes. Poverty researchers in Bangladesh dealt directly with senior officials in the bureaucracy; these officials had the power to execute policy, and the research team lacked strong affiliations lower in the government hierarchy. In Latin America, by contrast, trade policy researchers cultivated relationships with mid-level civil service professionals because their ranks remained stable while politically appointed superiors tended to change with every change of government. Setting determines who exactly researchers should try to influence and how that influence should be attempted.

Nor should research to policy strategies assume any linear logic in the ordinary course of policymaking. On the contrary, policy decisions over time generally display a complicated pattern of advances and reversals tied together in feedback loops of decision, implementation, second thoughts, and course corrections. New issues arise, decisions are taken and tested, and the issues shift (in part, by not only, as a result of the preceding decisions).

All of this suggests that researchers intending to influence policy have to anticipate, educate, and inform policy decisions and policymakers, more or less continuously. In Senegal, for example, poverty reduction researchers set up workshops for political leaders, including those in the opposition, to discuss economic developments before they emerged on the political agenda. They brought novel policy approaches to the policy people to educate them in advance of decisions, and they established their own credibility as helpful interveners so policymakers would seek out their advice when the moment arrived for a policy decision.

The only cases where policy influence seemed to occur as a one-off event were in the domain of ICT. In Nepal, a small project costing under $100,000, was quickly instrumental in the designing of a telecom policy for the country. But even here appearances can deceive. Although policymakers did turn to researchers for guidance on a particular policy question, the researchers and their research programme were already well known to the policy community, and they enjoyed a solid reputation. Once a decision was made to request policy advice (a relatively easy move when the subject is new), enlisting the help of familiar advisers would have seemed natural and risk free. Again, influence normally grows out of long-standing relationships.

Besides these matters of context, experience demonstrates that the probability of influencing policy is improved by the adroit management of three other critical factors: partnerships and networks, communication, and time. Each of these factors is discussed in detail.

Partnerships and Networks

The arguments for investing in development research partnerships and networks are by now well known, but they are no less valid for that. In many and different places, partnerships and networks have captured significant economies of scale, assembled diversities of knowledge and insight, mobilized public opinion and energy, and achieved influence with policymakers. Research by its nature is almost always a collaborative effort. Partnerships and networks help to organize these collaborations in shared undertakings of discovery and change. The distinction between partnerships and networks eludes any hard and fast rule. A network is an organizational form; a partnership, operational or strategic, gives expression to a cooperative plan or intention.

Building and maintaining research partnerships and networks will never be effortless, or free. They require commitment of resources, including time. And success demands a certain strategic coherence—a plan of action, membership, and purpose reflecting both the available resources, and the surrounding political-economic circumstances. With these elements in place, partnerships and networks have served to alter public policy and advance development.

International Development Research Centre's (IDRC) evaluation has identified four operational considerations especially important in determining whether a partnership or network exercises real influence on policy.

The first determining factor is the deployment of adequate skills and resources in all aspects of the research enterprise, including public advocacy and governmental engagement. Policy influence is frequently more effective when researchers themselves carry out the work of advocacy and engagement with policymakers. The SRISTI project in India presents a persuasive model in which network members were personally and extensively involved in village-level consultations and governmental lobbying. In the copper mining case in Peru, the fact-finding and advocacy group, LABOR (Asosiación Civil Labor, http://www.labor. org.pe/info.php?id_seccion=1), applied its experience to galvanize international opinion, generate publicity, and induce policy change by the government.

The second consideration is the readiness of the project participants to form partnerships directly with decision makers. From economic research in Vietnam to ICT policymaking in Mozambique, progress was achieved when networks brought both researchers and policymakers to the same table, with the same objectives. In fact, these partnerships are often instigated first by the policy side, always a promising sign that policy is open to influence from good research.

Box 5.1: Building Negotiating Strength in Latin America

Developing countries typically suffer a chronic and damaging disadvantage when they try to bargain with the industrialized countries in trade negotiations. Whereas rich-country governments are endowed with well-informed policy ministries and independent think tanks, poor-country governments come to the table without any of these resources. As a result, they are commonly sidelined from the most complex of these negotiations—unable to take a full part in shaping agreements, but subject to their effects for years to come. As the reach of trade negotiations grows more comprehensive and intrusive (affecting labour and environmental practices, tax law, competition policy, and much else besides), lack of capacity for policy analysis grows all the more harmful.

That generally was the experience of Latin American countries in the long Uruguay Round of global trade negotiations that culminated in 1994. And it was that experience that led to the creation in 1998 of the LATN.

With IDRC's support, LATN set out with a three-part mission: to inform policy formulation on emerging trade issues from a Latin American standpoint; to mobilize research capacity for engagement in trade negotiations; and to strengthen regional institutional collaboration in pursuit of these long-term goals.

LATN eventually assembled about 35 researchers from more than 30 academic institutions, along with policy officials and colleagues in international NGOs, academic institutions, and intergovernmental organizations. Their studies tend to fall into three categories: issues of coalition-building and bargaining strategies in multi-party negotiations; substantive studies of emerging subjects; and country-specific studies identifying best outcomes for individual governments.

The aim overall has been to deliver timely, policy-relevant research to decision makers, in government as well as in the private sector. Subject-matter emphases have changed over time, as issues arise and recede. And middle-level bureaucrats are often the most productive audience for LATN's advice, because they preserve continuity better than the political ranks of ministers and their top-most deputies.

Evaluation shows LATN has achieved policy influence—strengthening institutional policymaking and negotiating capacity, educating the policy community, and opening decision regimes to more transparent, participatory procedures. In consequence, governments have entered negotiations better informed about Latin American interests, and better prepared to advance their own development priorities.

This leads to the third factor, that is membership and questions about who should be recruited into a partnership or network. Here the calculations can become tricky. Over time, it is generally good strategy to enlist all those with a stake in the issue to participate in the research and in the policy design and implementation. It is always sensible, at some point, to attract support from anyone who has the power to block a research to policy project. It can also be advantageous to include policymakers themselves in a research-centred partnership or network, although it is rare for decision makers in positions of authority to take part throughout. Harder questions arise when it comes to judging when, and how, these various actors should be brought into the partnership or network. In some situations—tobacco control programmes and conflict resolution, to name two—the right sequencing of recruitment and participation is crucial. IDRC has found over the years that research itself can contribute to dispute settling accommodations; new evidence can dissolve old prejudices, build trust, and break zero-sum deadlocks. This is why it is worthwhile to engage many participants in a research to policy partnership, not just the like-minded. In due course, all stakeholders should be included, but not necessarily all at once.

The fourth factor is about creating a common vision among disparate partners, and co-ordinating separate efforts with common goals. This is not easy. But it is essential for achieving the enormous multiplier effects of the best partnerships and networks—effects that could not be produced by any of the partners acting alone. Researchers commonly doubt their own abilities to inspire and sustain a common sense of purpose and zeal to proceed. It is often wise to recruit network partners with precisely those talents of attraction and inspiration.

Communication

One way or another, if research is to influence policy, the people who make and execute policy need to know about the research. This takes communication between researchers and policymakers. At its best, communication starts early in the research, designed into the research plan, and carried out as the project unfolds. Sometimes policymakers are personally engaged in planning and conducting the research, perhaps as participants in an informal partnership, or formally organized network. In Tanzania's research on health service delivery, government officials were involved from the beginning. More often, researchers report to policymakers, and others, as research yields results.

Dissemination of the implications and lessons of research occurs through two kinds of channels: in the exchange of information, and in the interchange of people between research and policy assignments. Information exchange includes anything from a policy brief for ministers to a nationally broadcast television programme. The interchange of researchers and policymakers describes what happens in the intermingling of the research and the policy communities. Both can have a powerful effect in bringing research into policy and action.

Information exchange embraces all the well tried approaches to inform policymakers: workshops, conferences, policy papers, reports in specialized or mass media, and personal contacts between researchers and policymakers. But even if these techniques look obvious, they are not always exploited successfully. Attention to key variables greatly improves the chances of achieving policy influence.

First, information needs to flow both ways. Important as it is for researchers to speak to policymakers, it is just as important for researchers to listen. This is the dialogue in which attentive researchers hear policymakers' question in their own words, and discern whether policymakers are absorbing the research advice that researchers are presenting. Understanding the policy problem as the policymaker sees it, then crafting a research-based answer in similar terms, speeds communication and influence.

Second, communication needs to be continuous. One-shot briefs or workshops will have little lasting impact, especially where turnover in government offices runs high. This is one reason why communication belongs in the research strategy throughout the life of the project. Long-term communication counts among the most valuable functions of research networks, particularly those that include policymakers in their membership.

Third, communication needs to be economical. Short papers, going straight to the policy issue, are more likely to be read and remembered than long demonstrations of scholarly learning. Experience shows that this is a hard truth for researchers to put into practice. But it is a truth.Busy policymakers, especially those in authority, have no time for elegant abstractions or richly detailed histories. A few routine workshops connecting policy people and researchers; timely reports of work in progress; occasional meetings to reflect on upcoming developments or mobile priorities—all these have proven useful in facilitating research-based policymaking.

Interchange of people between research and policy jobs comprise the second channel of communicating research to policy. In a striking number of cases, this happens when research project members move directly into government offices, where they share research knowledge with colleagues, and promote the application of research in policy decision and implementation. One member of the Asian fisheries research network eventually assumed leadership of a large bureau of agricultural research in the Philippines; a project leader in Syria was appointed minister of agriculture after the project ended. Other examples abound.

Dissemination through people can also occur when those who hold important societal positions become involved in research. In India's SRISTI case, the reputation of the project's principal researcher allowed him to excite the interest of senior government officials in the project's exploration of indigenous knowledge. A nationally known informatics scholar in Mozambique was able to interest government officials in the potential for ICT development. Well-earned prominence eases the transformation of research into policy.

Finally, personal interchange happens when researchers form their own alliances inside government, or with people who have influence inside government. In Jordan, researchers in greywater recycling projects developed relationships with officials in the Bureau of Statistics. When these officials realized they shared goals with the project, they posted project activities on their website, thereby distributing project outputs to other parts of the government, and enhancing the standing of the project itself. In Vietnam, the head of the country's premier research institution, who held membership in several decision-making bodies, is credited with popularizing the project's findings and promoting their implementation.

Such cases make another enduring point about researchers and policymakers: ultimately, they do not always constitute two separate communities. Rather, they are more often people occupying different roles at different times, with complementary needs and interests. This is true in rich countries; it might be even truer in many developing countries where research and policy communities must share the same limited number of highly qualified profes-sionals. When notions and expectations of division between research and policy are set aside, cooperation between researchers and policymakers can find its full potential.

Who's Listening?

Policymakers need not always be the sole or primary audience for communication of researchers. Other influential audiences can include NGOs; research institutions; university scholars; business, labour and farm organizations; local or regional authorities; and community leaders. As more than one case has shown, activating public opinion can help attract and hold the interest of politicians and senior government officials. (And this bears repeating: The best outcome of research is sometimes to inform and change the working lives of men and women in their own communities, irrespective of any formal governmental response.)

In any case, communication by researchers seems to pay off best when project managers identify specific audiences at the outset, and sustain a communication strategy during the whole project. Strong dissemination practice cannot guarantee influence; events and context can defeat even the best of communication strategies. But where conditions allow for any chance of success, communication well planned and executed can radically improve the prospects for influencing policy.

Time and Timing

It is obviously easier to influence policy when the research coincides with a governmental interest in the research subject. In Africa, as in Nepal, ICT policy research was undertaken, and it produced results at a time when governments were recognizing they had an ICT policy problem that needed solving. In other cases, policymakers developed an appetite for research-based advice when the research had already progressed for several years—a reminder that researchers should always be ready for the policymaker's sudden call for help.

But the passage of time itself can serve to strengthen researchers' capacity to inform policy decisions. Persistence is often repaid as researchers gradually increase their own understanding of a policy issue, and build their confidence and credibility as reliable experts in the subject. In the LATN, and in the AFSSRN, years of knowledge gathering built capacity and reputation for giving useful advice.

Time and patience can also permit the playing out of a supply and demand dynamic between research and policy. The supply side represents the more conventional approach to development research: design the project, do the research, analyze the findings, publish and circulate the results. The demand side approach starts with the policymakers asking for advice, eliciting a quick analysis and response from researchers, and moving on to the next problem. Each approach carries advantages and drawbacks. The supply side looks more to long-term outcomes and capacity building, but can miss transitory opportunities to exert real influence on policy. Focusing on the demand side can score some quick hits with policymakers, but risks trapping researchers in a confining cycle of short-term outputs with little growth of lasting capacity. With time and patience, researchers and policymakers can reach a mutually supportive equilibrium between these two sets of pressures, generating timely guidance from research while enlarging research capacity for the long run.

Donor Performance: Persistence, Opportunism, and Other Virtues

Supporting timely research, and staying for the long run will inevitably test the resilience of donor organizations. IDRC's experience in the field proves the value of a multi-year commitment to underwriting a sound research project. IDRC's support for the Asian fisheries research network lasted 14 years; support for G-24 policy research lasted 15 years. These and other endeavours were designed from the start as long investments in capacity building.

This sort of durable donor support can be decisively important in fostering the legitimacy and credibility of a research team, building its confidence, and facilitating uptake of research results by policymakers. But a long-run strategy imposes stresses of its own.

For one thing, donors need to exercise a determined modesty in their offers of support and the direction they give. Indeed, the more significant the donor's support is in the scheme of the research programme, the more modest it must be in prescribing policy research priorities. As outsiders, donors need to support relevant research without interfering in a country's own policy agenda. Sustainable development research, like sustainable development, must be decided by the people of the developing country itself.

For another thing, the desirable agility of a donor agency to respond quickly to new research opportunities and simultaneously promise support for the long term, operates in tension with the ordinary funding cycles that usually govern the donor's own budget. Parliaments and congresses typically authorize funding to national and international agencies one year at a time; they properly insist on accountability to tax payers for the plans made, and the money spent by agencies supporting research. But development research hardly ever falls neatly into these yearly budget calendars. Seizing sudden project opportunities means quickly moving funds between accounts; pledging stable funding for years into the future imposes commitments on future legislators and future governments. These frictions of time and timing need to be expected, and managed, if research is to meet short-term demands from policymakers while supplying long-term knowledge for sustainable development. As always, getting research into policy will demand powers of manoeuvre, invention, and tenacity.

IDRC's own experience as a research donor and advocate displays many of the rewards and difficulties typical of both short-term, project specific support, and longer running knowledge building commitments. With the right strategies, and good timing, either approach can work to influence policy.

How IDRC manages its own participation in any research enterprise has proven to be a critical factor in determining success. Quality of donor management inevitably includes staff stability; IDRC's contribution to a project is degraded, communication with project managers is disrupted, and chances for influencing policy are diminished, when IDRC's staff turnover is high. Management quality also includes the expertise of IDRC personnel; strong IDRC familiarity with the research subject and methods usually helped a project's own researchers to pursue their work and enter the policy discourse. And management quality is demonstrably a matter of patience; steadfast, long-term support from IDRC has reinforced research programmes with reliable resources, capacity to exploit opportunities that have arisen, and time to build sustainable capacity for influential research. In short, high quality donor management contributes to both research and influence. Deficiencies in donor management inhibit research and influence.

Usually, projects funded by IDRC as part of a longer overall strategy, or in partnership with other donors, enjoy a better likelihood of influencing policy than a one-off project. But jumping at an unexpected project opportunity with a well prepared intervention can also pay dividends. Again we see the importance of both persistence and opportunism. Donors in development research need to practise a mix of reliability and flexibility.

The distinctive advantages of opportunism and persistent, long-term support can sometimes combine with excellent effect. In the Jordan greywater case, an IDRC programme officer adroitly helped existing partnerships to conduct a series of projects in sequence—together creating a critical mass of information on water management that captured the attention of policymakers. Similarly, related ICT research projects in Uganda and Mozambique together enhanced the potential for policy influence in both countries.

Whether donor support is geared to a discrete, fixed-term project or a longer strategic partnership, what is lamentably true is that, donor bureaucracy and funding delays can harm results. In at least a couple of cases, delays in IDRC disbursements were judged to have hurt chances for policy influence despite early potential. In the case of ECAPAPA, late funding by IDRC hampered efforts to disseminate research findings to policymakers. In that same case, and in Guatemala, slow IDRC disbursements probably contributed to staff losses in the projects themselves. Researchers in developing countries are often in short supply; when faced with competing demands and offers, they tend to spend their scarce time on the projects that render prompt and regular payment.

But donor performance is not just about the money. Donors can bring specialist knowledge, credibility, and connections to a research project; all of which can strengthen the research and the policy influence it achieves. Specialist knowledge, deployed by donors with tact and judgement, can extend from subject matter expertise through research methods and operations to interactions with the policy community. In IDRC experience there is often a South to South learning effect, with lessons from one developing country or region, applied with IDRC's intermediary help, to another in like circumstances. A donor's credibility counts as well. Credibility opens doors in the corridors of policymaking, engages support from other donor agencies, and attracts academic interest and contributions. Nor should the worth of connections be altogether disparaged. Donor officers and representatives with international reputations and records of accomplishments can advise, and solicit the advice of others, with real value for a research undertaking. There is something to be said for being on the right committees, privy to authoritative information and opinion.

The lessons of experience are unmistakable. With persistence and opportunism, donors can propel the pace of research and enlarge the capabilities of researchers for significant and lasting effect on policy.

Conclusion

6

When all is said and done, influencing public policy is only a means to an end. The true purpose of development research runs much deeper. Its purpose is to improve lives, especially the lives of poor people, by advancing the course of a country's development. Informing better policy, and better governmental action, is a necessary means to that compelling end.

The record shows there are no universal 'best practices' for influencing policy with research. Every circumstance is different. Every situation presents its own complications of need and choice, danger and advantage for researchers and for policymakers. For researchers, influencing policy begins by forming some understanding of these complications, and understanding of how they interact.

More specifically, development researchers seeking influence will have to see their own work as one part of the policy process. When research influences policy, it is always in the turbulent confluence of factors that shape policy decisions and policy outcomes. Sensing the flow of these events, the interplay of personalities, the particulars of a political bargain or bureaucratic compromise, the political economy of crisis and transition even where the structures and procedures of government are reasonably stable and transparent, it is never easy to get a confident feel of the looping dynamics of policymaking.

IDRC's 23 case evaluation allowed an exploration of these variables. The research projects examined here were not all successful; some failed to demonstrate much or any influence on policy. But they teach us that influence is possible, if rarely certain. Influence does not always happen. Still less does it happen in ways that are fully expected. Influence nearly always demands patient diligence, observant responsiveness to changing conditions, careful networking, and luck.

More than that, the cases point to practical steps researchers can take to increase their prospects of influencing policy. Influence here does not simply mean having effect on a certain policy. Influence that is lasting, that results in real change, draws from research that expands a country's capacity for sound policymaking, broadens the policy horizon with new choices, and improves the ways in which governments make decisions. Expanding capacity strengthens the policy community's own powers of analysis and communication. Broadening the policy horizon means introducing new knowledge, and new solutions for thinking about and resolving pressing policy problems. Improving the procedures of policy decisions makes a government more open, informed, accountable, and effective. This is influence that endures by promoting development that is sustainable and democratic.

Devising and executing a strategy for influential research, therefore, turns on a few recognizable practicalities. At the bottom, the objective for researchers here is to understand the setting in which policy is made and to organize research strategy for best effect within that setting.

The first diagnostic consideration to bear in mind is the overall nature of the decision regime: routine, incremental, or fundamental. This matters, because different sorts of governmental decision regimes call for different approaches by researchers trying to influence policy. Generally, policymaking in most countries tends to be routine or incremental; decision makers in these settings are most receptive to research-based advice that looks to small changes along the familiar lines of logic, values, and expectations. Fundamental decision regimes are much more open to big questions, and big answers, that depart from conventional wisdom. Researchers will enlarge their chances for influence by realistically assessing the character of the prevailing decision regime, and its receptivity to research findings. Routinists and incrementalists are likely to favour prescriptions for change in small doses. Fundamental decision regimes (governing countries in transition, for example, or in economic crisis) might be ready for more radical policy change.

The next questions go to the actual interaction between research and policy in any particular policy/political context. Recalling the discussion in Chapter 2, Table 6.1 sets out five distinguishable categories of governmental readiness and capacity to absorb research, ranging from positive interest to outright hostility. Each of these categories carries its own implications for research design and execution.

Obviously, some of these policy/political contexts are more promising than others for researchers attempting to influence public policy. But even in the least hospitable contexts, system contingencies can open surprising opportunities for policy influence. Researchers, along with their sponsors and advocates, should continually scan the policy landscape for the emergence of these contingencies—and for the opportunities they present. Five specific questions deserve constant attention.

How Stable are Decision Systems?

Where the structures and processes of governmental decisions are erratic, or undergoing significant change as in reorganizations or budget-cutting campaigns, prospects for influencing policy may be weak. Still, it is sometimes possible to find a level within the decision regime that retains a comparative stability—lower in a bureaucratic hierarchy, perhaps, where personnel and practices are less exposed to political storms.

What is the Capacity of Senior Decision-makers?

When policymakers lack analytical skills or practice, or when they are distracted by competing agendas, it will be harder to make a sophisticated, evidence-based policy argument that registers. In these cases, researchers need to think hard about how to communicate

Table 6.1: Responding to Policy Contexts

Policy Context	What It Means	What to Take into Account
1. Clear government demand	A welcoming environment in which policymakers seek evidence to inform action they must take. Where researchers are credible, opportunities for influence are high.	A relationship of trust between researcher and policymaker is critical. Researchers need to anticipate issues so their advice is ready on short notice. This requires researchers to be working on issues before they trigger policy interest and to think through policy implications of their findings before getting the policymakers' call for help. It also requires clarity in communicating evidence and a reputation for delivering reliable work.
2. Government interest in research, but leadership absent	The issue is well known to government but structures or decision-making processes to use the evidence are not in place. Researchers need to exercise leadership in designing implementation. It is not enough merely to present evidence. Communication strategy is crucial, with attention to organizational and institutional mechanisms that will be needed (and realistic) for application of evidence. Potential for influence can be high.	To play a leadership role, researchers have to think about issues beyond the research itself. Directly or in collaboration with colleagues, consider the institutional and organizational implications of the evidence: if this evidence is going to be used, how will it be used? Where will decisions need to be made? What policy and regulatory changes might be implied and what effect can these have in other quarters? Researchers must focus on their communication with decision makers. They may also need strategies for ensuring that the interested public, that is people most likely to be affected by the use of the evidence, are fully engaged and able to assert influence on decision makers.
3. Government interest in research, but with a capacity shortfall	The issue is well known to the policy community, but resources are not available for adoption of research findings. Researchers need to assume leadership in identifying key advocates to raise the profile of the research and to attract resources for implementation. Cost implications demand pragmatic attention if research is to be converted into policy and action. Organizational mechanisms and low-cost solutions need to be presented along with the evidence to create momentum for influence. Risks of short-term failure are considerable.	Low capacity in policy analysis and execution means researchers have to be creative and realistic while coming up with policy options for the use of evidence. They can devise institutional structures that draw few resources, or identify an economic pay-off that meets a priority need of government, or secure other sources of funds for implementation. They need to exert special communication skills to turn the subject into a high priority issue, perhaps by mobilizing public opinion behind their efforts.

4. A new or emerging issue activates research, but leaves policymakers uninterested

This is the starting point for much development research, with researchers often aware of an issue—and the promise of research findings for solving a policy problem—before it reaches the general public or decision makers. Great effort must be invested to move the issue into the policy arena. Galvanizing political support for research implementation is essential. Risks of failure are high.

The research agenda, and its relevance to policy, must be strong and vigorously promoted by researchers. While they must be sensitive to the government's needs and priorities to capture any shifts in official thinking, researchers should be especially focused on other communities that can help to promote the evidence and its merits to decision makers. Economic and social rewards of research implementation deserve emphasis in placing the arguments before interested constituencies. These groups include, among others: advocacy groups, the media, affected communities, the private sector, and educational institutions. Both advocacy and communication are central to advancing the uptake of evidence in this context. Also, researchers need to give thought to institutional requirements of adopting their evidence; if the research does rise to higher priority, researchers should be ready with helpful implementation advice.

5. Government treats research with disinterest, or hostility

In this environment, policymakers resist listening to research advice, and may be hostile to the subject itself. Politics of the day might be working against researchers, or they might be just ahead of their time. They will most likely have to exercise patience and seize the moment when the issue comes to the fore. Pushing too hard in this environment generally fails. Odds against achieving policy influence are very high.

Researchers facing policymaker's resistance or hostility need to preserve a strong sense of purpose and commitment to the future. Their research is preparation for a potential change of political interest. While they should think about institutional implications of their findings, it may be counterproductive to advocate too strongly for a course of action fiercely opposed in policy circles. It is better to outlast the resistance and stand ready always to seize an opening for influence when it appears.

advice in terms and formats easily absorbed by policy people unfamiliar with the subject and busy with other problems.

Is the Decision System Centralized?

Evaluation demonstrates that research can influence policy even where decision-making powers are broadly decentralized to provincial or local authorities. But where powers are dispersed, researchers need to address the level of government making the decisions in the researcher's specific field of interest. Detecting where policy is made requires a reading of the country's constitutional structure—and a feel for its day-to-day politics.

Are any Special Conditions at Play (With Countries in Transition)?

Particularly where researchers are trusted and prepared, transitions give them a chance not only to influence policies but also to improve how policies are made. Similarly, the emergence of new policy challenges—like regulating and fostering ICTs for development—can open policymakers' minds to the guidance that research can offer.

Do Policymakers Confront an Economic Crisis?

The cases show that economic crisis (or inescapable economic pressure, at least) strongly favours researchers who are ready with helpfully relevant advice. For any researcher, these questions are worth asking: Can you impute economic value to your evidence or findings? Can you relate your evidence to the government's economic problems? If some in your country would benefit economically from the policy implications of your evidence, can you bring them into the discussion with policymakers? If you cannot identify direct economic value in your evidence, can you connect it nevertheless to national, subnational, or regional development? If as a development researcher, you cannot show any contribution your research might make to development, a reassessment of your work and objectives is overdue.

Whatever the policy context, and whatever contingencies arise, our evidence confirms the critical importance of researcher's responsiveness in three operational endeavours: establishing intent to influence policy, creating relationships between researchers and policymakers, and communicating with policymakers and the public. All three of these activities share this happy quality in common: Regardless of all the travails and frustrations of politics and policy-making, these three functions remain wholly within the power of researchers to undertake.

Intent Affects Outcomes

Researchers cannot just wish their work to influence policy. They need to build their intent to influence explicitly into the design and conduct of the research itself, and into the communication of findings to the policy community and the public. So researchers must first ask whether their project is really tied to change and development; what specific policies are targeted for change; and whether all the project elements coherently serve this explicit intent to influence. To repeat a point stressed in Chapter 4: Intent is not merely a state of mind. Intent that is expressly declared in the research plan and execution will inform the early questions, shape the operations of the project, and frame the language in which it is reported to policymakers. Even when intent is absent from a project's first phases, all is not lost; late-developing intent, vigorously expressed and executed, can make up for lost time in some cases. Generally, however, influence on policy is maximized when intent is explicit from the start. This general rule holds true even where the political or economic context looks unpromising. Under the worst conditions, the policy influence to be expected at the beginning might necessarily seem modest. But it is precisely in these hostile circumstances when intent needs to be made clear and remain robust.

Relationships with Policymakers and among Researchers Help Speed Research into Policy

In case after case, researchers in our evaluation emphasized the value of building relationships of trust and confidence with people in the policy world. This can sometimes develop informally, but it almost always has to develop intentionally. Researchers can connect personally with policy people; they can form alliances with local NGOs and associations of business, labour, and other economic interest groups; they can join or start research networks and partnerships to pool resources, share experiences and spread their influence within and beyond their own country or region. Partnerships and networks can overcome disadvantages of distance and isolation, and amplify the authoritative credibility of soundly based research findings. Throughout the life of a project or programme, researchers need to ask themselves: What decision processes are they trying to influence? Who are the key actors in these processes? How can those players be approached and engaged? Who are the natural allies in their work? And how can the participation of donors, other researchers, and other potential partners, reinforce the probability of exerting a meaningful effect on policy and action.

Communication is Essential for Achieving Policy Influence

Among our cases, communication contributed to every success. But communication is not confined to delivering information when it happens to emerge from research. Effective communication is a long-term, organized process of engaging with policymakers and with the public—heeding their concerns while keeping them abreast of the research under way, and highlighting its utility and pertinence to their interests. Researchers have to ask: Does the research design include a pragmatic communication strategy and operational plan? Have the researchers identified key communication channels, both formal and informal? Has the research team formed links with allies and potential advocates for the research—people who can help tell the story of its relevance to policymakers? Is the research team establishing genuine rapport in neighbourhoods and villages, with the people whose lives this research is meant to improve? Communication connects research to policy, in part by mobilizing interest and action. It belongs at the heart of any development research enterprise.

In the end, when development research succeeds in affecting a government policy or action for the better, something else can happen as well. The procedures for deliberation and deciding questions of public policy become fairer and more effective when they are fact-based, and reflect an open-minded tolerance. The scope and competence of governmental policy formulation grows stronger, and policy execution is more efficient. Citizens themselves secure new knowledge, a better informed understanding of public policy choices, and a wiser judgment about their government's performance. With these changes, lives improve. This is the defining imperative of development research—empowering people with knowledge to understand and decide their own futures.

The Case Studies

Introduction

The findings of this study are based on 23 rich case studies. As the interpretations and conclusions are inevitably based on the perspectives of the author and the other users and researchers who mined them, we thought readers would find it useful to have summaries of the cases to which to refer. The reader may find additional issues through reflection on these studies. For that reason, and for the benefit of those readers who would like to delve into the stories behind the findings in a bit more depth, summaries of all the cases are presented in this section of the book.

The cases are organized here around subject matter. Table 7.1 situates them by region for the benefit of the reader with a specific geographic interest.

We have attempted to cover the salient points in each case, but of course much of the rich detail included by the case study authors is necessarily truncated. For those who want even more depth, the longer studies can be found on the IDRC website at www.idrc.ca/evaluation-policy/ev-26606-201-1-DO_TOPIC.html.

The 22 case studies featured in this book show how research has and has not had an influence on policy.

Table 7.1: Summary of Case Studies by Region

Subject Area	Region				
	Sub-Saharan Africa	Middle East & North Africa	Asia	Latin America	Other
Poverty Monitoring	• An Interactive Policy Process Against Poverty (Senegal)		• A New Dynamic in the Struggle Against Poverty (Bangladesh) • Enlisting Communities in the Fight Against Poverty (Philippines) • Research and Policy on Parallel Courses (Vietnam)		
Trade and Finance				• Negotiating the New World Order of International Trade	• Influencing the Global Economic Agenda (global)
Resource Management	• Battling Brain Drain (East Africa)	• Sharing the Land, Shaping the Future (Lebanon)		• Changing the Face of Mining in Peru*	
Water Management		• Making the Most of Scarce Resources (Jordan) • Searching for an Interim Irrigation Solution (Syria) • Changing Water Policy by Degrees (Tunisia)			• A River Runs Through It (Ukraine)

			• Influencing Education Policy in Guatemala
		• Patience Brings Rewards (Southeast Asia)	
		• Promoting Traditional Knowledge (India)	
		• Nepal Struggles to Enter the Information Age	
Health and Education Reform	• The TEHIP Spark Leads to Better Health (Tanzania)		
Networks and Innovation			
Information and Communication Technologies for Development	• Bringing Information Technology to the Senegalese People		
	• Mozambique Enters the Information Age		
	• Information and Communication Technologies Come to the Rainbow Nation (South Africa)		
	• Bridging the Digital Divide (Uganda)		

Note: *This case study includes cases 7 and 11 as listed in Table 1.1.

Poverty Monitoring

8

A New Dynamic in the Struggle against Poverty: Researchers in Bangladesh Help Policymakers Find New Strategies to Reduce Poverty

This brief is based on a case study written by María Pía Riggirozzi and research carried out by Kirit Parikh.

Poverty has been an endemic problem in Bangladesh throughout the country's 33 year history, and remains so despite an encouraging annual economic growth rate of more than 5 per cent in recent years. Now researchers and policymakers are collaborating to better understand the root causes of this stubborn economic malaise and design practical solutions.

Bangladesh, with its population of 142 million, is by far the largest member of the group of the 50 so-called Least Developed Countries. Despite decades of sustained domestic and international efforts to improve the nation's economic prospects, Bangladesh remains one of the world's poorest countries.

It must be said that nature has not been kind to Bangladesh. About one-third of the country is flooded every year by the rains of the monsoon season, and catastrophic cyclones are common. This is a major impediment to economic development, and seriously affects the livelihoods of the two-thirds of the population who are employed in the agricultural sector.

By no means can all the blame be placed on the forces of nature. The causes of poverty are deep-rooted and complex. Even the definition of poverty can be hard to pin down. One dictionary defines it as 'the state of one who lacks a usual or socially acceptable amount of money or material possessions.' Economists, it seems, read dictionaries. They have traditionally measured poverty solely on the basis of income and consumption. Unfortunately these measures do nothing to suggest the causes of poverty, nor do they point to solutions.

MIMAP

The search for solutions based on a clearer understanding of the root causes of poverty led Bangladesh to become the second country to participate in the Micro Impacts of Macroeconomic and Adjustment Policies (MIMAP) Programme in 1992. Created by the International Development Research Centre (IDRC), the MIMAP network pioneered the application of economic modelling techniques and poverty monitoring (see Box 8.1).

Box 8.1: The MIMAP Network—Promoting Innovation and Understanding

The MIMAP approach is founded on the conviction that poverty reduction strategies and programmes will succeed only if reliable and timely information about poverty indicators is provided; and the belief that such programmes will not succeed without a comprehensive understanding of the impacts of macroeconomic policies on the poor.

MIMAP helps developing countries design policies and programmes that meet economic stabilization and structural adjustment targets while alleviating poverty and reducing vulnerability through research, training, and dialogue. Created by IDRC in 1989, the MIMAP network now connects developing country researchers, policymakers, NGOs, and international experts in a dozen countries of Africa and Asia. Specifically, the MIMAP programmes aim to:

1. Enhance the research capacity of developing countries to analyze the impact of macro-economic policies on their citizens;
2. Provide new instruments for policy and programme design and analysis by developing rigorously analytical tools and poverty monitoring systems;
3. Assist the development of community-based monitoring and local development mechanisms;
4. Strengthen the ability of policymakers to negotiate with international players such as the banks and other multilateral and bilateral organizations;
5. Bring together researchers, politicians, government officials, and NGOs in policy dialogue at the national and regional levels; and
6. Promote the exchange of research knowledge, tool, results, and policy dialogue among countries, institutions, and donors.

For further information visit www.idrc.ca/mimap.

The resources offered by MIMAP enabled researchers and policymakers in Bangladesh to work together in the search for policy solutions. The innovative research involved poverty monitoring that goes well beyond simply measuring income and consumption to include indicators such as health, access to drinking water and land, quality of housing, and a myriad of other factors.

The resulting knowledge-related production has become a key source of information for policymakers regarding poverty reduction, according to María Pía Riggirozzi, who prepared a report on an evaluation of the MIMAP project in Bangladesh for IDRC, based on the research carried out by Kirit Parikh. The report states: 'One of the most striking problems combating poverty in Bangladesh has been related to the lack of adequate sources of information on poverty-related issues.'

Access to information on poverty has been a critical challenge to the design of effective and sustainable economic policies that can have a positive impact on the poor. Access to adequate information on poverty-related issues and understanding the dynamics of poverty was considered a key priority in the government's antipoverty agenda.

Although Bangladesh has initiated a number of antipoverty programmes, sources of information were both outdated and unreliable. Authorities had traditionally relied on only one source of data collection, the Household Expenditure Survey (HES) prepared by the Bangladesh Bureau of Statistics (BBS). Dr Mustafa Mujeri, leader of the MIMAP team at the Bangladesh Institute of Development Studies (BIDS) in Dhaka, comments:

> This survey was of little use to policymakers because it was produced irregularly—every five or 10 years—and its results were published with a time lag of three or four years so the available data was out of date. Moreover, the HES offered limited, one-dimensional information as it looked solely at income and consumption.

New research tools

Researchers developed a new tool, the Poverty Monitoring System (PMS) which tracks a wide-ranging set of indicators. These include income, employment, health, education, housing, access to community services, access to land, and so on. Several rounds of surveys are conducted to assess the situation of the same set of households over time. New indicators were added over the life of the project as the system was refined. The system now includes a multi-dimensional core set of 12 indicators that are used to collect data in 21 districts through a continuous series of surveys.

> These surveys have emerged as a primary source of information on trends in poverty, with strong policy implications. As Riggirozzi says: The PMS results are available within a year of the survey allowing policy formulation to be based on reliable and timely information, enhancing efficiency in poverty-related policies. In this context, decision-making on poverty-related issues has improved as policies can be based on alternative scenarios, and their implementation monitored and adjusted along the process.

The PMS tool has since been adapted for use at the local level. This is a considerable challenge in a country that is divided into 64 districts with a total of 60,000 villages. Initially, the surveys were conducted at the district level, with the results made available to local NGOs and civil society organizations. A small number of village level surveys were conducted, and the Bangladesh Academy of Rural Development (BARD) expressed confidence that the experience could be replicated on a broader scale with the involvement of local NGOs.

Computers are an invaluable aid when dealing with the volume of complex data produced by such surveys. Two computer-based tools were developed as part of the MIMAP project. The Computerized Information System (CIS) was created for the development of an integrated database to process, archive, and disseminate poverty-related information. Riggirozzi reports that capacity building in the management of the CIS was important to ensure that users were able to take full advantage of the system.

In addition, the MIMAP team developed a Computable General Equilibrium (CGE) model, an analytical tool to help monitor and analyze the impact of macroeconomic policies on poverty. The model proved to be particularly useful as the country embarked on a process of structural adjustment and macroeconomic reforms, reports Riggirozzi. 'Antipoverty policies can be followed as the government implements necessary economic reforms, observing macro and micro aspects of economic impact, such as the consequences of macroeconomic policies on household welfare and income distribution.'

The MIMAP programme also included a series of focus studies designed to supplement the modelling and poverty monitoring efforts. These studies generated numerous working papers, technical papers, policy papers, and newsletters. These and other documents were widely disseminated as part of a strategy to keep those closest to the policymaking process up to date on the latest research results.

Policy influence

The point of all this information gathering and analysis, of course, is to influence government policy. Riggirozzi reports that:

> The objective of influencing policy has been implicit in the content of the IDRC-supported programme. Its key aim in this sense is to articulate research that has the potential to inform policymakers in a linear manner and to contribute to the formulation of sound policy options.

Dr Mujeri, former leader of the MIMAP team at BIDS, puts it more bluntly. 'At the end of the day,' he says, 'it is not whose research has got to the policymakers, but whether the policies have been developed or not—and if they are the right policies.'

According to Riggirozzi all these activities—the PMS surveys, computer modelling, capacity building, focus studies, dissemination—have been important in broadening the understanding of poverty. 'MIMAP activities not only filled the gaps in the existing knowledge of researchers and policymakers but also introduced new fields of policy inquiry, putting these issues on the agendas of policymakers,' she reports.

For example, she notes that, in one instance, information gathered by the PMS surveys was the main source underpinning the Finance Minister's budget documents. It is also an important input for the work of the Planning Commission. 'The Planning Commission has significantly relied on MIMAP modelling work.... Moreover, the fact that a CGE model was managed in the Planning Commission has enhanced the ability of government officials to use instrumental data on issues of micro impact of macro policy.'

Another example of the direct use of knowledge generated by MIMAP is the contribution of CGE survey data in the preparation of Bangladesh's Poverty Reduction Strategy Paper (PRSP). The paper was developed by the Planning Commission, and outlines a detailed five-year planning process. Dr Mujeri, who participated in the preparation of the PRSP, highlights the impact of MIMAP research inputs. 'Bangladesh is now allocating 26 per cent or 27 per cent of its total budget to social sectors. When we started, the allocations were 15 per cent to 17 per cent,' he says. 'MIMAP has stressed the importance of social development since the beginning.'

MIMAP findings have also proved useful in capacity building. Based on interviews conducted by Dr Kirit Parikh with many of the participants, Riggirozzi concludes that MIMAP has strengthened the professional capacities of researchers and research institutions to conduct high quality, policy-relevant research. It has also increased the ability of decision makers to use the research for poverty alleviation programmes on the ground. And because government agencies and MIMAP project members worked together on poverty monitoring activities, capacity building has significantly contributed to the skills of government officials.

Affecting policy regimes

The success of MIMAP-Bangladesh in influencing policy is based on the close links that developed between research producers and research users. This collaboration was something new, according to Dr Mujeri. He observed 'When the MIMAP project started there was no culture of informed research on policy in Bangladesh, no tradition of consulting researchers. We had to convince policymakers that they need research. One of the keys to bridging the research-policy divide lies in close relationships.'

Dr Mujeri believes that involving government officials in MIMAP activities helped to create a sense of ownership. Taking the PMS surveys as an example, he says, 'We could have carried them out ourselves and there would have been a report, but continuity would not have been there.' He believes that dialogue between the policy and the research communities has had a direct impact on decision-making processes.

Some Lessons

1. Adopting a coordinated approach to bridge the gap between the policymakers and the researchers helped to create a culture of research usage and ownership.
2. The collection and analysis of data on poverty-related issues was not relegated to academic experts, but was based on partnership as a practical principle.
3. The availability of reliable, timely data created a sense of ownership in government agencies and has been an invaluable instrument for policymakers in dialogue with multilateral donors and aid agencies.
4. 'Learning-by-doing' had a crucial impact on the researchers, strengthening their ability to participate in formulating and implementing strategies for poverty reduction.
5. The local level approach to poverty issues helps to increase public awareness and to empower local actors in the search for practical solutions that help to alleviate poverty.

Basic Data

Period of Operation: 1992–2001

Objectives:
1. To increase the understanding of poverty and to promote dialogue among researchers, politicians, government officials, and NGOs in the search of equitable and effective policies of poverty alleviation.
2. To develop an analytical framework to analyze the key macroeconomic and structural adjustment policies on the poor.

Research Outputs:
1. Poverty Monitoring System; first at national level and then addition of a local level system.
2. Computerized information system for data management.
3. Development of a CGE model and training on its use.
4. Focus studies on poverty related issues (*inter alia*, role of public expenditure, agriculture and rural poverty, efficiency of rural markets, human resource development, and the poor).

María Pía Riggirozzi supports that belief in her report, arguing that 'in Bangladesh a major contribution of MIMAP has been the development of dynamic channels and mechanisms in favour of greater research use by policymakers.' She adds that the main project outcomes have contributed to fostering policy change.

In effect, she writes, from the beginning the implementation of MIMAP, 'was based on coordinated work bridging the needs of policymakers in terms of policy instruments and the expertise of research institutions and experts in the development of new methodologies to approach the issue of poverty.'

As such, researchers and policymakers developed close links in the process of policy formulation, monitoring, and assessment. In the process, a culture of research usage and ownership in the development of economic policies was strengthened.

Enlisting Communities in the Fight against Poverty: Gathering and Analyzing Information Yields Results in the Philippines

This brief is based on a case study written by María Pía Riggirozzi and Tracy Tuplin, with files from Kirit Parikh.

Effectively reducing poverty requires timely, accurate information. But while poverty alleviation has been a major goal of the Philippine government since 1986, gathering the data to support poverty alleviation programmes has been difficult. IDRC's Micro Impacts of Macroeconomic and Adjustment Policies (MIMAP) programme has been helping to provide that information since 1990. As a recent evaluation noted, the research initiated by MIMAP was exactly what the country needed.

Tourist guides almost invariably refer to Palawan as the most 'enchantingly rustic' of the Philippine provinces. For the province's 750,000 people, however, 'rustic' is a euphemism for 'poor'. The poverty rate in Palawan is close to 50 per cent. Many inhabitants do not have potable water, adequate sanitation facilities, or electricity. Many are illiterate and malnourished.

When the provincial officials sat down to plan the 1999 budget, they were determined to change that reality. But the problems seemed insurmountable. Palawan, made up of close to 1,800 islands stretched over 650 kilometres, suffers from an inadequate infrastructure, an enormous obstacle to development. Education and health services desperately need huge injections of money. Also contributing to poverty is the rate of population growth—at 3.8 per cent, it is the highest in the Philippines.

Effectively reducing poverty requires timely, accurate information. But while poverty alleviation has been a major goal of the Philippine government since 1986, gathering the data to support poverty alleviation programmes has been difficult. In fact, data on poverty was irregular, infrequent, and unmatched from survey to survey, so no comprehensive profile could be drawn at any time. Regular surveys provide data on macro variables, such as the rate of inflation, the exchange rate, and the balance of trade. Surveys that measure income, housing, and the rate of malnutrition, however, are not conducted yearly, reducing their relevance and impact.

'We would know the impact of policies and programs only after three or four years,' says Dr Ponciano Intal, Executive Director of the Angelo King Institute for Economics and Business Studies (AKI) at De La Salle University in Manila. A case in point is the effect of the 1997–98 East Asia financial crisis and El Niño phenomena. Economist Dr Celia Reyes points out that 'We only had a 1997 national survey; the next survey would be done three years later in 2000, so we didn't have enough information to signal to policymakers and others that there were adverse social impacts on the population.' Yet the impacts were considerable: the Philippines gross domestic product contracted by 0.5 per cent, triggering a boom-bust cycle and loss of foreign investment. Years of gains in poverty reduction were wiped out.

A three-pronged programme

Also lacking was a systematic and regular collection of information on the 'human dimension'. 'We had planning exercises, but we didn't have a way of measuring the quality-of-life of households,' explains Josephine Escano, Chief of the Research and Evaluation Division of the Provincial Planning and Development Office in Palawan. 'We needed to find a way to measure that over the long haul so we could plan more efficiently and effectively.'

What they found was a Community-based Poverty Monitoring System (CBMS) designed by the MIMAP-Philippines team. MIMAP had begun in 1990 in the Philippines to sustain efforts to measure and analyze poverty, and to develop policy alternatives that minimize adverse impacts on the poor (for more information:http://web.idrc.ca/en/ev-6649-201-1-DO_TOPIC.html).

'There are many possible strategies for addressing poverty,' says Dr Reyes, leader of MIMAP's CBMS network.

I think one of the most important may be to put in place a poverty monitoring system. Why? Because it would provide information on the different dimensions of poverty. Good numbers from a poverty monitoring system also allow us to assess the impact of policies and programs, and can help us identify beneficiaries for targeted programs.

Poverty monitoring is one of the three main components of the MIMAP-Philippines project. The second component, economic modelling, consists of a series of economic model using estimated Philippine data, including macroeconomic models, household models, and a linking matrix that translates macroeconomic effects into household effects. These models have been used to analyze the impact of tax reforms, trade liberalization, foreign exchange liberalization and deregulation, among others.

The third component is policy advocacy and information dissemination. As Celia Reyes explains, 'It is only by effectively communicating the project's findings to the appropriate audiences that we can hope to influence policymaking.' Tools include publications such as a quarterly bulletin, research papers, and a website. Policy workshops and community dialogues bring together technical experts and practitioners from the academic and research community, and from policymaking bodies. MIMAP-Philippines has also participated actively in technical working groups on poverty and welfare monitoring, as well as on policy impact assessment.

Linking research to policy

According to the report prepared by María Pía Riggirozzi and Tracy Tuplin with files from Kirit Parikh, MIMAP could not have arrived in the Philippines at a more propitious time. Dr Marío Lamberte, President of the Philippines Institute for Development Studies (PIDS), says that the research initiated by the MIMAP project was exactly what the country needed in 1990. 'The Philippines had experienced a number of economic crises,' he says, 'and the government was concerned about how to respond.'

The success of MIMAP's modelling work was evident early on in the interest policymakers and government officials took in the results. Every forum brought more people to the table. Key, explains Dr Caesar Cororaton, Research Fellow at PIDS and MIMAP Assistant Project Director, was that everyone recognized the research to be neutral.

Broadening horizons, expanding capacity

Respondents interviewed in the course of the study pointed to two major contributions by MIMAP-Philippines that broadened policy horizons and expanded policy capacity.

First, analytical tools were developed to capture the consequences of various economic reforms, and to provide policymakers with good information on their possible impact. 'MIMAP-Philippines illustrates a case of improving knowledge and supporting recipients to develop policies and capabilities of policymakers,' note Riggirozzi and Tuplin. Simply put, the tools for collecting data, and the information gathered have enabled local decision makers to analyze the causes of poverty, track changes, and assess the welfare of the population. When MIMAP first started, there was little research to back up policies. As Lamberte bluntly commented, government analysts or policymakers would not bother with the micro impacts of macroeconomic policies because there was no way of checking on them—the analytical part was simply missing.

The Commission to Fight Poverty, created in 1993–94, has since adopted those tools. The MIMAP team has also helped government agencies to implement the monitoring system. The evaluation notes, however, that the Philippine policymaking bodies have not yet institutionalized the models.

Second, MIMAP developed and tested quantitative methods for policy analysis and simulation, including computable general equilibrium, macroeconometrics, income distribution, and household models. These affected the planning system, budgeting, and programme design at local and national levels. The modelling work and development of the indicators have clarified important policy issues and contributed to national debates on them, says the report. New development knowledge was brought to the table, as well as new insights into the process of development.

'The MIMAP project has played a crucial role in the analysis and forecasting of impacts of macroeconomic and adjustment policies in the Philippines,' say Riggirozzi and Tuplin. Not only were new ideas of poverty alleviation and new tools to monitor the consequences on the poor developed, but MIMAP's analytical instruments increased the quality and reliability of diagnostic work.

Affecting policy regimes

MIMAP's lynchpin, however, is the poverty monitoring system. First tested in two villages, the system is now being implemented throughout the Philippines, including province-wide in Palawan, and more recently, in Bulacan. In April 2003, the Philippine Department of the Interior and Local Government directed all local government units—at the *barangay* (smallest administrative unit in the Phillippines), municipal, city, and provincial levels—to adopt the system's 13 core indicators for measuring poverty. From its first home in the Philippines, CBMS has now spread, with IDRC support, to 12 countries.

Fundamentally modifying programmes and policies is not an easy task. But, say the evaluators, the implementation of CBMS in Palawan, 'is a shining success story'. Contributing factors include:

1. The involvement of policymakers at provincial, municipal, and *barangay* levels, as well as the vice-Governor and Governor, which contributed to the effective use of research outputs in the policy process.
2. MIMAP research and statistical activities fed a new way of approaching poverty-related problems in Palawan. At the core is the set of indicators that allows data collection and interpretation in an easy, focused way. 'CBMS gives you information about where you are now, where you should be, and how you're going to get there,' says the Honourable Joel Reyes, Governor of Palawan and a staunch CBMS supporter. 'It provides reliable, relevant, and comprehensive data on welfare conditions and development status across the province.'
3. The research results were transferred to local people who now have a sense of ownership of the CBMS.

This last factor is crucial. Community members participate in the collection, processing, and use of the data, and in validating the data after collection. This empowers communities by providing them with information and a process through which they can actively participate in planning, explains Dr Reyes. *Barangay* residents thus develop a keen sense of their priorities and are better able to articulate their needs to city planning officers. Armed with hard information on their condition, they are able to play a direct role in allocating budgetary resources. And they can demand accountability and transparency on the part of government officials.

'The MIMAP project has changed the way of making policy in that research gave new understanding to define a manageable, relevant set of indicators, as well as it gave credibility to policy formulation. In this sense it made it possible to test ideas, to adjust policies, and to improve them along the process of implementation,' say Riggirozzi and Tuplin. Equally important, CBMS' successful implantation in Palawan facilitates its replication in other Philippine provinces.

Keys to success

MIMAP's success in influencing policy in the Philippines is not serendipity. Riggirozzi and Tuplin note that the project was conceived 'to influence policymakers directly by generating problem-solving knowledge.'

Other factors also contributed. Important were the close relationships established by the research team with government bodies such as the Presidential Commission to Fight Poverty (now the National Anti-Poverty Commission), the Department of the Interior and Local Government, the Department of Social Welfare and Development, and the National Economic and Development Authority. In fact, senior government officials participated in the project's advisory board from the outset. Since then, the National Anti-Poverty Commission has invited Dr Reyes to collaborate in proposing mechanisms to diagnose poverty before an inter-agency committee working on institutionalizing a local poverty monitoring system. This close collaboration with government agencies resulted in further networking exercises among governmental and non-governmental actors at different levels.

The sense of ownership by local government units, such as in Palawan, and by communities themselves, contributed strongly to MIMAP's success. Says Celia Reyes: 'It is important to work with local governments at the outset since they will ultimately bear the costs and benefits.'

Building capacity by doing

Influence was further assured by building the capacity of both policymakers and researchers through workshops and by networking. For instance, training was provided for government officials in newsletter writing and preparation so that the results of the CBMS survey could be disseminated more widely. This, says the evaluation, helped broaden policy debate among the population.

Lamberte also recognized that the capacity of researchers themselves to understand and advise policy was increased. According to him, this affected the growing maturity of the researchers, deepening their understanding of the issue, and providing better and more credible policy advice.

The next challenges for MIMAP are to scale up and ensure that national statistical agencies coordinate the generation of data. This would enable CBMS to go nationwide, says Celia Reyes. Also needed is technical assistance to local government units, and a central repository for the data. And as Carmelita Ericta, administrator of the National Statistical Office, pointed out, all government units need to recognize that information gathering is not a cost—rather, it is an investment.

Basic Data	
Period of Operation: 1990–2002	
Objective:	To develop poverty modelling and monitoring capacity to inform poverty alleviation strategies.
Research Outputs:	1. Different economics models such as CGE (computable general equilibrium).
	2. CBMS poverty monitoring system designed.
	3. Provincial database and poverty monitoring maps of Palawan Province; and research reports and focus studies.

An Interactive Policy Process against Poverty: Researchers and Policymakers in Senegal Create Home-grown Strategies

This brief is based on a case study written by Tracy Tuplin with research by Fred Carden.

Like most countries in Sub-Saharan Africa, Senegal has struggled unsuccessfully to provide a better life for the majority of its people. Now a new approach to the underlying issues of poverty offers hope for policies that will finally bring about real change.

Senegal is among the poorest countries in the world. In the past decade the proportion of the country's population living below the poverty line has increased from about one-third to more than half. A 2001 survey estimated that two-thirds of the people were 'poor'. In the rural areas that number increases to about 80 per cent. These are grim statistics indeed for a nation of 10 million that had high hopes when it became independent from France in 1962.

Evidence of the economic problems surfaced in the 1980s. Low economic growth, strong internal demand, instability in public finances, and a chronic balance of payments deficit combined to bring about a serious deterioration in the quality of life for many Senegalese. A short-lived federation with neighbouring Gambia never fully got off the ground: the union was dissolved in 1989.

In the 1990s the Government of Senegal attempted to turn things around by launching an ambitious economic reform programme with tough measures that included devaluing its currency, and dismantling price controls and subsidies. The reform programme produced results—from 1995 to 2001, the country's Gross Domestic Product (GDP) grew at an annual rate of 5 per cent, and inflation declined.

On the other side of the ledger, however, the number of poor people continued to rise despite the increases in GDP. Seventy per cent of the workforce is employed in agriculture, and this sector remained stubbornly stagnant despite the support of the international donor community. Industrial development and the private sector have not expanded as envisioned.

The micro impacts of macroeconomic and adjustment policies (MIMAP) approach

As it has been seen in many of the world's least developed countries, poverty is a complex and persistent problem that is not easily eliminated. Increases in GDP do not automatically translate into improvements in the lives of the poor. To design programmes that will alleviate or even eliminate poverty, economists and policymakers first need to understand the root causes of the problem, and how the poor are affected by government's economic strategies, or indeed, if they are affected at all.

Providing answers to those kinds of questions is the role of the MIMAP programme. The programme was created in 1989 by Canada's IDRC and now comprises a network of a dozen countries in Asia and Africa (see Box 8.2). Senegal is a recent member of the MIMAP network.

IDRC had been active in Senegal since the 1980s. One of the institutions it had been supporting, the Centre de Recherches Économiques Appliquées (CREA), was chosen to undertake the MIMAP-Senegal research. This brought about a notable change, according to Dr Abdoulaye Diagne, who is the director of CREA and was appointed coordinator of the

Box 8.2: The MIMAP Network—Promoting Innovation and Understanding

The MIMAP approach is founded on the conviction that poverty reduction strategies and programmes will succeed only if reliable and timely information about poverty indicators is provided; and the belief that such programmes will not succeed without a comprehensive understanding of the impacts of macroeconomic policies on the poor.

MIMAP helps developing countries design policies and programmes that meet economic stabilization and structural adjustment targets while alleviating poverty and reducing vulnerability through research, training, and dialogue. Created by IDRC in 1989, the MIMAP network now connects developing country researchers, policymakers, NGOs, and international experts in a dozen countries of Africa and Asia.

MIMAP programme in Senegal. 'Previously, Senegalese academics did not work on poverty,' he says. 'Many studies were done, but by foreign consultants. Thanks to MIMAP our institute was able to carry out research on poverty.'

The MIMAP-Senegal programme is one of the number of projects selected by IDRC's Evaluation Unit for study to determine how effective the project has been in influencing policy and policymakers. The study report, prepared for IDRC by Tracy Tuplin, is based on an original document by Fred Carden and points out that, at the time MIMAP-Senegal was getting underway, a second event occurred that had a significant impact on the original project design.

The project had barely started when Dr Diagne was made aware of the country's requirement to produce a comprehensive PRSP. This paper was a requirement to determine Senegal's eligibility for the initiative for the Heavily Indebted Poor Countries (HIPC) led by the World Bank and the International Monetary Fund (IMF) to alleviate debt and benefit from new loans. To be eligible, a country must submit a proposal on how the various national actors intend to use newly available funds to reduce poverty.

Just three months into the MIMAP project, CREA was selected as the technical partner of the Ministry of Economics and Finance to develop the PRSP. The goal was for the paper to reflect a consensus among government bodies, local experts, development partners, and civil society organizations. Given the pivotal role of CREA, it was inevitable that there would be considerable overlap between the two initiatives—MIMAP and PRSP.

Dr Diagne sees it as pure serendipity. 'We produced a document that served as the launch pad for the consultative process leading to drafting the PRSP,' he says. 'The barriers fell very quickly, and we now have joint teams involving our researchers and those of the administration. Now it's as if there is no one involved but ourselves. I don't see consultants any more.'

The turning point

MIMAP-Senegal began in June 2000 with the overall objective of improving CREA's capacity for research that would lead to a better understanding of the microeconomic effects of macroeconomic decisions, and how they impact on poverty issues. The CREA research team of 10 included professors and doctoral students from CREA, as well as representatives from the Bureau of Statistics. They had four specific goals:

1. Construct a profile of poverty in Senegal and develop a monitoring system;
2. Develop tools to analyze the impact of macroeconomic policies on income distribution;
3. Study poor people's access to financial services, the gender dimension of poverty, and the relationship between education and poverty; and
4. Encourage dialogue among development actors (researchers, policymakers, NGOs, and financiers) in the fight against poverty.

In November 2000, seven members of the CREA team attended a workshop on poverty analysis. This was the turning point, according to Tuplin who writes:

To a large extent the originally planned MIMAP activities were put on the back burner. The bottom line is that the PRSP process made active use of CREA data and studies—a contribution that was praised on a number of counts. The PRSP recommendations are based on CREA findings, illustrating the importance of the work in influencing policy, particularly in Senegal's poverty reduction strategy.

The report adds that CREA's help ensured that the PRSP document was written by Senegalese, establishing ownership that is expected to make implementation easier. In fact, CREA's collaboration with various government ministries brought about an important change in the policy community. As Carden noted, 'Before the PRSP, national researchers were largely ignored by policymakers and economic policy research was directed primarily by staff of the World Bank and the IMF ... the involvement of national researchers in the PRSP is a critical case of change in the policy community.'

The fact that several of the CREA team members were also public administrators resulted in a policy process that was much more interactive—it became a two-way process. Not only did the administration make their needs known, now they were also advised by the researchers as to what was needed. And after decisions were made, the researchers continued to be involved in monitoring and evaluating the results. Tuplin writes:

Perhaps the most striking aspect of this policy influence is the fact that it was unintended. While the final result was likely more than the project hoped to achieve, there was a sense of apology that the MIMAP team was not able to keep to the original calendar of activities as planned at the outset of the project.

Types of policy influence

Despite that 'sense of apology', Tuplin reasons that the MIMAP project has achieved most of its original goals to a greater or lesser extent. Expanding policy capacity was a key element of the original proposal. This was achieved through a number of training events, as well as the development of a Computable General Equilibrium (CGE) model. This is an analytical tool to help monitor and analyze the impact of macroeconomic policies on poverty. Development of the model required a review of available poverty data, and resulted in new and more relevant national data on poverty.

Several government officials commented on the impact of the project. Daouda Gueye, with the Ministry of Education's Office of General and Economic Administration, noted that

CREA's continuing requests for information forced some government departments to improve their information collection methods in order to be able to provide what was needed. Also, Thierno Niane, coordinator of the Cell to Fight Poverty in the Ministry of Economy and Finance, commented that the project was able to 'work on the levers that work in Senegal to understand which ones do work in order to better identify the links between economic growth and poverty reduction.'

Tuplin adds that visibility and trust grew with the research. 'The team became known for its abilities, establishing CREA as a credible research centre for government work. The researchers trained within the framework of the MIMAP project are now considered as being among the most qualified resource persons in the region.'

The report points out that the MIMAP project also broadened policy horizons for a wide range of people—from students and researchers to economic planners and administrators, as well as donors. Even researchers and administrators who are no longer associated with the MIMAP project continue to work on other initiatives in the fight against poverty in Senegal, using the experience and contacts they have gained.

In terms of the project's effect on policy regimes, Tuplin states that it was key in redefining research-policy linkages in the country.

> Before the project, the Senegalese administration did not have the habit of integrating researchers, except for the occasional consultancy. Collaborative efforts here resulted in recognition that researchers increase the quality and speed of the work and of the team. This in itself translates into a new framework for collaboration.

Factors affecting policy influence

Key people are a significant factor in affecting policy influence, and Tuplin has praise for CREA's Dr Diagne as project leader, as well as others who played important roles in the MIMAP–PRSP projects. However, the report also points out that 'In Africa, human capacity is overextended ... national experts are too few in number, creating a bottleneck in the supply-and-demand chain. This affects not only the quality of work but also presents problems for institution building.'

Dissemination of research was seen as less critical in the MIMAP–PRSP project than in some other research programmes, although there were numerous activities aimed at communicating more effectively and reaching a broader audience. For example, CREA organized a 'Day of Reflection on the Economy of Senegal', which was very well received by policymakers.

Tuplin writes that, because it was interactive, the research had direct access to policy circles.

> Dissemination as a concept has a passive connotation that is contrasted with how mainstream MIMAP-Senegal became. Policymakers were a standing constituency of MIMAP as MIMAP unfolded into PRSP. This is in stark contrast to other research projects that are particularly dependent on dissemination to reach policymakers.

Institutional issues also affect policy regimes. Although institution building was not an IDRC policy, at the time it was felt that support through CREA could eventually have a significant

Some Lessons

1. Flexibility is essential—in this case in accepting the opportunity to work on the PRSP rather than the planned MIMAP outputs.
2. Linking the project to a specific policy process created a favourable environment for the work to be translated into concrete policies.
3. Institutional support is sometimes necessary to create greater visibility, which leads to improved credibility and interaction with policymakers.
4. Data that is compiled by competent national experts, rather than foreign consultants, results in a greater sense of ownership and improved implementation.

Basic Data

Time Period: 2000–2002

Objectives:
1. Construct a profile of the poverty in Senegal and develop a monitoring system.
2. Develop tools to analyze the impact of macroeconomic policies on income distribution.
3. Study: poor people's access to financial services, the gender dimension of poverty, and the relation between education and poverty.
4. Encourage dialogue among development actors working in the fight against poverty (researchers, policymakers, NGOs, and financiers).

Research Outputs: The research outputs were largely blended with the overall research outputs of the research centre involved. The core recognized output from the MIMAP team was its leadership in the development of the PRSP for Senegal (a paper required by the World Bank as part of programming), not a research output per se. The volume and importance of this work to the national agenda sidetracked the original research agenda.

impact in the region. Tuplin reports that this was an investment that is paying off, adding however that some believe CREA should have more formal links to government. To date, the links are informal and personal, with government researchers involved in MIMAP activities as experts, but not as representatives of their ministries.

CREA's director, Dr Diagne, is attempting to establish some institutional arrangements to sustain partnerships. As an example, he cites a three-year contract with the Ministry of Education to conduct a number of studies and prepare a report. There is also the possibility that CREA-MIMAP could serve as the research base for activities related to the New Partnership for Africa's Development (NEPAD).

Ultimately, Tuplin concludes, 'the most striking aspect of the project is that the PRSP was not part of MIMAP's original landscape. A number of internal and external factors created a significant policy window that was critical in joining these two efforts, and making the result so successful.'

Research and Policy on Parallel Courses: The Challenges of Measuring the Influence of Research on Vietnam's Economic Policies

This brief is based on a case study written by André Saumier.

Since the early 1990s, Vietnam has embarked on a radical overhaul of its economic system. The country aims to open its economy to market forces, but without changing its socialist political structure. During this same period, IDRC has sponsored three large research programmes in Vietnam. Have these projects influenced Vietnam's policies?

Despite its considerable economic and social problems, Vietnam has made important strides. In less than 12 years, it has succeeded in raising itself from the bottom of the World Bank's list of least developed countries to the status of 'simply' a developing country.

Some 80 per cent of the Vietnam's 80 million citizens live in rural areas. Economic development, however, is concentrated in the two main cities, Ho Chi Minh City in the south and, to a lesser extent, Hanoi in the north. This creates increasingly large and growing disparities of opportunities, employment, and income. Not surprisingly, illegal migration from the countryside to the cities is growing. Nevertheless, Vietnam's progress is impressive. GDP per capita increased from US $114 in 1990 to an estimated $423 in 2002, despite a population increase of 14 million people. During the same period, seafood exports rose from $239 million to $2 billion, and rice exports doubled. Vietnam is now a leading exporter of rice, coffee, footwear, and other products.

None of these developments have happened by accident. Since 1991, Vietnam has pursued an ambitious programme of economic reform and modernization called Doi Moi, or 'reconstruction'. Doi Moi aims to introduce into Vietnam's socialist system some elements of a market-oriented economy—a 'market socialism', in effect. Doi Moi has an unusual and distinctive characteristic: the determination to change the economic components of the communist system without changing the political system. Since this has not been attempted before, except in the People's Republic of China, there is no roadmap, no recipe to follow.

André Saumier, who assessed the influence of research on policy in Vietnam on behalf of the IDRC, notes:

> ... few in the leadership had much, if any, even superficial familiarity with either the theory, the practice, the measurement or the development and deployment of such policies. Since none of these could come from within, at least for an initial period of undetermined length, they had per force to come from without.

IDRC's presence in Vietnam

It is in this context that IDRC began supporting research in Vietnam in 1991. A study commissioned by IDRC's Evaluation Unit in 2002 sought to determine if, to what extent, and by what means, the work it sponsored has had a degree of policy influence. As André Saumier points out in his report, 'The "policy impacts" one is searching for here are neither trivial nor marginal. We are indeed looking at the root and branch redesign of an economic system; that redesign is unfolding within the extremely severe constraint of the continuation in power of a totalitarian Party [...].'

André Saumier's report was compiled on the basis of a literature review and interviews with Vietnamese researchers and senior government officials, in particular leaders of advisory and research bodies. His survey focused on three IDRC programmes.

Vietnam Sustainable Economic Development (VISED)

In 1993, IDRC and the Canadian International Development Agency (CIDA) supported a major effort to increase Vietnam's capacity in environmental economic research through the Vietnam Sustainable Economic Development (VISED) programme. By its close in 1997, it had supported 50 relatively small-scale, somewhat disparate investigations in 25 institutions. It examined such varied topics as special economic zones, shareholding companies, credit funds, and state-owned enterprises.

IDRC's counterpart organization was the new Ministry of Science, Technology, and the Environment. Although the Ministry was less involved with economic issues, it had a strong, well connected advisory group.

Vietnam Economic and Environment Management (VEEM)

In 1997, both IDRC and CIDA contributed to VISED's successor, the five-year VEEM programme, which built on the past experience in a more tightly structured manner. VEEM aimed to enhance the government's capacity for policy development in economic integration and natural resource management, and to conduct policy-oriented research in those areas. Says André Saumier: 'VEEM had a clear and upfront policy thrust from day one.'

VEEM's economic component focused on only two interrelated areas: trade liberalization and the competitiveness of export industries. Five major reports, published in 2001, were supported by a comprehensive computerized trade database, the first and only one of its kind in Vietnam.

Micro Impacts of Macroeconomic and Adjustment Policies (MIMAP)

The MIMAP programme (1995–2001) had two somewhat autonomous components: poverty monitoring and modelling issues. Poverty alleviation and hunger elimination have for years been stated policy objectives of the Government of Vietnam.

The poverty monitoring component sought to develop a community-based monitoring system offering 'richer' and quicker data on actual poverty than large traditional surveys. MIMAP proposed and tested a methodology calling for bottom-up measurement on the basis of simple questionnaires administered by local people. Such an approach ought to lead to social programmes better tailored to the needs of each community.

The other MIMAP component supported the development of econometric models capable of analyzing the broad consequences of various policy stances or proposals, a first for Vietnam. The areas analyzed were the distribution and equity effects of fiscal policy (that is, VAT rates) and of trade reform (tariff rates).

Assessing policy influence

Research can influence public policy in different ways, for example, by expanding policy capacities, broadening policy horizons, and affecting policy regimes.

Expanding policy capacities

Research can support the development of innovative ideas and the skills to communicate them, and develop new talent for doing issues-based research and analysis. In other words, research can improve the institutional framework surrounding policymaking.

When IDRC started supporting research in Vietnam, the policy capacities of Vietnamese institutions and scholars were weak. As Vietnamese economists in important policy advisory positions had studied orthodox Marxist doctrines in Soviet capitals, they were unacquainted with Western economic concepts. The kind of economic analysis required in a market economy is fundamentally different from that called for in a centrally planned economy. All economists therefore had to be retrained in capitalist economic theory and models. But who would do the retraining, and how?

It is at this level 'that the three IDRC programmes [...] made an outstanding and singular contribution through their adoption of an innovative approach which no one else was using at that time,' writes Saumier. The approach was to let the Vietnamese researchers themselves select the issues to be investigated, to entrust the research to Vietnamese institutions and researchers, and to provide senior academic advisors who came periodically to Hanoi to advise their colleagues and to review progress. Also, IDRC encouraged the formation of inter-institutional networks capable of working cooperatively. This approach proved extraordinarily fruitful, and gradually a cadre of competent researchers emerged.

The effectiveness of that method was evident from the start, with the VISED programme and its varied small projects. But the scenario holds particularly for the components of VEEM, which were major undertakings calling for the gathering and analysis of large quantities of hard data. The preparation of the computerized trade database, for example, was a complex exercise hitherto unheard of among Vietnamese researchers.

The scenario applies also to the modelling component of MIMAP. Here again, Vietnamese researchers, assisted by outside scholars, carried out the complex work. Similarly, when the time came to actually use the model to analyze policy proposals, the issues were selected by Vietnam's Ministry of Finance.

Another innovation, encouraged especially by VEEM and MIMAP, was the creation of teams of institutions and researchers working together, a rare collaboration in Vietnam.

The IDRC projects showed that it was possible to jointly carry out complicated endeavours requiring a range of skills.

Broadening policy horizons

Research can introduce new ideas to the policy agenda, ensure that knowledge is provided to decision makers in a form they can use, and nourish dialogues among researchers and decision makers. To put it another way, research can improve the intellectual framework surrounding policymaking.

As André Saumier notes, Doi Moi was launched when the limitations of the communist economic doctrine became increasingly obvious. Therefore, he writes, 'The initial challenge to policy and decision makers was less one of broadening existing policy horizons than one of exploring a true "terra incognita" of economic policy and of finding one's way around there.' At the beginning of this process, Vietnam enjoyed great success: the country was heralded as the 'new tiger' because of the rapid growth of its economy. 'A certain complacency had taken hold,' notes Saumier, 'based on the view that sufficient reform had by and large already been implemented, that success was basically in hand.' But the Asian financial crisis of 1996–97 was a brutal wake-up call. The urgent question then became: How to restore the momentum?

As these issues arose after VISED had ended, the programme's role in broadening policy horizons is unclear. It is true that most of the projects supported by VISED did break fresh ground, such as its contribution to new thinking on regional development. On the other hand, VISED's impact on senior level advisors remains poorly documented.

By contrast, the VEEM programme helped the Institute of Economics address two urgent questions: trade policy and competitiveness policy. The Institute's research showed that the vaunted export orientation policy of the government was actually one of import substitution and, in effect, a legacy of the centrally planned economy. It also showed that the tariff policy worked to the detriment of rural areas. In addition, the research revealed that measures to maintain the competitiveness of the key export sectors of garments and textiles were based on flawed analyses. Undoubtedly, such findings had important policy implications.

The conclusions reached by the Institute were shared by other key policy groups, and as Saumier points out, these were 'in the air', although it is not possible to fully document the mechanisms employed for the diffusion of the results to senior policy levels. But the economic component of VEEM was managed by three senior government advisors who could bring those findings to high places. And as several persons interviewed during this evaluation argued, the president of the Institute of Economics played a key role in his capacity as a member of the Party Central Committee and of the Standing Committee on Economic Affairs of the National Assembly.

One of MIMAP's overt purposes was to broaden policy horizons, since it proposed a new definition of poverty and a novel method to document it. 'It is clear', writes Saumier, 'that MIMAP has had an important impact on the thinking and methodology of PHERP [the National Program for Hunger Eradication and Poverty Reduction].'

MIMAP's modelling component has also had a clear broadening effect on the taxation side of the Ministry of Finance. The Ministry's lack of econometric models was remedied by the development of a CGE model with the assistance of IDRC provided experts. The Ministry has since taken 'ownership' of this model and has been using it for many purposes. It is also continuing to expand it.

Affecting policy regimes

Finally, research can sometimes influence public policy in a direct way: findings can modify the development of laws, regulations, programmes, or structures. In actual fact, such a process is rare and normally circuitous, and only in a few instances can change be attributed, visibly and directly, to the inspiration of research alone.

As Saumier argues, because the implementation of Doi Moi called for a fundamental redesign of programmes and policies and the development of new ones,

> ... it would certainly not be illegitimate to argue that the various components of VISED and VEEM did inevitably affect the Vietnam policy regimes, if only by the fact that they expanded the Government's policy capacities and broadened its policy horizons in a context of strong demand for policy and of very scarce supply thereof.

Clear paths are difficult to trace, but in the case of VISED, one can at least observe that many important policy decisions did conform, ultimately, to the recommendations of some research.

VEEM, meanwhile, came to far-reaching conclusions, but paradoxically had less perceptible direct effect on policy regimes. Among factors contributing to this were academic style reports that were not operational in policy terms. Also, the reports became available only in late 2001, and so insufficient time may have passed for their influence to be felt.

MIMAP did not set out to replace current poverty indicators. However, the government may well adopt MIMAP's approach to poverty measurement. Thus, that programme will have enjoyed far-reaching policy consequences. And its modelling element has led to interesting theoretical conclusions, for example concerning the failure of trade liberalization to 'trickle down'.

Some Lessons

1. All three of IDRC's programmes have had an impact on policy, particularly on the expansion of policy capacities and the broadening of policy horizons.
2. Timing contributed strongly to achieving policy influence: Vietnam was transforming its economic system and was therefore in need of research to guide its reforms.
3. In Vietnam, more than in most countries, institutional and personal links were crucial to achieving influence on policy and measuring this impact later. Strong, well-connected project advisory groups contributed.
4. IDRC's general approach of fostering an indigenous and autonomous research and policy capability through capacity building, institutional development, and network creation contributed to its success. Persistence and perseverance were key.

Basic Data

Time Period:	1993–2001
Objectives:	1. VISED: Strengthen research capacity to support the national research programme under four themes: environment, economy, legal, and small grants. 2. VEEM: Strengthen capacity for knowledge-based policy development in economic integration and NRM. 3. MIMAP: Develop and apply a poverty monitoring system; and develop econometric (CGE) models for analysis at the national level.
Research Outputs:	1. VISED: (*a*) Four studies: 'Foundations for regional development', 'Organizations and management of export processing zones', 'Formulation and organization of shareholding companies' and 'Establishing a system for credit funds'. (*b*) Various small grant research reports; highly varied. 2. VEEM: (*a*) Five reports in 2001 on trade liberalization and its impacts; and on industrial competitiveness in textiles and garment industry. (*b*) Computerized trade database (one of a kind in VN). 3. MIMAP: CBMS; CGE models; analysis using these models were distribution and equity impact of fiscal policy and trade reform.

Trade and Finance

9

Influencing the Global Economic Agenda: Developing Country Economies are Growing in Importance

This brief is based on a case study by Diana Tussie.

The World Bank estimates that the developing countries will account for more than half of global consumption and capital formation by 2010. Yet, in the esoteric world of international economic and monetary policy, developing countries must fight to make their voice heard over their Northern industrial neighbours.

The voice of the developing world in discussions to set the global economic agenda is the inter-governmental Group of 24—better known simply as the G-24. Created more than 30 years ago, the G-24 faced a daunting task in attempting to ensure that their issues were heard in deliberations of the larger G-77, dominated by the wealthy Northern industrialized nations, the World Bank, and the International Monetary Fund. Both the G-24 and the G-77 are creations of the United Nations Conference on Trade and Development (UNCTAD) and they continue to operate under the UNCTAD umbrella. Their role is to help set the policies of the Bank and the IMF in issues of international finance. However, from the beginning, the G-24 found itself disadvantaged at the conference table, lacking the capacity to research the complex issues in order to make its case effectively.

Initial technical support for the project, administered by UNCTAD, was provided by the UN system through the United Nations Institute for Training and Research. Financing was arranged though the United Nations Development Programme (UNDP), but because of a UNDP provision that prohibits financing beyond 10 years without parallel funding, UNDP funds came to an end in 1986. The Group turned to IDRC for assistance. The objective of the original three year project in 1988 was to 'assist developing countries in building up their capacity in international monetary negotiations and to strengthen their technical preparedness and their ability to participate in and contribute to all phases of discussion and negotiation within the framework of the IMF and the Bank.'

A wide-ranging programme

Officially the project was called the Technical Support Service (TSS), although within the G-24 it was more generally known simply as the Research Programme. The primary aims of the G-24 TSS are:

1. To continue to strengthen the capacity of the G-24 to meaningfully contribute to the ongoing deliberations of the international financial institutions.
2. To enable developing countries to effectively participate in various fora in the debates on reforming the international financial architecture.
3. To reinforce developing countries' capacities to design policies to help create a stable financial environment conducive to investment, and to reduce vulnerability to external shocks, particularly those arising from volatile world markets.
4. To enhance the understanding of developing country policymakers of complex issues such as the functioning of international markets and the inter-relationships between trade, investment, and finance.
5. To raise awareness outside developing countries of the need to introduce a 'development dimension' into discussions of international finance and institutional reform.

IDRC's original commitment was for three years, but the Centre's involvement with the TSS project has continued through four phases for close to 15 years. During that time, the Research Programme became, in the view of most of the stakeholders, 'the glue that held the G-24 together.' Other support, either financial or in kind, now comes from UNCTAD, the governments of Denmark and the Netherlands, and from the governments of the G-24 countries themselves.

The TSS has undertaken more than 100 research studies over the past 15 years. Among the more tangible products of the programme are 11 volume set of *International Monetary and Financial Issues for the 1990s*, and dozens of research papers published in the *G-24 Discussion Paper Series*. The aim of the studies was to provide solid technical analysis from a Southern point of view in the ongoing dialogue with the IMF and the World Bank—the type of research and analysis that previously had been almost the exclusive domain of those international financial institutions. The publications were also intended to alert members of the G-24 to emerging issues.

In addition to providing development-related research, the programme has served as a source of fresh ideas for the international public policy community at large, as well as for academics and research institutes. From IDRC's viewpoint, the programme raised its visibility and reach among senior policymakers, and institutions working in this specialized area of development.

Reaching out to policymakers

The renowned economist G.K. (Gerry) Helleiner, currently Professor Emeritus of Economics at the University of Toronto, was the research coordinator for the TSS for eight years, starting in 1991. Dr Diana Tussie, the lead evaluator of the project for IDRC, comments that Helleiner was 'a very active project director', attending meetings of the G-24 deputies and ministers, as well as its Governing Council. He was also a strong advocate for a larger role of developing countries in world financial affairs.

Helleiner pointed out that in the mid-1990s, the developing countries accounted for 44 per cent of the world output in purchasing power parity terms. 'Developing countries as a group are generally projected to grow at roughly double the rate of the industrial world during the coming decade,' he said. 'The developing countries (and other non-G-7 members) are economically as well as demographically important, and they are very rapidly increasing their importance in the global economy.'

As an example of this importance, Helleiner pointed out that 'during the 1991 recession in the industrial world, three-quarters of the increase in world exports, which buffered their problems, went to developing-country markets.'

While he was effective at making the case for an enhanced role for the G-24 countries, Helleiner faced some more mundane problems in the day-to-day operations of the Research Programme, particularly in the area of communication. It was found that the mailing lists used to distribute the research output were often out of date. Thus, material was not reaching the right people. Dr Tussie also points out that there was 'an erroneous assumption that by distributing the products to the Executive Directors, the rest of the national machinery would be in contact with the outputs.'

Many of these issues were overcome during the second phase of the project, from 1993 to 1996, and from the outset important steps were taken to increase 'ownership' of the G-24 programme by the member countries themselves. This included countries contributing to the funding, and the creation of new mechanisms for guiding research and gauging policy needs. Under this heading, the Technical Group (TG) was a key development, says Dr Tussie.

> By bringing the researchers together with the G-24 representatives in a formal setting, the TG acted as an intermediary between the Research Programme and the G-24. It was a mechanism in which dialogue was expected to bridge the gap between research and policy.

Changes in approaches

Further attempts to bring about closer contact between researchers and policymakers were made during the critical third phase of the project from 1996 to 2000. These included the establishment of a Liaison Office with the goal of providing better access to the Executive Directors. In addition, informal meetings between researchers and policymakers from the G-24 countries provided opportunities for direct policy input to the Research Programme.

This phase of the project also saw Helleiner's retirement and the appointment of a new research coordinator, Dani Rodrik, Professor of International Political Economy at Harvard University's John F. Kennedy School of Government. Rodrik set out at once to improve the dissemination and outreach of the Research Programme's output. Dissemination by way of the Internet was implemented—a major step in making the Research Programme's product globally available. There was also an attempt to make the material more accessible by complementing some of the detailed research papers with shorter position papers on strategic topics. Papers were no longer published as volume sets because of the lag time involved; instead they were published jointly with UNCTAD and Harvard as stand-alone discussion papers.

Equally significant was a change in approach—an attempt to reach a wider audience and influence public policy at the global level, while also contributing more to the academic debate on international monetary and financial issues. As the proposal for the fourth phase put it, future studies would be published 'with a view to contributing to the wider international discussions on financial and monetary issues from a development perspective in political, intergovernmental, and academic circles, and the civil society at large.'

This was a key departure from the previous nine years, when the focus of the Research Programme had always been on the executive directors of the G-24 countries as the primary target audience, says Dr Tussie. The change in emphasis resulted in some tension between the research coordinator, who advocated long-term change, and the Liaison Office, which favoured more demand driven research.

Even more fundamental, the extent of the research coordinator's responsibilities, and the roles of the other actors in the project—never formally defined—became a matter for debate. Unlike Helleiner, who stressed the G-24's ownership of the project, Rodrik saw himself as accountable primarily to UNCTAD that, for its part, saw the project as a technical assistance project to the G-24, similar to other technical assistance it provides.

The differences stem in part from differing perceptions of the policy process, Dr Tussie believes. 'Traditionally, policymaking is viewed as a linear process where papers and positions are prepared and presented to policymakers who use them in negotiating and taking policy decisions', she says, adding that it is a view that has largely been discarded today. In the early years many of the G-24 stakeholders had faith in a linear approach, believing that research papers could directly influence policy. Even today there is still 'at least some hope that the Deputies and Ministers would read them and be influenced in their position by what they read.'

The alternative to the linear approach to influencing policy is what has been termed 'enlightenment', where research indirectly influences the 'circulation and percolation' of ideas over a period of time. Helleiner compared this approach to the action of water that drips and drips on rock until the rock slowly gives way. Rodrik, on the other hand, commented that while the linear approach is more immediate, 'enlightenment' is oriented more towards policy change as a result of changing perceptions.

The actual use of the Research Programme's output is unclear, and various participants have differing views on who used it, and how. Aziz Ali Mohammed, with the G-24 Liaison Office, felt that the papers produced by TSS were most likely to be read by those at the lower levels of the policymaking machinery. On the other hand, Rodrik believed that executive directors and assistants were primary users of the material. A former Executive Director from Nigeria, Patrick Akatu, thought the papers were of high quality, but did not penetrate the policy community at the level of the Bank and the IMF. He says the research 'is helpful to understand the context in which policy is made, but not helpful at the time to negotiate specific issues that are in the daily agenda.' However, Dr Tussie concludes that the G-24 having an official Research Programme lends a certain seal of approval to developing country issues.

Further, the fact that the Managing Director of the IMF and the President of the World Bank attend G-24 meetings gives the issues they raise more legitimacy than those raised by other international bodies. And finally, the fact that the Research Programme receives funding from multinational donor institutions lends it a further seal of approval.

Assessing policy influence

The study of the Research Programme's influence on policy, carried out by IDRC, identifies three types of policy influence:

1. *Expanding policy capacities*—this includes improving knowledge, supporting, the development of innovative ideas and the capacity to communicate them, and developing new talent for research and analysis. Requests for detailed policy briefs are cited as one indication of the need for additional knowledge on specific issues.
2. *Expanding policy horizons*—similar to the 'enlightenment' approach as a means to influence policy, the resulting form of influence is often in terms of new concepts being introduced, new ideas on the agenda, and researchers and others educated to take up new positions with broader understanding of issues. This is considered to be one of the most important forms of influence attributed to the Research Programme.
3. *Affecting policy regimes*—referring to a fundamental redesign of modification of programmes or policies. This is considered to be a long-term goal for the Research Programme, although there are few instances where change can be seen to have been brought about through the influence of the Research Programme alone.

Basic Data

Time Period: 1988–2003

Objectives:
1. To assist developing countries in building their capacity in international monetary negotiations.
2. To strengthen their technical preparedness, and their ability to participate in and contribute to all phases of discussion and negotiation within the framework of the Fund and the World Bank.

Research Outputs:
1. Web and traditional dissemination of research papers in two main areas:
   (a) Technical economic research
   (b) Normative research (that is, on role and performance of international financial institutions)
   Ph I: 32 research studies
   Ph II: 36 research studies
   Ph III: 27 research studies
   Ph IV: 15 research studies
2. 11 volume set of International Monetary and Financial Issues for the 1990s
3. 24 papers in the G-24 Discussion Paper Series

Negotiating the New World of International Trade: Research Helps Latin America to Cope with an Expanding Trade Dialogue

This brief is based on a case study by Luis Macadar.

During the late 1990s, in the wake of the Uruguay Round of international trade negotiations, Latin American nations found themselves literally lost in a plethora of issues that until then had been foreign to the discourse on foreign trade. They risked becoming mere spectators in a game that was crucial to their continued survival. That was when researchers, with IDRC support, got involved, seeking to bring together different sectors and countries in the region to begin writing a new chapter in the history of policymaking in the developing world. It's a lucid and interesting, if still unfinished, chapter.

The year was 1997. Three years had passed since the exhaustive Uruguay Round had formally ended and the resultant agreements signed. But in the minds of thinkers such as Rohinton Medhora, the then team leader of the IDRC's Trade, Employment, and Competitiveness programme initiative, the ink was taking a long time to dry. Something was wrong.

The trade negotiations, named after the Latin American country where they had begun in September 1986, had revealed major weaknesses in the region's negotiating capacity. It seemed to validate the thesis, expounded a quarter century earlier by economist and educator Albert Hirschman, that some countries, Latin American ones prominent among them, had lost the liberty enjoyed by sovereign states to set their own policy agendas. They had become mere 'coping states'. They spent more time reacting rather than acting.

Seven and one-half years of trade talks helped highlight this regional inadequacy. After Uruguay, trade negotiations were no longer just about the selling of sugar, cars, and textiles, but according to the World Trade Organization (WTO) website, covered everything 'from toothbrushes to pleasure boats, from banking to telecommunications, from the genes of wild rice to AIDS treatment.'

Those talks, recalls Medhora, 'were the first where the trade agenda was expanded to include what we now call behind-the-border subjects.' These include international investment, competition policy, trade in services, telecommunications, financial services, export promotion, intellectual property rights, special and differential treatment, labour policy and, of course, the environment. In this expanded discourse, developing countries often found themselves on the sidelines, unable to participate fully, uncertain how to respond to this plethora of issues. The distinction between domestic and international policy had been blurred and, says Medhora, the need for 'extremely specialized and sophisticated analytical ability on the part of trade negotiators' became evident.

Medhora and other participants at a 1997 brainstorming session in Buenos Aires, Argentina, were moved by another piece of evidence of Latin America's lack of preparedness for engagement in the growing international trade policy dialogue. Part of a World Bank study questioning the performance and effectiveness of Mercosur—a regional trade arrangement established six years earlier by Argentina, Brazil, Paraguay, and Uruguay—appeared in the *Financial Times*. A well-reasoned response to the publication came not from Latin America, but from the desk of an official in the Washington-based Inter-American Development Bank.

'In the industrialized countries,' says senior foreign trade expert Luis Abugattas, 'there are hundreds of think tanks producing policy papers that are analyzed by the authorities and then used as inputs for negotiating positions. In my own country, Peru, there is no university or think tank doing this kind of research.' He characterized the Latin American situation as one of 'gambling with our countries' future every day at the negotiating table.'

There were other problems: the sheer lack of technical expertise, particularly among the smaller countries; a 'disconnect', in some cases, between policymakers and the research community; and poor coordination among various institutions within the same government. Something had to be done. The Buenos Aires session led to an unprecedented mobilization of the research community to generate the information needed to influence Latin American trade policymaking and international trade dialogue in a new and positive way.

The researcher comes to the table

So, this is how the LATN was born. Just as developed country think tanks and research groups were represented at the negotiating table through the reception of their insights into their countries' policymaking processes, the time had arrived for researchers to find their place, so to speak, on the Latin American side of the negotiation room. By December 1997, a project proposal had been drafted. The following March, IDRC approved a CA $1.32 million grant to the Latin American Faculty of Social Sciences (FLACSO) to establish LATN.

Consulting economist Luis Macadar recalled the objectives of LATN in a recent case study undertaken to discover whether and how the project had begun to influence public policy. LATN, says Macadar, aimed to:

1. Support agenda building and policy formulation in Latin American countries in response to the emerging trends and issues in the international trade system;
2. Harness the existing research capacity in Latin American countries to engage in international trade negotiations and contribute to human resource development; and
3. Strengthen collaboration among the participating institutions with a view to sustaining the long-term goals of the Network.

Many of the people interviewed by Macadar in the preparation of the case study envision the pursuit of a regional approach to trade negotiations as an important complementary objective. In terms of the research process itself, they stress the importance of LATN's coordinating role in drawing upon the expertise of various national and regional institutions and in finding 'common ground' by bridging the much discussed divide among governments, researchers, and the private sector.

Studies undertaken to meet these aims fall into three groups.

1. Group 1 comprises wide, overarching issues. These include the preconditions for the formation of trade coalitions, and the challenges of bargaining in the context of ever-changing coalitions.
2. Group 2 involves the study, from a Latin American perspective, of emerging issues, including the expanding menu of items on the trade negotiation agenda that has made the Uruguay Round such an eye-opener.

3.   Group 3, says Macadar, 'consists of country case studies that aim to identify optimal or feasible national responses in the context of the current international trade relations regime for Argentina, Brazil, Chile, Colombia, Mexico, Peru, Uruguay, and Venezuela.'

The Network that set about fulfilling this ample mandate in the spring of 1998 comprised a dozen researchers. Today, it brings together some 35 researchers from more than 30 academic institutions. The Network also includes policy officials from Latin American countries, and colleagues working with a number of international agencies—academic, non-governmental, and intergovernmental. Most LATN researchers are experienced academics—many, such as the Network's director, Diana Tussie, having already achieved international renown—with broad experience in the issues addressed by LATN. There are also a number of young researchers, mainly Masters or PhD students or graduates of FLACSO.

Perfecting the LATN trademark

LATN's focus is simple and pragmatic. It seeks to deliver policy relevant research that meets the needs of the region's decision makers—those in government, but often those in the private sector as well. An example of this approach is the research by Tussie and LATN Deputy Director Miguel Lengyel on export subsidies. That study was valuable, given the long-standing importance of subsidies to key Latin American industries, and the complaints from other countries that such subsidies conferred an unfair advantage.

Following the Uruguay Round, which defined the term subsidy and clearly listed acceptable export promotion practices, reports Lengyel, 'countries now have their hands tied when it comes to export promotion policies.' The study identified 'margins for manoeuvre' that survived the agreements signed as part of the Uruguay Round, and that were consistent with other bilateral and multilateral obligations. The two experienced researchers discovered that measures such as reimbursing indirect taxes on items like energy costs and such policy initiatives as research and development or training support, continued to be legitimate.

LATN's focused approach has also meant following up on the output of other researchers and academics in the field of international trade, rather than yielding to the temptation to generate brand new research. Macadar describes what he calls 'the LATN trademark', the Network's particular way of looking at problems, which 'involves taking approaches from the literature and prioritizing them in a certain way, applying them to a specific issue related to the trade negotiations.' This combination includes technical, legal, juridical, and economic elements. This unique LATN approach may be summarized as 'academic knowledge applied specifically to a concrete sphere.'

Also, LATN has seen the need to combine firm focus with creative flexibility. While the objectives in the original IDRC project proposal remain, emphases have been adjusted to meet the changing multilateral agenda which has represented a shifting and confusing picture. Agriculture has emerged as the key issue, followed by competition policy, internationalization of the multilateral trade rules, safeguard issues, anti-dumping, and services.

Also, emphasis was placed on the policy formulation process within individual governments, and the importance of adapting it to the needs of negotiators. The project was also tweaked to place greater emphasis on education. 'The authorities were much less well informed than had been assumed in the original proposal,' says Macadar. The emphasis on education was particularly important in view of the emerging need to conduct multiple and simultaneous negotiations, and because of the paucity of published material on relevant topics in Spanish and with a Latin American perspective.

Flexibility also required a change in the level at which LATN's research output would be targeted. Given the frequent changes at the ministerial and deputy ministerial levels, LATN began to gear its material towards the middle level bureaucrat. The Network recognized the control of information, the capacity to influence policymaking in subtle ways, and the responsibility to provide policy continuity that resided at this middle level.

A dream fulfilled?

Asked whether the dream, that motivated him and a number of Latin American colleagues to come up with the LATN concept, had been fulfilled, Medhora, now IDRC vice president, Programme and Partnership Branch, answers: 'Capacity building is a slow process and we had no illusions that anything dramatic would happen overnight. But I think if I were to assess where LATN is today, I would have to say I am extremely pleased.' As an evidence of LATN's success, Medhora noted that the Network had helped spawn similar networks. These include networks, also established with IDRC support, in Latin America itself, and in South Asia and Southern Africa.

This positive assessment is reflected in the results of Macadar's case study, specifically in terms of the effectiveness of the project in influencing policy. An overall study by IDRC's Evaluation Unit, of which Macadar's case study is a part, identified three major forms of policy influence: expanding policy capacities, broadening policy horizons, and affecting policy regimes. Macadar found evidence of influence in all three areas, but particularly in the first two.

1. *Expanding policy capacities:* LATN has demonstrated success in this area, not only by the quantity and quality of its work, but also by the innovative ways in which it has targeted its research activities to ensure that specific needs in the area of international trade negotiations and international trade policy are addressed and that the education, information, and strengthening of Latin American negotiators can be achieved. The initiation of a new generation of academics—many of whom may well end up as policymakers later in their careers—into this aspect of social science research is another example of expanding capacities.

2. *Broadening policy horizons:* This 'enlightenment approach' encompasses the research, information dissemination, and training through which the Network has helped to better equip policymakers, negotiators, middle level officials, and private sector representatives to undertake effective international trade policy analysis and decision making. Various Latin American governments—those of Argentina, Paraguay, Peru, and several Central American countries—have approached the Network for assistance. Argentina's Secretary of Trade, faced with complaints from the footwear lobby about competitive imports from Brazil, resolved the dispute with the help of a paper by LATN's deputy director, and through the author's direct participation in the discussions.

Regional bodies, including the Andean Community and the Inter-American Institute for Cooperation in Agriculture, and Brazil's National Confederation of Industries, have also sought LATN's assistance in trade negotiations. LATN has helped the World Bank Institute customize its trade policy courses for the region in an effort that has also been supported by UNCTAD's Trade Diplomacy Programme. UNCTAD and the WTO, both of which are linked to LATN, have identified the Network as a vehicle through which to strengthen regional collaboration between their two organizations. The United Nations Economic Commission for Latin America and the Caribbean (ECLAC) has also associated itself with LATN's work. Workshops conducted by LATN brought together negotiators from various governmental agencies of the same country, as well as representatives of various countries and of the private sector, in a non-competitive environment—often for the first time.

3. *Affecting policy regimes:* This 'fundamental redesign or modification' of policies or programmes is more difficult to demonstrate at this early stage. However, some examples are beginning to emerge. In developing negotiation approaches for liberalizing services, governments, at least in part as a result of the Network's input, have been accepting the need to go to the negotiating table with a number of options, rather than with a single inflexible position. The importance of the Network's studies and of its websites in the preparation of the background analysis for Argentina's anti-dumping and subsidy countervail legislation was rated very highly. And following an agricultural seminar organized by LATN to equip policymakers for upcoming international negotiations, Argentina's Ministry of Agriculture prepared a series of studies that were transformed into manuals that are now found in every decision maker's office.

Some Lessons

1. Timeliness of the research question is a crucial element in policy influence.
2. Political and institutional factors (including in LATN's case, the fact that the same person may be researcher, negotiator, and decision maker simultaneously or over time) need to be taken into account.
3. Success may be hastened or hindered by the structure of linkages established by the Network and also by the approaches to dissemination.
4. Clarity of objectives must be balanced by flexible responses either to changed circumstances or to the recognition of gaps in the original project proposal, as in LATN's switch from publishing research results in book format to the use of briefing papers when the need for quick, 'real-time' information was realized.
5. At least in LATN's case, the fact that policy research responded to policy needs and focused on meeting those needs was a defining success factor.
6. The use of public media as part of the dissemination effort may help not only to increase policy influence but also to establish what may be called policy transparency.
7. Constructing a single model or approach that is applicable to all countries or even to all those within a single region is difficult, at best.

Basic Data

Time Period: 1998–2002

Objectives: To conduct policy oriented research on emerging issues in international trade relations to:
1. Support the process of agenda building and policy formulation in LAC (Latin America and the Caribbean) countries in response to emerging trends in the international system;
2. Harness existing research capacity in LAC countries to engage in international trade negotiations; and
3. Strengthen collaboration among participating institutions with a view to long-term sustainability of the network.

Research Outputs: Working papers and policy briefs on:
1. Overarching issues such as preconditions for trade coalitions, bargaining and relationships between multilateralism and regional integration initiatives.
2. Emerging issue from a LAC perspective, such as international investment, competition policy, financial services, telecoms, IPR, dispute settlement, etc.
3. Country case studies to identify optimal or feasible national responses in international trade relations.
4. Website, newsletters, conferences.
5. Training courses.
6. Meetings with officials.
7. Consultancies.

Resource Management

Sharing the Land, Shaping the Future: In Lebanon, Social Consensus and Institutional Revival were Key Ingredients in the Search for a Sustainable Land Use Strategy

This brief is based on a case study written by David Brooks.

A major accomplishment of the 'Sustainable Improvement of Marginal Lands in Lebanon' project was to help communities in Lebanon's poor Arsaal district overcome social strife and chart a new course towards the sustainable use of an overstretched resource. But in the process, it had unexpected impacts—contributing to the revival of a moribund municipal government and prompting Lebanese researchers and international donors to adopt a new approach to environmental research.

There is a strong sense of history that clings to Arsaal, a sparsely populated, semi-arid highland area that stretches across 36,000 hectares in northeastern Lebanon, up to the Syrian border.

The town of Arsaal (the surrounding countryside goes by the same name) was first recorded some 350 years ago, and monuments in its cemetery date back to 100 years. In recent memory, it was a town mostly of tents, although most have now been replaced by stone houses. Many residents of the area still earn their livelihood from animal herding—indeed, goats and sheep outnumber the people by nearly two to one. But change has been coming to Arsaal, bringing both good news and bad. Stone fruit trees—introduced in 1952 by a local known as the Cherry Man, who brought the first cherry sapling—were not expected to thrive in this parched area. In the half-century or so since, however, orchards have flourished. This means, paradoxically, that at a time when deforestation is a major concern elsewhere, one of Lebanon's driest places is getting greener. Arsaal now has some two million trees, mostly cherry and apricot, that provide a major source of income for 60 per cent of its population.

Yet the underside of this economic surge has been intensified social conflict and environmental uncertainty. Fruit farmers have 'enclosed' some of the best lands for cultivation, disrupting and shortening the herds' migration patterns, and denying herders the use of lands they had relied upon during the driest periods. Local institutions have not been strong enough to resolve the differences between herders and farmers, who come from different families and social classes. And this social divide has been exacerbated by deepening income disparities, since fruit growing families are able to earn more, with less effort, than herders.

Looming ecological problems

The growth of the fruit industry also raised concerns about soil degradation. An Arsaali schoolteacher laments that: 'The people don't know how to look after their land properly; they were shepherds before. The soil is becoming weak, and now there is less common land for the remaining shepherds to use' (Hamadeh et al. 2006).

Added to these problems is a further layer of conflict that emerged when outsiders began quarrying rock in the area. Since the practice started during Lebanon's civil war when Arsaal had no functioning municipal government, quarry operators did not need to worry about permits or community oversight—often they just grabbed the land and shut out traditional users. Today, the dust from these quarries smothers nearby fruit trees, and truck traffic is a significant cause of road accidents.

A need for overlapping solutions

Dealing with this interlocking web of environmental, economic, and social challenges has required wide-ranging multidisciplinary research, undertaken in close contact with communities over a number of years. A two-phase project supported by IDRC, named Sustainable Improvement of Marginal Lands in Lebanon, had a complex mandate. One of its objectives was to help communities find and practice more sustainable forms of land use management. But before it could do that, it had to help create and nourish the institutions through which communities could work out their differences and establish some common goals.

The authors of *The Cactus Flower*, who also collaborated as researchers on the Sustainable Improvement project, note that the simultaneous challenges unfolding in Arsaal required a multitude of tools. 'Our repertoire,' they write, 'included participatory geographic information systems, blending community participation with state of the art satellite imagery; different forms of institutional bricolage, such as a local users' network, cooperatives and communication platforms; and new paradigms for development research, such as a sustainable livelihood approach and embedded research.'

The IDRC-supported researchers—who were based at the American University of Beirut (AUB) but who would, in many cases, live in the community for long periods—worked closely with the Arsaal Rural Development Association (ARDA), a local NGO. ARDA functioned like a kind of surrogate municipal government during the time when formal structures did not exist. It later helped to restore strength to the reinstated local council by creating the means for citizens to participate in the decision-making process.

One example of this is the local users' network, which ARDA and the AUB researchers designed along the lines of the Arab *majlis,* or councils that facilitate face to face dialogue as a means of dispute resolution. This traditional form was augmented by modern methods such as the use of video cameras. The researchers believed that making videos allowed for a more candid and thorough exchange of information: people expressing their grievances on video would speak their minds more directly than in a formal town hall setting, while citizens who watched the videos had more time to consider the others' point of view.

Other aspects of the work relied on similar marriages of modern technology and participatory methods. For instance, GIS modelling and satellite photos mapping soil types and water run-off patterns have helped community members plan for the construction of a reservoir—a lynchpin in the community's plan to shift to a more sustainable style of management.

Real benefits for communities

David Brooks, a water expert who authored an evaluation of the Arsaal project for IDRC, is unequivocal in his assessment of the project's community level impact. 'The two phases of work in Arsaal were successful by almost any standard,' he writes. Community members were deeply involved in the research programme, and have often seen tangible benefits as a result. For example, ARDA and AUB staff helped institute several cooperatives, a women's food-processing business and carpet weaving enterprise that continue to function. Farmers and pastoralists have tapped into new information sources that have helped them reduce the high losses associated with the pests, water stress, and poor roads typical of their area. In general, community members made use of the resources that became available. Over 500 farmers, for instance, have participated in agricultural workshops associated with the project.

The project's success is also reflected in its favourable reception outside the immediate area. Within Lebanon, the Arsaal experience has become a point of discussion in other communities, with aspects of its work being replicated in other areas. For example, four other herder cooperatives have been created based on the Arsaal model. Further afield, the UNDP has cited the Arsaal project as an example of 'best practice in sustainable development'. Meanwhile, an official with the German aid agency GTZ, which adopted the Arsaal approach for its work against desertification, has praised the project for the 'enormous intellectual investment' it brought to Arsaal.

An unexpected policy dimension

Influencing policymakers and the policymaking process was not an explicit objective of the project at the outset. However, Brooks finds that it did make itself felt in the sphere of public policy in a variety of different ways and to differing degrees. He categorizes the project's three levels of policy influence as: (*a*) 'upward' (influencing national institutions); (*b*) 'horizontal' (influencing the practices of researchers and research institutions); and (*c*) 'downward' (influencing local institutions and local people). Ranking the extent of influence in these three areas, Brooks found the greatest impact was horizontal, the second greatest was downward, and the least was upward.

A primary explanation for the relative lack of impact on national institutions is that the sparsely populated Arsaal region has been, historically, largely invisible to national authorities. The area's poverty, and inadequate transportation to the area have contributed to the long-standing marginalization of Arsaal.

Brooks comments: 'Over and over I heard the Arsaal region described as isolated. This is a remarkable way to describe a region that one can reach in a morning's drive from the capital, Beirut. Yet there is no question that the feeling of isolation is real.'

This situation has not changed much since the project ended in 2004. 'The Ministry of Agriculture as an institution has remained relatively impervious to both the process and the results of the Arsaal study,' reports Brooks. For example, the major concerns in Arsaal, notably pastoralism and land range management, remain well down on the national ministry's list of priorities. But there are some positive signs: 'Extension officers now attend workshops given in Arsaal, and members of parliament from the region do take issues on a one by one basis to high levels for action.'

This tepid impact on national policy does not mean, however, that the project has not had a significant overall influence on how environmental policy is made. The municipal government has identified strongly with the Arsaal project and has adopted its goals. This is important because municipalities have much of the mandate to enact environmental legislation, though they often lack the resources to act on that mandate. Indeed, some current municipal officials previously held positions with the NGOs involved in the Arsaal project. Brooks also notes that local community organizations that grew out of the project have cultivated links to the political process, particularly at the municipal level.

Changing the research agenda

The Arsaal project's biggest impact was felt at the points where research and policymaking intersect. The Arsaal example seems to have persuaded researchers and donor organizations in Lebanon to approach resource-use issues in new ways.

For example, one of the project's primary influences over AUB—already one of the strongest research institutions in the Arab world—was to reinstate the role of fieldwork. Previously, most work had been conducted in the lab or on the AUB farm. Now, AUB researchers favour working in close contact with communities, in a way that links research findings with development outcomes. In addition, the Arsaal experience prompted AUB to create, in 2001, its multidisciplinary Environment and Sustainable Development Unit (ESDU). The unit is now delivering programmes in research, education and training, and outreach in two other areas of Lebanon. There are plans to eventually transform the ESDU into a regional centre of excellence in sustainable development.

Officials with the governmental Lebanese Agriculture Research Institute (LARI) also indicate 'that the Arsaal projects have had an enormous influence on how they see their role and how they structure their research,' recounts Brooks. Among the most prominent changes is the adoption of a more participatory model in LARI's own research projects. International agencies like the regional International Centre for Agricultural Research in Dry Areas and Germany's GTZ have also adopted major aspects of the Arsaal model.

While these changes at the institutional level may seem sudden and dramatic, back on the ground in Arsaal, change comes slowly and more incrementally. The work of new local organizations shows that there is a greater capacity at the community level, and this is being noticed, to some extent, at the national level.

Some Lessons

1. In situations of conflict, it is important to work closely with communities, local NGOs, and councils.
2. A multidisciplinary approach is key to resolving complex problems.
3. There are multiple advantages to mixing modern and traditional methods.
4. Political stability and concrete economic gains are often mutually reinforcing goals.

Basic Data

Time Period: 1995–2004

Objectives: **Phase I:** To evaluate the sustainability of major farming systems, and to examine the viability of establishing a network of users to improve sustainable community development.
Phase II: To evaluate options developed in Phase I, and to increase focus on gender analysis as key to sustainable resource management.

Research Outputs: The Arsaal project led to the creation of the Environment and Sustainable Development Unit in 2001, a new multidisciplinary group at the American University of Beirut.
Maps of Arsaal on land use, degradation hazards and land capability; one professional article; 14 MSc theses; several brochures, videos, newspaper articles, and tools for rural development in arid areas were developed; and a book, *Research for Development in the Dry Arab Region: The Cactus Flower*, Shadi Hamadeh, Mona Haider, and Rami Zurayk, published by Southbound/ IDRC (2006).

'Arsaal is on the map, though still considered remote and unimportant,' concludes Brooks. 'The marginalization of Arsaal will not end quickly, but it is less marginal today than at the time the projects were started, and that is an important indicator of policy influence.'

Changing the Face of Mining in Peru: The News is Both Good and Bad for Miners and Mining Communities

This brief is based on two case studies by Fernando Loayza Careaga.

Mining is a dirty, dangerous occupation, but never more so than when multinational mining companies set up shop in developing countries. Since these countries desperately need the foreign currency that the mining industry brings, they do not always enforce environmental and health regulations. Two projects in Peru, where mining is a major industry, illustrate the difficulties, and in one case show how the effective use of research can influence the policies of both business and government.

The Pacific coast town of Ilo in southern Peru has for neighbours two of the largest mines in South America, Cuajone and Toquepala, operated by the American controlled Southern Peru Copper Corporation (SPCC). For most of the past 50 years the mines have been very bad neighbours.

Ignoring the protests of municipal officials and the farmers in the nearby valleys, the mining company polluted the region's air, fresh water, and coastal zones with impunity. Untreated mine tailings were discharged into the ocean, destroying marine life in the nearby Bay of Ite, and polluting the ocean as far as 11 kilometres offshore and at depths up to 60 metres.

Tens of thousands of tonnes of slag were dumped on beaches, extending into the sea at a rate of 40–60 metres every year. Sulphur dioxide gases from the smelter caused health problems for the local people, destroyed more than 20 square kilometres of the surrounding natural coastal pastures, turned the area into a desert, and damaged farmers' crops inland.

Worse, the mines extracted high quality water in the high Andes, reducing the quantity and quality of water available downstream for domestic and agricultural purposes. Geological studies showed that the company's extraction of water was responsible for a decrease in the flow of local rivers, as well as an increase in salts in the river basins.

Mobilizing for change

Things began to change in the 1980s when a local NGO called LABOR decided that international pressure was needed to redress the balance of power between the community and the company. In the words of Doris Balvín Díaz, a lawyer and a LABOR organizer: 'Social and environmental conflicts in developing countries such as Peru do not take place under equitable conditions. Investors have more power than local communities and are supported by the state because they bring resources to the economy.'

LABOR looked for an opportunity to level the playing field. They found it in the form of the second International Water Tribunal (IWT II). The IWT II, supported by more than 100 European environmental organizations, has no legal authority, but has successfully relied on international publicity to get results. Supported by the local authorities, LABOR's case was accepted by the Tribunal, which then asked IDRC to support the detailed research LABOR would need to present its case.

The Centre's expectations of the project's policy impact were fairly low, says Fernando Loayza Careaga, who evaluated the project for IDRC. 'The feeling was that if they could assist LABOR in making a well-researched presentation to the IWT II, then the ensuing publicity might convince SPCC to improve their environmental behaviour.' LABOR and its supporters, however, were much more ambitious. Balvín Díaz believed that a favourable finding would make the national government pay attention to the complaints of the local people, and change its lenient attitude towards SPCC.

LABOR had worked closely with the municipality of Ilo since the mid-1980s, and by the start of the 1990s had become the local government's main environmental advisor. Two successive mayors supported LABOR's cause. LABOR's case was also supported by the Multi-sector Permanent Commission on Environment (MPCE), made up of representatives of local munici-palities and state government departments, as well as unions and civil society groups. And it just happened to be chaired by the mayor of Ilo, Ernesto Herrera Becerra. It was MPCE's role to oversee SPCC's compliance with environmental recommendations. The Commission members wanted to see concrete action from the mining company, and they were not getting it.

A victory

Edmundo Torrelio, of the Ilo Valley Commission of Irrigators, pointed out that the valley farmers also had a stake in the management of the scarce water resource. The farmers' persistent complaints eventually got the attention of the General Inspection Office of the Republic, and resulted in a major coup—the General Inspector agreed to testify before the Tribunal.

This brought the project national media attention. Three days before the IWT II hearing, the newspaper, *Onda*, reported, 'The General Inspector of the Republic, Dr Luz Aurea Sáenz, said yesterday that during the last three decades some factors, such as lenient legislation and bad public servants, have allowed SPCC to impose its terms, to do nothing to solve problems, and to misuse water resources.' Another newspaper, *La Republica*, quoted Dr Sáenz as saying that, while a favourable ruling from the IWT II would be only a moral victory, it would be acknowledged at the United Nations Conference on Development and Environment, held later that year in Brazil.

LABOR was able to put together a strong coalition of local and regional forces to support its case against SPCC before the IWT II. That case included the IDRC funded study. Additional evidence was presented at the hearing in February 1992, including a video and live testimony from Dr Sáenz and Mayor Becerra.

But Balvín Díaz and her colleagues realized that local support and a victory at the IWT II might not be enough. They would need political support at the national level to guarantee action. And they got it. Immediately after the Tribunal's decision was announced, 50 members of congress came out in support of its findings. This was the result of intense lobbying in the preceding months by two local members of the congress, Cristala Constantiñidez and Julio Díaz Palacios, who was mayor of Ilo during the 1980s.

In its findings the IWT II jury condemned SPCC for its abuse of freshwater resources, its negligence in disposing of toxic slag, and for emitting enormous quantities of sulphur dioxide gases. It accused the company of taking advantage of lax enforcement of environmental laws and regulations, and of increasing its profits at the expense of the local community.

Concrete results

While the jury's findings were everything that LABOR and its coalition had hoped for, it was in one sense anticlimactic. Just two months before the IWT II hearing, anticipating a negative outcome from the Tribunal, SPCC signed an accord with the national government committing an investment of US \$200 million for environmental projects, and a further US \$100 million for new technologies and equipment.

Since that time the company has built an earthquake-proof tailings dam so that tailings are no longer discharged into Ite Bay. The bay itself has been reclaimed, and the flamingos, fish, and shrimps have returned. Slag dumps on the shore near Ilo have been removed.

The company compensates farmers for damage to crops, and has established a fund for agricultural loans and technical assistance. Water recycling has been increased and SPCC no longer exploits water wells in the Ilo valley. A three-stage project to reduce sulphur dioxide emissions by 92 per cent was scheduled for completion at the end of 2004, but the government recently approved a two-year extension.

There have also been changes in public policy. Most significantly, the Government of Peru adopted a new environmental regulatory framework for mining activities. How much this

Box 10.1: High Altitude Mining—An Occupational Hazard?

In 1990 Cerro de Pasco, 4,300 metres above sea level, was the largest and highest mining town in the world. About one-third of its population of 71,000 are miners, and their families—according to Dr Alberto Arregui of the Centro Medico San Felipe, were dying too young, much younger than people who lived at sea level.

The main cause of death was Chronic Mountain Sickness (CMS), which is essentially a process of loss of adaptation to high altitudes. Preliminary research carried out by the Universidad Peruana Cayetano Heredia, at the request of the miners' trade union, had suggested that a combination of factors led to the high incidence of CMS among the miners of Cerro de Pasco. Many smoked tobacco, drank alcohol, and chewed coca leaf. But more than bad habits, the research suggested that shift work and the severe working conditions in high altitude mines increased the incidence of CMS.

In 1989 IDRC funded a study to explore these results with a view to gaining recognition of CMS as an occupational illness by the government and the International Labour Organization. However, the project included no formal strategy to lobby policymakers or other social agents.

The 18 month study did find a higher incidence of CMS among the miners than among the general population, and concluded that 'the highly exhausting physical activity of miners in general, and mining drillers in particular' accelerated the symptoms of CMS. The results of the study were outlined in a presentation to the miners' trade union. Leaflets were published and distributed in other high altitude mining centres in Peru. The results were also published in an award-winning book, *Desadaptación a la Vida en las Grandes Alturas* (loss of adaptation to life at high altitudes). However, there was no concerted effort to meet with the government, the mining industry, or community-based organizations. The effort to gain recognition for CMS fell far below what was expected, according to Dr Arregui and researcher Marcel Valcarcel (1990).

This was in part because of the threatening presence of Shining Path guerillas in Cerro de Pasco, which forced the research team to keep a low profile. Then both the Ministry of Health and the mining industry representatives challenged the project's findings because they contradicted the 'traditional assumption' that people born at high altitudes are 'well adapted' to these conditions. In addition, it was suggested that the findings of the initial study were biased, that the miners had been 'induced to express perceptions of health discomfort.'

Thus, despite some positive findings, the study has had a negligible impact on occupational health and safety or mining policies in Peru, says Fernando Loayza Careaga, who evaluated the project's policy impact. Among officials at both the National Institute of Occupational Health and the Ministry of Energy and Mines, as well as among representatives of industry associations, he could find no one in 2002 who was aware of the study. Union officials, however, were aware of the study, but they now had other priorities.

Since the study was conducted, Peru, like many other Latin American countries, has undergone major economic reforms, including labour market reform and the privatization of state companies. This has resulted in a rapid increase in the number of miners working on contract, and a subsequent weakening of the miners' union. The weakened unions have largely lost their ability to influence policy, says researcher Marcel Valcarcel.

was influenced by LABOR's campaign depends on whom you talk to. LABOR staff and both the current and former mayors of Ilo believe that the Ilo case was critical in determining the new framework.

On the other hand, officials such as Luis Alberto Sanchez at the Ministry of Energy and Mines, attribute the reforms more to the privatization process and pressures from multilateral financing institutions. He concedes, however, that the mining industry's legacy of pollution and environmental degradation played a role.

Assessing policy influence

Concluding his evaluation of the two projects, Fernando Loayza Careaga assessed the type of policy influence each project had, the factors that affected policy influence, and IDRC's role in the project's ability or inability to influence policy. Some of his conclusions are:

1. The overriding purpose of the LABOR case against SPCC before the IWT II was to influence corporate policies towards the environment, and to change the Peruvian government's

---

Some Lessons

1. Influencing policy is not a spontaneous by-product of good quality research; when a project is part of a broader strategy to influence policy, its effectiveness improves significantly.
2. Empowering local communities by providing technical and specialized information breaks through their isolation and enables them to influence policy.
3. Careful planning and analysis—from project design to project implementation and dissemination of results—are needed to close the gap between research and policy.
4. Small things can make a big difference: providing LABOR with a fax machine enabled them to be in touch with activist groups nationally and internationally.

Basic Data

1. Copper Mining Project

Time Period:	1991–93
Objectives:	To assess the impact of mining activities on water resources in southern Peru and present the results to the IWT II, February 1992.
Research Outputs:	A report to the IWT II which led to the findings against the practices of the mining company.
	Not research output, but SPCC (the mining company) changed its policies and practices and started some environmental projects addressing environmental degradation.

2. High Altitude Mining

Time Period:	1990–93
Objectives:	To gain recognition of the incidence of Chronic Mountain Sickness in high altitude mining and to influence national policy.
Research Outputs:	Book was published and recognized—two studies.

lenient attitude. LABOR correctly saw the IWT II hearing, and the attendant national and international media coverage, as an instrument to bring about change. In the case of the high altitude mining study, however, government officials remain convinced that CMS is not an occupational disease, and there has been no organized attempt to use the evidence provided by the researchers to confront this perception and identify the need for further action.

2. Two main factors account for the LABOR project's success at influencing policy: the development from the outset of a strategy to disseminate the research results among key national and international stakeholders, and the ability to build community support around the issue. While the high altitude study did publish its results, there was insufficient follow-up, and neither the mining community nor the unions was actively involved in promoting a dialogue on the causes of CMS.

3. In both cases, the projects might have had a greater policy influence if IDRC had had a framework in place to assess a project's impact after its completion. For example, disseminating LABOR's study to a broader group of research institutions supported by IDRC could have had a great influence on the environmental regulatory framework in Peru, and possibly in other mining countries in the region.

Battling Brain Drain: East and Central Africa Needs More Sustained and Relevant Research to Succeed in Agriculture

This brief is based on a case study by Chris Ackello-Ogutu.

Policymakers in East and Central Africa face major hurdles as they try to create sound agricultural policies to fuel economic growth. Their need for good quality research is clear. But frayed lines of communication and the frequent departure of researchers mean project results sometimes don't reach officials who could use them.

The road to a better future for East and Central Africa (ECA) runs through its member countries' rural heartlands, where enhanced food production provides the best hope for alleviating domestic poverty and providing much needed export income. Although in the recent past several nations in the area have set ambitious plans for industrialization, 'agriculture remains the most dominant sector in almost all the economies' of the region, explains Chris Ackello-Ogutu, researcher with the Resource Management and Policy Analysis Institute (REMPAI), based in Nairobi, Kenya. This central role means that agriculture is key to achieving the economic gains upon which food security, poverty reduction, and social stability depends.

Warns Ackello-Ogutu: 'Neglect of the sector in terms of national economic development strategies and in terms of coherent policy direction will lead not only to a weakening of agricultural institutions ... but also to a decline of economic growth.'

The crucial role of research

This places significant weight on the shoulders of the ECA's research community, which possesses the tools, and potentially the knowledge, to enable the region's policymakers to wade through the complexities and arrive at workable plans for improving rural livelihoods. This responsibility is especially onerous given the multiple challenges facing ECA's agricultural sector:

1. In the area of markets, recent trade reforms have increased farmers' risk while not yet providing promised access to external markets. The region's producers depend on a narrow range of low-value commodities, and have historically been hurt by price fluctuations and an over-reliance on rainfall for successful harvests. Now, under liberalization of domestic markets, they have become more dependent on agents, some of whom may take advantage of them. Meanwhile, implementation of new trading regimes promising open markets across eastern and southern Africa has been stalled, while access to developed country marketplaces remains limited.

2. Agricultural productivity remains low. This is due partly to low levels of innovation. There is a pressing need for new technologies (seeds, fertilizers, etc.) and new methods of dealing with constraints like water shortages. New institutional models (co-ops, marketing and extension services, etc.) are required to enable farmers to improve practices. Alternative models of agricultural finance would also offset the limitations of commercial banks and public lending institutions.

3. Upgraded infrastructure such as rail and road networks, storage facilities, electric power, and telecommunications would also boost productivity. Finally, higher levels of productivity also hinge on sustainability. Sometimes, resources have been degraded to the point where they cannot sustain livelihoods. The need for new resource sharing mechanisms is illustrated by the situation in Kenya, where the traditional formula for land division has reduced the size of holdings below the point where farming is viable.

4. Civil strife and government failures have diminished productivity, disrupted trading opportunities, created costly flows of refugees, and channelled aid money towards disaster relief and away from long-term development initiatives.

Leaks in the research pipeline

Given these and other stresses, policymakers at all levels need sound research to help them navigate through the maze of technological, economic, ecological, and social factors facing ECA's agricultural sector. But the links between researchers, policymakers, and farmers are fragile.

'We lament the high number of technologies that lie in the shelves un-adopted by farmers,' writes Ackello-Ogutu. 'Similarly, adoption of recommendations coming out of agricultural policy analysis by researchers … remains at levels that are not acceptable.' How can this picture be improved? To generate potential solutions, Ackello-Ogutu conducted a multipart evaluation.

One part examined six sample IDRC funded projects in three countries (Kenya, Uganda, and Tanzania), hosted by the Eastern and Central Africa Program for Agricultural Policy Analysis (ECAPAPA). These projects' policy-related outcomes were measured against stated goals and the requirements of governments and communities. Then, 'key informants' analyzed the project experiences as well as general trends on the ECA research landscape. They drew out themes affecting relationships between research and policy.

The sample projects were divided into two groups. Projects in the first group were geared to assess the viability of specific agricultural technologies. The following sketches provide the details.

The role of technology in poverty alleviation: Determination of farm household financial profitability in bean production in Kenya

The researchers highlighted a number of means for dealing with farmers' low yields and bottlenecks in the bean marketing system. The remedies included providing farmers with information on fertilizer and certified seeds, arranging seed-sharing arrangements among farmers, and improving marketing. All team members left the project before the dissemination stage, so the project's final report did not reach government agencies and was not acted upon.

Farm household profitability of Irish potatoes in Uganda

The project focused on the high cost of improved quality seeds. A series of recommendations outlined the need for cooperation between government agencies and the private sector, particularly in relation to the promotion of more and better seeds. These conclusions were disseminated in a workshop attended by legislators, NGO representatives, farmers, seed producer associations, and researchers. Influence over policy was exerted at several levels. For example, the private industry agreed to take part in new collaborations, and the government—on the basis of research produced by the project—selected potatoes as a strategic export crop.

Farm household financial profitability of maize/beans intercropping technological packages: A case study of northern Tanzania

One goal of this project was to inform policymakers and other stakeholders about the profitability of different patterns of intercropping using different inputs. Two workshops disseminated information to farmers, NGO representatives, and others, but did not include policymakers. Ackello-Ogutu found it difficult to discuss the results of the project since none of the researchers, including the team leader, wanted to take ownership of the project report. Although collaborators said that the recommended agricultural technologies have been adopted, discussions with farmers contradicted this claim.

Countering conflict

The final three projects in the case study dealt with conflicts involving natural resource management issues. Those projects are listed below.

Minimizing conflicts in natural resource management and use: The role of social capital and local policies in Kabale, Uganda

This project was an extension of other initiatives in Kabale aiming to support newly decentralized local governments, and build other forms of social capital to diffuse conflicts over resource use. Although the project had not ended by the time of the evaluation, project researchers report that findings were being implemented as the project progressed. A lack of progress reports, however, made that difficult to substantiate. The participatory, community-based approach involved and informed community members through focus groups, interviews, workshops, and meetings. Additional dissemination was accomplished through email, publications, and reports. The evaluator notes that one weakness of this project (like others) is its lack of a focused definition of the level and type of policy engagement it strove for.

Pasture and water use conflict between Karamoja (Uganda) and the neighbouring districts: Impacts and potential conflict minimization strategies

Chris Ackello-Ogutu describes Karamoja as 'a region of constant social hardship, droughts, famine, livestock epidemics and general insecurity.' A local preference for cattle has led to overgrazing. Modern weapons are now entering the area, and conflict has intensified. Using participatory methods, the project sought conflict minimization strategies and suggested natural resource management solutions. One conclusion is that an attempt by the central government to enforce disarmament of combatants would only worsen conflict; what is needed is local level resolution brokered by third parties such as NGOs, and common property regimes as a means of resource allocation. Due to deteriorating security, the intended dissemination workshops have not taken place.

Conflicts in access and use of water resources in the Tana river basin, Kenya

Competition for water (for horticulture, food production, and hydro-electricity) is a major concern in the Tana River Basin. The project produced policy briefs that outline the nature of those conflicts, examining the potential for a regime of plural water rights and summarizing users' views of tradable water rights. Those briefs are intended to inform government's new policies on the water issue. With the project not yet completed, key collaborators either emigrated, or took on other work within Kenya. Despite this, researchers said they made plans for a future dissemination workshop in Nairobi.

Seeing the trends and opportunities

Examining the sample projects—and also surveying broader trends in the ECA region—a panel of 'key informants' identified some important themes affecting the relationships between research and policy.

First, they suggested that donor organizations' more direct role in supporting and helping to shape research projects in the region may have created a disconnect between policymakers and researchers. As regional governments have withdrawn funding from research institutions, international agencies have taken up the slack, creating closer links between donors and ECA institutions while possibly removing policymakers from the equation. This increasing donor influence may be framing research questions in ways that governments—which are hard pressed to deal with the immediate demands of poverty reduction, HIV/AIDS, and new global trading arrangements—may perceive as out of line with their own priorities.

Putting researchers and policymakers into direct contact at the design stage would not only ensure that policy concerns are factored into research design, but might also help overcome an apparent mistrust between the research community and the government.

One consistent problem is the glaring absence of gender considerations in any of the projects, despite gender being a critical issue in agricultural policy. This may be symptomatic of wider, systemic problems. Capacity may be one contributing factor, with economists and others who undertake agricultural research in the region lacking training to approach gender issues. Other daunting problems facing Africa may also cause policymakers to see gender as secondary, and to subsequently 'put it on the backburner.' The effects of 'brain drain' were apparent in many of the sample projects. As researchers move out of institutions in search of employment, the stability of research projects suffers, particularly at the latter stages (at which dissemination should take place) when most project staff may have migrated to other roles.

Financial considerations also factor into the stability of the research community. Individual projects generally receive a low level of funding, creating an incentive for researchers to quickly move on to other work when opportunities arise. Overall, there is a feeling that funding is divided among too many projects, a practice that also limits the scope of research and diminishes its appeal to policymakers. Modestly funded research often can only deal with smaller problems with a geographically limited impact, 'thus making it difficult to come up with the generalizations that capture the big picture that a policymaker usually needs,' writes Ackello-Ogutu.

Timely delivery of research results is also key to affecting the policymaking process. In this regard, the informants pointed out that ECAPAPA needs the increased institutional capacity, and specific policies in place to enable it to set benchmarks and accelerate the completion of time sensitive research.

Some Lessons

1. Steps need to be taken to counteract the 'brain drain' that often damages prospects for disseminating research results.
2. Funding bigger research projects rather than a wide range of low-funded projects may better capture the 'big picture' that policymakers need to see.
3. Increased institutional capacity is needed to generate research results more quickly.
4. Involving policymakers in the design of research projects may lead to more policy-relevant research.

Basic Data

Time Period:	1997–2002
Objectives:	To improve the policy environment for the purpose of enhancing agricultural technology generation and adoption to reduce poverty and environmental degradation.
Research Outputs:	Only three projects were completed, so outputs were limited. No dissemination materials of note produced.
	Final reports are available from three projects, interim reports from the others.

Water Management

11

A River Runs through It: Cleaning Up the Dnipro River Basin in Ukraine

This brief is based on a case study by Iryna Lyzogub.

In the aftermath of the collapse of the Soviet Union, Ukraine had the dubious distinction of being the most environmentally degraded of the former USSR republics. Efforts to alleviate the situation were hampered by an ingrained reluctance of officials and decision makers to share information or to take initiative. Overcoming such attitudes was one of the major obstacles faced by IDRC researchers when they undertook a programme designed to clean up the Dnipro River Basin. Patience, perseverance, and the willingness of key Ukrainian actors to adapt to new ways of thinking brought fresh hope for the rebirth of a historic waterway.

At almost 2,300 km, the Dnipro River (also called the Dneiper) is one of the longest rivers in Europe, and for more than half of its length it runs through Ukraine. More than 2,000 years ago the Greek historian Herodotus described the Dnipro as ' ... by far the biggest and the richest river in nutrients... with the exception of the Nile in Egypt.... The water is clean and it tastes well. It is by far the most beautiful river.' The modern Dnipro is no longer a natural source of fresh and clean water according to the authors of the book *Preserving the Dnipro River* (Shevchuk et al. 2005*)*. They write, 'Each year, industry, agriculture, and municipalities discharge enormous amounts of contaminated wastewater into the Dnipro. Every year, 5.5 million cubic metres of sewage are dumped into the water bodies of Ukraine, which includes 4.2 million cubic metres of contaminated sewage, 2.8 million of which is raw waste.'

Together with neighbouring Russia and Belarus, some 33 million people in 50 cities depend on the waters of the Dnipro River Basin. But they must share those waters with industrial and agricultural needs, as well as hydro-electric and nuclear power facilities. In only a few places does the river still retain the bucolic appearance described by Herodotus.

It was against this background that IDRC's newly created Office for Central and Eastern Europe Initiatives (OCEEI) undertook the Environmental Management Development in Ukraine (EMDU) programme in the summer of 1994, in collaboration with the UNDP, and the Global Environment Facility (GEF). The programme was funded by the Canadian International Development Agency (CIDA).

A formidable task

From any perspective IDRC's task was a formidable one, involving a wide range of activities from environmental education and training in project, and environmental management to trans-boundary pollution issues.

There were six components to the EMDU programme, which continued through a second phase until 2001. They were:

1. Water pollution control: a baseline water quality study conducted in collaboration with three Ukrainian institutes. This included some short-term training by a Canadian specialist and the provision of some critical lab equipment.
2. Water toxicology: demonstrating six simple, inexpensive but effective tests for the presence of toxins.
3. Information systems development: including national and regional systems as well as a national atlas of Ukraine.
4. A series of pilot projects: ranging from drinking water treatment technology to groundwater protection and shoreline rehabilitation.
5. Environmental audits and entrepreneurship: including both large and small industries.
6. Public outreach: developing various forms of media, including videos and television programmes to raise public awareness of environmental issues.

It was an ambitious capacity building programme, but if it was to succeed, the IDRC team needed to first overcome another kind of environmental issue—an attitudinal one. Ukraine in the early post-Soviet years was in a deep economic crisis, and the government was reluctant to pursue economic and political reforms. This was also 'a period of psychological crisis,' according to Vasyl Shevchuk, former Minister of Environmental Protection and Nuclear Safety, who served as chairman of the programme's Ukrainian Management Committee (UMC).

Expanding policy capacities

During Soviet times, people learned that 'initiative is punishable', and this lesson proved to be difficult to forget, especially under conditions where the political situation remained uncertain. 'People are inert, passive, and scared. They always lived in fear. It is difficult to change our generation,' explained Kostantyn Chebotko, Head of the Hydrochemistry Department at the Ukrainian Scientific Research Institute. Adding hopefully, 'The next generation might be more efficient.'

There were other hurdles to overcome in addition to what many referred to as the 'Soviet caution'. A law dating back to 1937 decreed that information about the water supply of cities was secret. Participants in the programme who revealed this information to foreigners faced possible legal action. Some Ukrainian research institutions were reluctant to share information, or insisted on being paid for it. And when it came to paying for anything, there was initially no functioning banking system. Transactions were made in cash or barter.

Ukraine was newly independent at this time and just beginning to change its political structures and processes. Not surprisingly, there were constant changes at all levels in the Ministry of Ecology and Natural Resources, including several ministers. With every change new people appeared, with new views about what should, or should not be done.

Remarkably, despite all of the obstacles and the constraints, the programme achieved all of its objectives, and in the process established a lasting relationship between Ukrainian and Canadian scientists. It also had a positive influence on environmental policy and legislation in Ukraine. The key factor in the programme's success proved to be the UMC, which from the outset involved senior decision makers from both the government and the research field. This was important according to Grygory Semchuk, a UMC member who was First Deputy (equivalent to Deputy Minister) with the State Committee on Construction, Architecture, and Housing Policy.

'The work of the Committee was not given to people who did not have power, who did not have influence. This provided a positive result. There was a psychological aspect as well. While considering a project, we discussed it and expressed our views with no fear,' Semchuk said, adding that discipline and a systematic approach were also important.

> The Committee worked systematically, therefore there was a positive result. Everyone knew that each last Friday of the month the meeting at Shevchuk's office should be attended. If a person did not attend a meeting he would be removed. There was a discipline.

As chairman of the UMC, Vasyl Shevchuk was credited by many of the participants for the much of the programme's success.

Almost all the projects as well as the EMDU programme as a whole, presumed policy influence from the very beginning. The active participation and involvement of decision makers was important, and resulted in a higher potential of influencing the relevant policies. And just as the involvement of government increased the potential for policy influence, the involvement of senior research people facilitated the links between researchers and decision makers.

Affecting policy regimes

One important effect of the projects funded through the IDRC programme was the revival of institutions that were failing because of lack of government funding. The protracted economic crisis in the Ukraine had seriously affected scientists—salaries were not paid, equipment was not purchased, and in winter many worked in offices that were only a few degrees above freezing. 'The international programs, and the IDRC program in particular, gave us hope. These programs allowed us not to fall into despair' said Konstantyn Chebotko.

Another participant, Olexander Kolodiazhny from the Space Research Institute, added that 'This program allowed us to achieve a higher level of professionalism. We had to study GIS technologies and the Internet more precisely, and we learned remote sensing.'

The programme also brought together institutions that had never before collaborated, says Anatoly Yatsyk, a UMC member and director of the Scientific Research Institute for Water and Ecological Problems. 'Everyone worked separately—my institute was working on water issues, other institutes dealt with different issues.... Within the IDRC program all of us united to provide a complex approach to resolve the problems of the Dnipro River,' Yatsyk says.

The revival of the scientific institutions also stimulated an influx of postgraduate students and resulted in the publication of a series of textbooks based on the work done under the programme. The textbooks continue to be used in universities, and for training and retraining professionals in the field, according to Vasyl Shevchuk. For example, a textbook on hydro-ecology that is now widely used in university programmes in Russia and Belarus, as well as in Ukraine, was prepared and published as a direct result of the EMDU programme.

For more general audiences, a series of videos was prepared illustrating the problems facing the Dnipro River Basin and the work that is being done to clean up the river. Several of these have been broadcast on national television, and at the instigation of Dr Shevchuk hundreds of copies of the videos have been distributed to schools and ecological centres for young people across the country.

Broadening policy horizons

The programme also provided support for some innovative projects, such as the production of organomineral fertilizers from the sediments that result from drinking water treatment. Many countries burn these sediments, or dump them into the ocean, but Ukraine became the first country to develop a technique to convert them to fertilizer, according to Konstantyn Chebotko, who managed the pilot project. The project would not have been successful without IDRC's financial support, and the high level of professionalism required under the EMDU programme, he adds.

Bringing the results of such projects to the attention of the international scientific community initially presented difficulties because Ukrainian research institutions did not use internationally recognized standards. Working with IDRC on the EMDU programme reinforced the necessity of introducing international standards in Ukraine. Learning international standards also enabled Ukrainian researchers to enter the international scientific community. Several researchers who were active in the EMDU programme have had their work published in international scientific journals and presented their results at international conferences.

Closer to home, the researchers have had the satisfaction of seeing the results of their work used as the basis for two pieces of national legislation: the National Programme on Ecological Rehabilitation of the Dnipro Basin and the law on Drinking Water Improvement. The programme was recently adopted by Ukraine's Supreme Council, the *Verhovna Rada*. 'This was our greatest political achievement,' says Anatoly Yatsyk.

In addition, numerous regulations supporting the National Programme, such as the one for estimating surface water quality, were developed within the EMDU projects. And the work of implementing the National Programme continues as an increased environmental awareness brings closer cooperation between Ukraine's scientific and government institutions.

Summing it all up, the programme's then Regional Director in Kyiv, Myron Lahola, comments:

What I know for sure is that IDRC left a legacy here that Canadians are people that are easy to work with, are not only friendly but also diplomatic ... who do things using a process of consensus building. I have heard this not only from Ukrainians but from other donor organizations. On a global scale, one of the most important things you can develop is trust and friendship between countries.

Box 11.1: The Canadians are Coming! The Canadians are Coming!

The perils of lack of communication were illustrated during an early phase of the EMDU programme when Canadians were briefly seen as unscrupulous invaders. It happened during a riverbank stabilization project. In true soviet style there was no public involvement. The project manager simply brought in heavy machinery and set his crew to work on 5 kilometre of riverfront. He did not even bother to inform the local authorities. Somehow the word got out that 'Canadians are buying up our land here ... soon they are going to build buildings and we will never get to the river anymore.' The furious locals turned out with pitchforks to defend their land, the Ministry received official complaints, and the resulting confusion delayed the project for almost a year. It was a valuable lesson on the importance of public outreach.

Basic Data

Time Period:	1994–2002
Objectives:	**Phase I:** To help establish the capacity of Ukrainian institutions to manage the Dnipro water system and its uses.
	Phase II: To strengthen environmental reforms in Ukrainian institutions and industry; heighten environmental awareness among scientists, decision makers and the general population.

Research Outputs:

1. National Environmental Management information system connected to 19 provincial offices along the Dnipro river.
2. Regional Management Information System.
3. A body of Ukrainian environmental legislation was collated, published, and made available to NGOs, and public and educational institutions.
4. Baseline water quality survey completed.
5. Health risk assessment of drinking water quality.
6. Various surveys and audits on water quality and other water issues.
7. The training of 90 individuals.
8. Changes in factories emission systems along the Dnipro river.
9. *Preserving the Dnipro River: Harmony, History, and Rehabilitation*, V.Y. Shevchuk, G.O. Bilyavsky, V.M. Navrotsly, and O.O. Mazurkevich. Mosaic Press/IDRC (2005).

Making the Most of Scarce Resources: Wastewater Recovery and Urban Farming in the Middle East

This brief is based on a case study by Eman Surani.

Population growth, rapid urbanization, and the shortage of water have led to rising food insecurity in the Middle East and North Africa. People in the region address this complex set of problems by encouraging urban agriculture and by using recycled water to feed it. In Jordan and other countries, city farms are irrigated with 'greywater' drawn from showers, bathrooms, and sinks. This innovative response, supported by IDRC, has had a wide-ranging influence on public policy.

Although 'urban agriculture' has been practiced for as long as cities have existed, only in recent years has the world awakened to the importance of city farming in ensuring that people have enough to eat.

In fact, urban agriculture is booming. The UNDP estimates the number of city farmers at about 800 million worldwide. Most are poor or middle-class people who raise livestock and grow produce to feed their families and to generate extra income. In the process, they recycle waste, reuse water, and put idle land to productive use.

In the Middle East and North Africa, already one of the planet's most arid regions, the amount of water available to each person is actually decreasing. This is due mainly to the rapid rise in population. The inventory of water is expected to decline to 725 cubic metres per capita per year (m^3pcpy)—far below 1,000 m^3pcpy, the benchmark indicator of severe water scarcity.

This dire situation is aggravated by increasing urbanization in the region. As more people move to the cities, more water is likely to be diverted away from agriculture and channelled into built-up areas for drinking and domestic purposes. Thus, the region may suffer increasingly from the related problems of food insecurity and water scarcity. This crisis is particularly severe in Jordan.

Jordan is a small country of about 5.2 million people. Its economy has been in decline for years. About 7 per cent of the population earns less than the international poverty line of US $1 a day. According to the UNDP, 'Jordan's high population growth and unprecedented urbanization rate threaten its recent economic gains. Its population growth is 2.7 per cent, and the proportion of its population living in urban areas, already 73 per cent, is expected to reach 80 per cent by 2015.'

These economic and demographic trends jeopardize the food and water security of Jordan's poor, more and more of whom are found in towns and cities. According to the World Bank, high population growth over the past 20 years has pushed Jordan's per capita water availability to below 198 m^3pcpy. Clearly, water scarcity on such a dramatic scale is sufficient to impede development and to harm human health.

As a result of this crisis, attitudes towards water management in Jordan have undergone a radical shift. In the past, water was viewed as a free public good, but now everyone accepts that it has an economic value. Conservation, as well as wastewater treatment and reuse, are considered priorities, and so is research into these measures.

The IDRC's urban agriculture programme has been supporting research and development activities that bolster the food security and incomes of the poor, while maintaining public health and a clean urban environment. As part of this initiative, during 1998–2003, IDRC sponsored a series of research projects to investigate the use of greywater in urban agriculture. These studies have had an important influence on water management policies in Jordan and elsewhere in the region.

What was done: The urban agriculture and greywater projects

The initial study was mainly a data gathering exercise. It compiled for the first time reliable information about the nature and extent of urban farming. Researchers focused on the capital city, Amman, and examined a range of issues with a view to suggesting policy changes.

Among the more interesting findings were that one in six Amman households practiced urban agriculture, that gender parity prevailed and the sexes performed equal portions of the work (unlike the men, however, most women went unpaid), and that untreated greywater was already being used by 40 per cent of farming households. Significantly, the study found that no policies or regulations specific to urban agriculture existed in Jordan, indeed that there was little official recognition of its benefits for strengthening food security.

A second project, conducted in the West Bank (Palestine), was primarily technical in nature. It sought to improve the design of a small-scale trickling filter for treating greywater for reuse in home gardens. The researchers tested 'domestic wastewater treatment plants'—essentially, recycled plastic shampoo barrels with a filtration media of valley gravel and recycled plastic soft drink bottles. Using such cheap and readily available materials, an impressive average of 56 per cent greywater recovery was achieved.

Incidentally, this project also responded to cultural and religious concerns about the use of recycled wastewater by engaging local sheiks to advise the community on the advantages of greywater.

Meanwhile, during 1997–99, CARE Australia carried out a very successful pilot project in southern Jordan to test soil and water conservation techniques of 'permanent agriculture' or 'permaculture'. An IDRC funded evaluation identified this project's broad economic and cultural impact: it raised the income of participating families, promoted cooperation, enhanced a sound sense of home economics and marketing, and formalized awareness about water conservation and reuse. Notably, female participants reported feeling more independent and proud because of the income they generated, the skills they gained, and their enhanced ability to feed their families.

Finally, the ambitious Greywater Reuse Project in Tafila, Jordan, was inspired by the promising outcomes of the earlier three programmes and was designed to build on the lessons learned from them. It was carried out during 2001–03.

The immediate goal was to improve a system for reusing greywater in home gardens in Jordan. Its broader goals were to help the peri-urban poor preserve fresh water, achieve food security, and generate income, all the while protecting the environment.

The project's achievements were far-reaching. It increased greywater recovery, and made greywater easier and safer to handle. It minimized environmental impacts by encouraging the production and marketing of cheaper organic soaps. It improved permaculture practices by enhancing irrigation systems, and by fostering the adoption of new crops more tolerant of greywater. In particular, it promoted policy changes that will encourage wider greywater acceptance in Jordan.

What was learned: The influence of research on public policy

In 2001, IDRC launched a strategic evaluation of the policy influence of the research it has supported. To assess the influence of the greywater projects, the Centre engaged Eman Surani, who surveyed the work done and outlined six concrete instances of 'policy influence'.

Revision of housing codes and launch of national committee to formulate Greywater Reuse Guidelines

The initial project, the data gathering exercise, had a direct influence on public policy, as one of its startling discoveries was that laws and regulations governing city farming were non-existent in Jordan. This finding helped spur the process of policy setting that is underway.

The Greywater Reuse Project has gone a long way towards filling this policy gap. This effort led, for example, to a proposal to modify domestic building codes to allow greywater use without the need for plumbing modifications. In addition, it prompted the establishment of a new National Committee to formulate Greywater Reuse Guidelines.

Policymakers become communicators

In a form of indirect policy influence, government officials who were not involved in implementing these research projects, nonetheless became enthusiastic communicators of their findings. Specifically, officers with Jordan's Department of Statistics, charged with designing its website, decided to add the results of the initial project to the home page for broader dissemination to the donor and research communities.

Replication of the model

The Jordan and Palestine projects were built stepwise, one upon the other, and in their turn they fostered similar efforts elsewhere in the region. Dr Murad Jabay Bino of the Inter-Islamic Network on Water Resources Development and Management (INWRDAM) observes, 'The projects in Palestine and Jordan are now spreading to Lebanon, and Syria has expressed its interest as well.' This replication effect is encouraged by a continually evolving project structure adapted to the cultural context of each country.

Within Jordan, replication has occurred because of key partnerships between INWRDAM, the recognized technical expert, and other agencies:

1. CARE Jordan installed the greywater system in all its projects. In five communities, 53 units were put in place by INWRDAM on behalf of CARE, in a scheme funded by the European Union.
2. INWRDAM signed a memorandum of understanding with the Regional Centre on Agrarian Reform and Rural Development for the Near East for cooperation in training people in the application of greywater.
3. Drawing upon INWRDAM's expertise, a 'water demand management unit' is being established at the Water Authority of Jordan to help coordinate water issues for the country.
4. Again drawing upon INWRDAM, codes are being revised so that greywater can be used for the beautification of tourist attractions.

Hyderabad declaration

In November 2002, an important international meeting on the topic of wastewater use in agriculture, sponsored by IDRC and other organizations, took place in Hyderabad, India. Two major breakthroughs occurred.

The first was a commitment by the World Health Organization to consider new evidence—including IDRC's reports on its greywater projects—in reviewing its guidelines for wastewater use in agriculture.

The second was the *Hyderabad Declaration on Wastewater Use in Agriculture*, a document drafted by researchers and practitioners representing 27 international bodies and national institutions from 18 countries. This statement expresses worldwide concern about ensuring safe water reuse, and sets out a common global agenda of building a wastewater 'community of practice'.

Networks formed

These projects brought together, for the first time, governments, the private sector, and the research community. Naser Faruqui of IDRC observed that Jordan is a small country and so 'all the individuals in the Jordanian research, engineering, and policymaking communities know each other and invite each other to workshops.'

While it is unusual for government officials and farmers to meet openly and to discuss issues of common concern, networking has occurred also at the local level, among policymakers, researchers, and beneficiaries.

Capacity building of policymakers

The IDRC-supported projects have trained, educated, and raised awareness levels of policymakers about greywater reuse.

For example, Jordan's Ministry of Social Development is adapting lessons learned from the projects, and teaching new trades to the poor. In addition to plumbing skills and agricultural techniques, these include expertise in financial and administrative management, communications, and networking.

In addition, researchers have spread knowledge about their projects widely, and have briefed government officials, non-governmental organizations (NGOs), and other scholars and researchers.

Why it works: Factors affecting research influence on policy

Surani went to considerable lengths to analyze why these projects have been so successful in influencing policy, and also to identify the remaining challenges.

Indeed, work remains to be done. In Surani's view, some factors that may have hindered the policy influence of these projects are: the failure to focus explicitly on gender equality as a core research theme and policy goal; the scarcity of funds for project evaluation; the 'lack of a learning environment' in some sectors of the Jordanian government; the insufficient use of the mass media; the administrative weakness of the Palestinian authority; and, initially at least, religious beliefs unsympathetic to the idea of wastewater reuse.

Despite these obstacles, the policy influence of these projects is clear. Many factors gave rise to this success: the strategic use of limited resources, in that lessons learned in one project were applied to subsequent projects; the warm personal links between IDRC and Jordanian partners; the awareness that these were not 'ivory tower' research projects, but that they offered immediate answers to pressing human problems; the sympathetic political environment in Jordan, long worried about the water crisis and receptive to scientific solutions; the reputation and credibility of the highly respected individuals and organizations involved in implementation; and the wide dissemination of research findings using different formats appropriate to different audiences.

Surani highlighted two particular factors leading to success. First, much of the research demonstrated the politically attractive link between environmental sustainability and economic development, that is to say, between wastewater recovery and poverty alleviation. Second, IDRC took care to develop a long-term strategic plan and sponsored successive projects each built upon earlier work. According to INWRDAM's Dr Bino, having carried out 'a well-defined project with clear objectives ... IDRC has good capacity to improve on the lessons learnt in future for follow-up projects.'

Basic Data

Time Period: 1998–2005

Objectives: A series of projects focused on aspects of facilitating policy development in support of urban agriculture at municipal and national levels in order to enhance urban food security, including technical research and capacity building.

Research Outputs: 1. Research into policies and practices on greywater reuse.
                   2. Installation of on-site treatment plants in Ramallah.
                   3. An evaluation study leading to:
                      — increased demand from households for greywater kits;
                      — workshops on irrigation requirements;
                      — workshops to train plumbers and electricians on management of systems;
                      — proposed building code revisions; graduate research on greywater reuse;
                      — revision of national housing codes;
                      — a national committee to create greywater reuse guidelines;
                      — replication of the greywater treatment kits in the Middle East and North Africa;
                      — ratification of the Hyderabad Declaration; and
                      — creation of a network of policymakers, researchers, private sector and beneficiaries.

Searching for an Interim Irrigation Solution: Researchers in Syria Investigate Whether, under Some Conditions, Brackish Water Can be Used for Irrigation without Damaging Soil

This brief is based on a case study by Bryon Gillespie.

Economically dependent upon agriculture and facing a deepening water crisis, Syria needs to find ways to make its limited water go further. As farmers turn to irrigating with saline water, IDRC-supported researchers proposed that perhaps they should be allowed to continue—if guidelines for using brackish water can be established. But who are most likely to pay attention to the researchers' findings: government officials, farmers, or regional agencies?

In Syria—as in neighbouring Middle-Eastern countries—access to water is a daunting problem.

The World Bank classifies the Middle East and Northern Africa (MENA) region as one of the driest areas of the world. With a current region-wide availability of water estimated at 1200 m^{3}pcpy, this group of countries hovers only marginally above the Bank's benchmark of 1,000 cubic metres of available water per capita per year—a cut-off point below which countries are considered to have a serious water shortage. By this definition, Syria, one of the most severely parched countries within the MENA group, can already be considered to be in crisis: its current water availability is calculated at 432 m^{3}pcpy—far below the World Bank's demarcation point for water scarcity. And the situation appears destined to deteriorate further. Pressure from a young and growing population and the demands of an economically crucial agricultural sector are expected to lower Syria's available water to a mere 160 cubic metres by 2025.

Given the pressures that are already being felt, Syrian farmers have been implementing several adaptive measures that, in the long run, may make matters worse. For example, the digging of new wells—most of them illegal—has contributed to a decline in ground water levels, as wells are pumped faster than they can be renewed. Farmers are also increasingly using brackish water to irrigate their crops, a practice that is likely to increase the salinity of the soil and in turn lower agricultural productivity.

Farmers' survival tactics

Higher salt levels in the soil are normal in the arid climatic conditions typical of Syria's deserts and steppes. Crystallized salts are left at the soil surface—at the interface between the land and air—as water is drawn upward through the soil and evaporates into the atmosphere. In the past this has not posed serious problems: under the traditional Syrian system of crop rotation, which leaves the land fallow for extended periods, levels of salt in topsoil have remained relatively low.

Recent changes in agricultural practices, however, have altered the picture. Intensive agriculture involving more frequent crop rotations has increased the volumes of water moving through the soil, thereby boosting its salinity. The salt content of soil and groundwater have also been increased by the growing practice of 'flood irrigation', whereby large volumes of water are pumped onto fields, creating standing pools that eventually percolate down through the soil. This has resulted in more salt finding its way into underground reservoirs and wells. In turn, the increasing salinity of groundwater, which is used for irrigation, has become a key contributor to the elevated salt levels in the soil.

The implications of this trend are profound and disturbing. Syria sees a robust agricultural sector as central to its plans, both for food security and for future economic growth. Those plans would fall apart, however, if increased soil salinity led to decreased productivity of agricultural lands.

Yet at the same time, it would be unrealistic to expect farmers to simply stop irrigating with brackish water. For some, it is the only type of water they have. It is estimated, for example, that over 70 per cent of Syrian farmers use flood irrigation and that many continue to do so after their wells have become saline.

Given that these practices are so firmly established, the Brackish Water Project set out to investigate if there were circumstances under which saline water could be safely used for irrigation. The group hoped to establish parameters that would instruct farmers and government on how to use brackish water without threatening the environment, or significantly diminishing the productivity of the soil (and, by extension, farmers' livelihoods). In doing so, they would formulate a 'bridge' strategy where current practices could be continued, in a modified form, until more permanent solutions to MENA's water crisis are found. Such a strategy would be of interest not just in Syria but across the region.

Water, public policy, and IDRC

For IDRC, supporting the Brackish Water Project was a natural fit, because the project's goals intersected with at least two of the Centre's ongoing thematic interests. First, IDRC has a history of supporting research on water that focuses on small-scale, decentralized, local level solutions. IDRC's small-scale orientation meshed with the approach of researchers from the International Centre for Agriculture in Dry Areas (ICARDA), Syria's University of Aleppo, and Canada's McGill University, who undertook the research. The Syrian government had also expressed its interest in small-scale, demand-side approaches to water through its promotion of efficient sprinkler and drip irrigation technologies.

Another long-term interest for IDRC is the question of how research can inform and influence government policy. On this front, however, it became increasingly clear that the project's potential was constrained by the nature of the Syrian political system, and by a policy formation process that some of the foreign researchers connected with the project described as 'opaque' and difficult to understand.

In the best of circumstances, policy-oriented research can stimulate vigorous public debate, allowing for different options to be aired with, it is hoped, the best choices filtering upward to the attention of the bureaucrats and politicians who set the national agenda.

But this is unlikely to happen under a political system such as Syria's. As Bryon Gillespie, who evaluated the policy influence of the project for IDRC, states, 'Policy decisions are made at the top, and are not offered for public scrutiny.' Any opportunity to influence how top officials make their decisions comes through the apparatus of the ruling Ba'th party, rather than through the country's six-party, 250 member elected legislature (which is generally taken to operate as a 'rubber stamp'), or civil society organizations.

Since the current regime came into power in 1970, Syrian agricultural policy has reflected the country's Soviet-inspired, centrally managed economic model. Recently, however, President Bashar Al Asad, who assumed power in 2000, has instituted limited economic reforms. The bureaucracy's role has changed from simply commanding that quotas be met, to providing farmers with technical advice and offering financial incentives, for example, by having marketing agencies buy strategically important crops at preferential prices.

What kind of research role?

Despite such cautious steps towards liberalization, policy formation in Syria remains largely insulated from outside input. This appears to have limited the scope of the Brackish Water Project. Gillespie observed, for example, that, 'I saw no social research, nor any research which looked into agricultural policies.'

More broadly, the role and value of research within the Syrian system remains an open question. Gillespie noted, for example, that several experts he had spoken to remarked that 'in Syria it is frequently the case that the technical reports [produced by the government's own research agencies] get shelved and go unread at higher levels.' Others, however, say that research can be effective when it is targeted to questions that officials are actively considering. While researchers will generally not be invited to contribute to the actual formation of policy, they are sometimes enlisted in a supportive role, providing technical advice on what means will be most effective in achieving already formulated goals.

'Influencing the policy comes as you find technologies or recommendations that respond to the needs of the decision makers at the time when they want to formulate policies,' says Dr Theib Oweis, Senior Water Specialist with ICARDA.

Oweis suggests that donors sometimes place too much emphasis on the direct impact of research on policy formulation. 'Not everything requires policy changes,' he says, 'although we know that policies are instrumental in making changes.'

Researchers also have to make sure that even the terminology they use aligns with the government's broader political objectives. For instance, the phrase 'water demand management'—commonly used by IDRC sponsored researchers—is problematic in Syria. The government believes it shifts focus towards domestic consumption and away from issues of international access to water. The phrase is therefore seen as undermining Syria's case for access to water that has brought it into competition with Turkey, Iraq, and other neighbours.

Practical and political influence

Despite the apparent impenetrability of Syria's policymaking process, there was one occasion where the Brackish Water Project's research did appear to have a direct influence on policy. Research examining the variables that affect the impact of saline water on soil indicated that salt accumulation is most severe in heavier clay soils. After these findings were presented at a conference where Ministry of Irrigation officials were present, a decree was issued forbidding farmers to irrigate high clay content fields with drainage water, which is likely to have high levels of salt.

Other than that, the project's influence has so far been felt outside the sphere of formal policymaking. Researchers reported, for instance, that after the findings of a master's thesis funded by the project—which showed, among other things, that the *sham 6* variety of wheat is most resistant to the effects of salt—the demand for *sham 6* on the black market increased in the area where the experiments took place. This indicates that the research helped change farmers' outlook and influenced their practices.

Gillespie suggests, however, that the most significant impacts of the project fall under the rubrics of 'expanding policy capacities' and 'broadening policy horizons'. For example, several young Syrian researchers, whose research and graduate studies were supported by the project, are now employed by the ministries of agriculture and irrigation. Bringing their knowledge and experience to their current positions, their presence indicates an effective expansion of research capacity within Syrian institutions. It also promises to bring new perspectives into the culture of the Syrian research community. For example, the researchers' experience of conducting experiments in farmers' fields—rather than at isolated research stations—was new in Syria.

Some signs of change?

A similar expansion of capacity took place when one of the senior participants in the project was appointed—coincidentally, rather than as a direct result of the project's work—to the position of Minister of Agriculture and Agrarian Reform. In his new role as minister, Dr Noureddin Mona instituted a series of reforms intended to elevate the stature of research within the ministry. While Mona was minister only for a short time, it is possible that the ascent of members of the research community into decision-making roles may lead to a new reality where research becomes a stronger contributor to policy formulation.

Gillespie considers the most important impact of the Brackish Water Project to have occurred on the regional stage. The creation of the International Centre for Biosaline Agriculture (ICBA), headquartered in Dubai, speaks volumes about the growing currency of the idea that standards can be established for the safe use of brackish water—an idea that was not part of the debate on the mid-east water shortage before the project first held it up to scrutiny.

Key Lessons

1. Political context can limit the scope and types of research that are possible.
2. Research can have an impact even if it does not change policy. In this case, for example, farmers acted on research results.
3. Expansion of domestic research capacity and shifts in understanding at the international level are longer term forms of policy influence.

Basic Data

Time Period:	1997–2001
Objective:	The formulation of long-term management strategies for the suitable use of brackish water in supplemental irrigation of field crops in the dry areas of Syria.

Research Outputs: 1. Six Master's Theses
2. One PhD dissertation
3. One peer-reviewed article (Hagi-Bishow and Bonnell 2000)

Changing Water Policy by Degrees: A Project Initially Ignored by Government Has become Part of a Paradigm Shift

This brief is based on a case study by Tracy Tuplin.

When Tunisia set its sights on averting an approaching water crisis, it concentrated overwhelmingly on increasing supply. An IDRC-supported research project with a focus on demand did little to change this. But the project seems to have contributed to a longer-term shift in outlook. Today, it also provides a reminder of the need to communicate technical findings in ways policymakers understand.

Tunisia is an economic success story—but excessive demands on the country's limited water supply may compromise that success.

With annual growth rates reaching as high as 5 per cent, Tunisia saw its per capita income increase more than five-fold between 1960 and 1997. Meanwhile, the proportion of its population living below the poverty line dropped from 22 per cent to 6.2 per cent between 1975 and 1995.

Advances such as these have catapulted Tunisia out of the ranks of underdeveloped countries. Now considered an 'emergent economy', three-quarters of Tunisia's population are classified as middle class. This positive economic portrait and generally equitable distribution of wealth have also helped Tunisia avoid the political instability that has plagued many other countries in the Middle East and Northern Africa. One remarkable feature of Tunisia's accomplishments is that they have occurred despite a water shortage. With an annual water supply of 430 cubic metres per person, Tunisia is well below the World Bank's definition of a water-scarce country, that is, one with less than 1,000 cubic metres per person.

Now, there are clouds on the horizon. Agriculture and other sectors that have propelled Tunisia's growth have been developed with little regard to water efficiency, raising the prospect of a depletion of water stocks that could trigger a crisis. The government took aim at this problem in a policy paper released in 1990, but its solutions focused mainly on the costly process of developing new supplies. References to water conservation remained vague and unconnected to the government's broader strategy.

Expanding the equation

IDRC saw an opportunity to broaden the policy debate in Tunisia. Around the same time that Tunisia released its policy paper, the Centre began a research programme on Water Demand Management (WDM) strategies, that is, looking primarily at demand rather than supply.

Researchers believed that Tunisia clearly stood to benefit from this kind of approach. Since most of its new water supplies had been identified or developed, the potential for Tunisia to meet future demand by boosting supplies was limited. More promising were the avenues being opened up by researchers like Professor Mohammed Salah Matoussi of Tunis University, a rising academic star who was beginning to explore the roles that economic mechanisms, such as tariffs, could play in promoting water conservation.

In supporting Professor Matoussi's research, IDRC saw the potential for Tunisia to benefit both environmentally and economically. An IDRC study of the project (written by Tracy Tuplin, based on research by IDRC's Sarah Earl and Bryon Gillespie) recounts that: 'The principal objective of the *WDM in Tunisia* project was to develop an integrated water demand management strategy in Tunisia that would result in more effective use of limited water resources, prevent rationing in the face of eventual shortage, and delay heavy infrastructure investments to increase supply.'

IDRC also hoped that any success it achieved with WDM in Tunisia would serve as an example to other countries in the region.

An intention to influence policy

From the outset, the plan was to achieve those goals by directly influencing policymakers. Tuplin writes that, when the project's parameters were first defined, 'significant time was spent on ... reviewing strategies to ensure the work would inform water policy in the region.' It was clearly understood that there should be 'more focus on policy implications rather than the development of economic models.'

For a while, it appeared that the project would make its mark in Tunisia's policymaking arena. Partway through the project's lifespan, internal IDRC documents showed considerable enthusiasm for results such as the citation of the project's research in government reports, and an apparently new interest by bureaucrats in issues like tariff systems. One report concluded that: 'This has been a highly successful project that physically succeeded in drawing attention to the demand side of water management.' Yet entering the home stretch, much of the optimism faded. It became apparent that the primary result of the project would be the publication of academic papers, to which policymakers paid little attention. What caused this dramatic shift? Years after the project ended, Earl and Gillespie's interviews both with the project researchers and the Tunisian officials shed some light on the matter.

The interviews reveal researchers' critical view of their counterparts in government—with government officials similarly disdainful of the researchers' approach. This state of mutual distrust conforms to theorist Nathan Caplan's 'two communities' hypothesis, which holds that the research community and the bureaucracy are often separated by significant differences in behaviour, expectations, and perceptions.

One Ministry of Agriculture official acknowledges that such a cultural divide does exist in Tunisia. He suggests that the rift could be mended if there was more contact between the two groups at dissemination events, and if both sides modified their approaches. Academic researchers, he says, need to do a better job at summarizing their research (so that busy bureaucrats can read them), and should take on more applied research. Policymakers, on the other hand, should communicate more clearly the problems they need to have answered.

Indirect impacts on policy

Does the failure of the researchers to forge a direct link with policymakers mean that the project was a failure?

The way that events have unfolded since the project ended suggests that the likely answer is 'no'. Within Tunisia, water demand management has become a supporting plank in the government's water policy—one of the three interlocking approaches to managing this critical resource. More broadly, the Water Demand Management Forum (WDMF) has moved the issue to centre stage, through conferences involving participants from eleven countries in the region. A cornerstone of WDM is the role of economic analysis and economic instruments in promoting conservation. While this approach is now widely accepted, it was new when Professor Matoussi championed it in Tunisia in the early 1990s.

All this indicates that, in the longer term, the Tunisian researchers' ideas did filter into the policymaking sphere.

Evert Lindquist has examined the ability of research to influence policy through circuitous, indirect means. One of those means is expanding policy capacities, that is, facilitating the creation of knowledge or competence in individuals or organizations that can later be put to use in some other context.

The *WDM in Tunisia* project clearly created such an expansion of capacity by allowing Professor Matoussi, a leading innovator in the application of economic theory to water management, to refine his approach and methods. The project also supported a number of graduate students examining the same issues. Cumulatively, this support led to Professor Matoussi's ideas having a sustained presence in the country and in the region. Writes Tuplin: 'IDRC support to this project helped to create the first group in Tunisia with the capacity to analyze water issues from a quantitative economics perspective.' Lindquist also notes that research can have a longer-term influence over policy by broadening policy horizons. In other words, researchers can put new concepts into circulation that may stimulate policymakers to frame issues in different ways or engage in different types of debates. Again, there is evidence that WDM in Tunisia did this. As David Brooks, the IDRC project officer during the latter part of the project observed, its emphasis on water demand brought policymakers into contact with an approach that seemed radical at the time it was first raised.

Through their involvement in water networks, however, project participants were able to advance the idea that water demand is not a fixed factor, as it had been assumed, but a variable that would respond to economic pressures. Within Tunisia, team members have interacted with the National Society for Water Exploitation and Distribution (SONEDE), while regionally Professor Matoussi has been active in the Water Demand Management Forum, which has made policy influence one of its major concerns.

Looking for direct links

But are these indirect influences on policy the best that researchers could have hoped for? Was it inevitable that WDM in Tunisia would fall short of its goal of directly influencing policymakers during the project's tenure?

Earl and Gillespie's post mortem of the project provides some instructive ideas about how productive links between researchers and policymakers can be cultivated. Their findings indicate that this project's failure to reach policymakers in the short-term was likely not because the task was too daunting, but rather because the right strategies were not followed.

There was, for example, no clear plan on how to communicate the research findings. Highly technical documents were not translated into popular language that would have made project results understandable to non-mathematicians. Although workshops were held, they were aimed primarily at academic audiences. Similarly, the researchers' papers were published in academic journals, some of which were not available in Tunisia. All this was compounded by restrictions on internet access, which scuttled plans for a project website.

In turn, the failure to develop a communications plan appears to have deeper roots in the project's design. The team was dominated by specialists, and lacked a member specifically responsible for dealing with policymakers. Additionally, since researchers were offered minimal compensation, the ability to publish academic papers became a more important reward for their work. Translating their findings into policy-friendly language was not something the researchers saw as their role.

Tuplin writes that norms have changed since WDM in Tunisia was launched. Now, IDRC and its partners pay more attention to the policy and communications dimensions of projects. 'Today,' she suggests, 'IDRC may look for "policy entrepreneurs" or people able to advocate change and adept at reading the environment both inside and outside government.'

Overall, what has become clear is that drawing out the policy implications of research, and communicating them to the people who steer the ship of public policy are not things that will happen on their own. Rather, they are crucial tasks that must be planned and budgeted for, from the outset of research projects. Writes Tuplin: 'Research alone, no matter how good, is not enough to draw policymakers' attention to important and relevant issues.'

Some Lessons

1. There are long-term and short-term ways to influence policy. A research project that lacks a direct and immediate influence on policymakers may have an impact over the longer term. For example, research could contribute to expanding the capacity of policymakers to integrate new approaches and practices. It could also broaden the horizons of other researchers, so that they will be able to bring new knowledge to bear on the problems they are studying.

2. A research team should include members who can express results in policy-friendly ways.

3. Communication efforts should be planned and budgeted for—they will not happen on their own.

4. Projects should provide researchers with incentives to focus on the policy implications of their research. It is important that researchers have a better understanding of the role they can play in the creation of a sound public policy.

Basic Data

Time Period: 1992–2000

Objective: To design a comprehensive strategy for managing the country's water demands in order to prevent any rationing due to a potential shortage, while delaying the major supply investments under consideration.

Research Outputs: 1. Five papers on resource allocation and decentralization.
                    2. Four papers on residential water demand estimation.
                    3. A mathematical model for determining optimal cropping in dry areas.
                    4. A model on integrated water-environment management and a paper on the same (based on willingness to pay).

Health and Education Reform

12

Influencing Education Policy in Guatemala: Groups Seek to Improve Education Opportunities for Indigenous Peoples and Women

This brief is based on a case study by Bienvenido Argueta.

Increased funding for education is a key component in the efforts of the government of Guatemala to put the country back on its feet. Ensuring that indigenous groups and women get their fair share of any increases was the goal of concerned civil society groups. With support from IDRC, they researched and published a proposal for a more equitable distribution of education funding that would overcome systemic discrimination.

Guatemala's Peace Accords were designed to lay the foundation for a lasting peace, ending 36 years of domestic armed conflict. Under the Accords, the guerillas agreed to disband and the government committed to constitutional and electoral reforms, resettlement projects, and recognition of the rights of Indigenous peoples, among other things. It also committed to increase spending on public education.

Education is of critical importance for Guatemala, where over 40 per cent of the population is under the age of 15, and the population is growing by more than 2 per cent annually. The Peace Commission and the Parity Commission confirmed the need for increased education funding in order to transform the country's education system to reflect, for the first time, cultural differences in the population. Indigenous communities have traditionally been seriously under-represented in education spending, and as a result they have the highest illiteracy and dropout rates in the country.

Education became a major issue during Guatemala's 1999 general election that saw the ruling National Advancement Party (PAN) defeated by the Guatemalan Republican Front (FRG). A diverse collection of civil society organizations launched the *Gran Campaña Nacional por la Educación* (Grand National Campaign for Education) and circulated a nationwide petition calling for a large increase in the education budget. The petition gathered some 150,000 signatures. Subsequently the government did increase the education budget, but by about half the amount demanded. The petition may have had little effect on the national budget, but it did have an impact on public opinion, and concerns over education policy.

Twenty-year plan

Those concerns were reflected in the new government's 2000–2004 Education Plan, which included an explicit policy of increasing the Ministry of Education budget to 3 per cent of GDP. This policy was adopted by the Consultative Commission on Educational Reform (CCRE), which includes representatives of the government, universities, schools, teachers, churches, Indigenous peoples, and the private sector. The Commission was also tasked with drafting a National Education Plan for the next 20 years.

Among the members of the Commission were two organizations that had played key roles in the *Gran Campaña*: the Coordination Office of Mayan Organizations in Guatemala (COPMAGUA) and the Standing National Commission on Education Reform (CNPRE). Both also served on the CCRE Executive Council. Working together, CNPRE–COPMAGUA were determined that the perspective of Guatemala's Indigenous peoples should have a prominent place in the discussion of education funding. They turned to Canada's IDRC for support in generating a proposal for a more equitable distribution of educational expenditures from an Indigenous perspective—'considering the exclusion, poverty and discrimination that the Mayan people of Guatemala has historically suffered.'

The project had three broad objectives:

1. To analyze the planning and execution of the education budget from the perspective of the Indigenous peoples. To meet this objective, the project called for a research report that would identify weaknesses in the education budget structure and pinpoint target population sectors and geographic areas for educational investment.
2. To formulate a proposal, based on the Indigenous perspective, to influence budgetary planning and execution in the context of education reform and the long-term National Education Plan.
3. To influence policy by enhancing the quality of the proposals submitted by CNPRE and COPMAGUA delegates, and by reinforcing Indigenous participation in the education reform debate.

Broader perspective

Although the original emphasis of the project was on ethnic discrimination in the education system, during the course of the project its perspective was broadened to include gender equity. This constituted a fundamental amendment to the concept and design of the project.

Ethnic discrimination in Guatemala's school system can be observed through various educational indicators. For example, the illiteracy rate for the Guatemalan population as a whole is 31.3 per cent. Breaking that number down, however, reveals that for the non-Indigenous population the illiteracy rate is 21.4 per cent, while for the Indigenous population it is almost double at 42.5 per cent. Statistics on academic failure—a particular problem in rural areas—show the highest incidence in the regions with the greatest percentages of Indigenous people.

The education statistics also revealed another inequity to the researchers. The gross school enrolment rate for boys from 1993 to 1998 was 93 per cent, but for girls it was 82 per cent. The composition of the student body for the same period was 54 per cent boys and 46 per cent girls. These statistics convinced the researchers to add a gender perspective to their research. There were some objections, particularly from Indigenous people, who felt that it would be more important to generate strategies and actions to eliminate ethnic discrimination than to worry about the gender issue.

On the other hand, the government and private sector research centres felt that both these issues should be subordinated to the traditional budget categories, and to a more global poverty reduction strategy. They argued that any special treatment for one group must necessarily come at the expense of the rest of the population.

Many obstacles

Dr Bienvenido Argueta, who evaluated the policy influence of the project for IDRC, following its completion, says that once the project got underway the researchers ran into a number of obstacles. First was the difficulty in accessing reliable sources of information. 'Databases, education statistics and budget figures generally take no consideration of ethnic and gender issues,' he says. The second problem was the limited time available to complete the study in order to have an impact on the education budget. He points out that it takes time to build alliances, to inform and mobilize key sectors of the population, and to present proposals properly.

Finally, simply identifying decision makers in the field of education finance policy was difficult. This was 'because of the dynamics of national politics in recent years, with the constant turnover in senior government positions, and a steady shift of power from the executive to the legislative branch', according to Dr Argueta. The Planning Unit of the Ministry of Education, for example, had seen four directors come and go in the space of 18 months. The Ministry's draft budget was not only scrutinized and cut by the Ministry of Finance, it was also completely overhauled by the Finance Committee of Congress.

Despite these issues, the project team produced and published a report entitled 'Financing of Education in Guatemala'. It included several analyses of education budget planning and execution, and projections disaggregating—to the extent possible—investment by gender and ethnic group. Accompanying the report was the 'Proposal for the financing of education in Guatemala with an emphasis on ethnic and gender equity.' The report and the proposal were delivered at a public event in the presence of the Minister of Education and the CCRE.

Strategy was weak

The CNPRE–COPMAGUA team recognized that their dissemination strategy for these publications was weak, says Dr Argueta, and that they did not have an adequate plan to forge broader partnerships with the various Indigenous groups in Guatemala. This was true of the alliances in the CCRE and in the *Gran Campaña*, where the proposals were more easily negotiated with the teachers' union and the University of San Carlos of Guatemala.

This situation was due, among other things, to the lack of experience, and the technical and financial limitations of CNPRE–COPMAGUA. Also, the research team itself did not feel that it was involved in the dissemination strategies.

The weaknesses in terms of outreach and dissemination were further highlighted by the fact that there was no specific strategy targeted at women's groups, or any attempt to build a broader alliance on gender and ethnic equity, according to Dr Argueta. 'The communications strategy placed no particular emphasis on women's groups. In general, the absence of strategies for reaching women's groups was repeated with respect to men's groups.' And most seriously he notes: 'It is obvious that there was no proper approach made to the Congress, or to officials of the Presidential Office for Planning and Programming (SEGEPLAN) and the Ministry of Finance.'

Most of the attempt at policy influence was directed towards the technical staff of the Ministry of Education. At the same time, people who bring pressure on the government through civil society organizations, such as members of the CCRE and the *Gran Campaña*, were made more aware of the need to incorporate ethnic and gender issues into the education budget.

Dr Argueta's evaluation concludes that the major changes during the project were of a technical nature, especially in the institutional strengthening of CNPRE and COPMAGUA. 'The study and the proposal took about one year, which means that the political, economic and social impact was not evident in the short run,' he says. 'Nevertheless, the fact that marginalized sectors of the population are participating more actively in the public policy debate is recognized as a step forward for Guatemalan democracy.'

Some lessons

The analysis of policy influence in this case study is based on Evert Lindquist's typology of policy influence, as presented in his paper *Discerning Policy Influence: Framework for Strategic Evaluation of IDRC-supported Research*.

Expanding policy capacities

The greatest learning was represented by the acquisition and strengthening of the capacities of CNPRE, COPMAGUA, and the research group, for justifying and preparing anti-discrimination policies. As a result they were able to generate information and produce knowledge, both in the research and in the proposal. They learned to introduce new concepts and issues on the agenda for debate by players who had previously little to say about the issue. In this respect, says Dr Argueta, they were able to influence other research centres with the capacity to do research, and to propose courses of action to the government relating to public policy. Even IDRC programme officers involved with the project say that they learned some fundamental lessons especially about working with the grass-roots Indigenous organizations.

Broadening policy horizons

The researchers point to a growing understanding of the rationale underlying financial programmes and qualitative programming in education. The qualitative analysis of the education sector required the establishment of goals and effective financial programming, which in turn demanded new concepts and new approaches. In addition, with respect to education funding, there was a favourable environment for communication and negotiation with various players in civil society. The research group also noted that it was very difficult, but at the same time very instructive, to address financial analysis from the gender perspective.

Affecting policy regimes

One of the fundamental lessons had to do with the process of giving legitimacy to policy by making it responsive to the national interest, and not only to sectoral and party groups. This required skills of a different kind in order to have political influence. In turn, this involved a process of learning how to simplify the communication of complex qualitative analyses and hard data taken from the budget and education statistics. The team also learned to prioritize issues, to identify the 'who, what, and how' of preparing and executing the budget. They also deepened their skills in preparing 'power maps' for influencing policy, although these still have to be refined.

Basic Data	
Time Period:	2000–2002
Objectives:	To influence educational policy in Guatemala, by formulating a proposal from an Indigenous perspective that could influence the planning and execution of the education budget in the context of the Education Reform and the National Education Plan (2000–2020).
Research Outputs:	Background research studies that resulted in a Research Report on financing education in Guatemala.

The TEHIP 'Spark' Leads to Better Health: Integrating Research and Development was Key in Tanzania

This brief is based on a case study by Terry Smutylo and Stephanie Neilson.

The Tanzania Essential Health Interventions Project (TEHIP) is a research and development partnership involving Tanzania's Ministry of Health and Canada's IDRC. It was established to test innovations in planning, priority setting, and resource allocation at the district level. The results make a powerful case that using research to make health spending more proportional to the prevailing burden of disease can have a significant, positive impact on health outcomes.

With a per capita income of CA $370, Tanzania is one of the poorest countries in the world and, like other countries of sub-Saharan Africa, has seen a series of grim health indicators worsen. Conditions such as malaria, tuberculosis, malnutrition, anemia, and HIV/AIDS have cut a deadly path across the continent, and national health systems have buckled under the strain. In Tanzania, as in other countries, economic deprivation and the health crisis feed off each other. The lack of resources makes Tanzanians more vulnerable to the effects of illness, and diminishes the government's ability to fund health services. Succumbing to sickness, in turn, reduces citizens' capacity to generate income. This dual burden does not make Tanzania unique, but it does make the country a fitting home for a demonstration project that has sought to determine if finding better ways of allocating health care resources could help revive moribund health systems and save lives. Originally known as the Essential Health Interventions Project (EHIP), the project found its initial inspiration in a hypothesis—contained in the World Bank's 'World Development Report' of 1993 (WDR '93)—that quite modest new investments in health care could have significant impact if those funds were applied to cost-effective health interventions targeting the most significant causes of death and disability. WDR '93 proposed that merely raising developing countries' health care spending to around $17 (US $12) per capita (an infinitesimal portion of the $3,900 per capita spent each year on health care in Canada, for example) could lower the burden of disease rate by 25 per cent, if the new funds were applied where they would have the greatest impact.

Tanzania, which was in the midst of health care reforms involving the devolution of planning responsibility from the centre to the district, applied to become the host country to test the WDR '93 hypothesis. With that, EHIP changed its name to TEHIP, and the programme was reoriented as a collaborative joint venture between the Republic of Tanzania and IDRC, housed within Tanzania's Ministry of Health (MoH), and combining the efforts of local researchers, international advisors, district health planners, health facility clinicians, and whole communities.

Local level action

The TEHIP team focused its work in two districts: Rufiji and Morogoro. TEHIP's primary functions were to facilitate the generation of research, and to develop a series of tools and strategies that would help those districts' District Health Management Teams (DHMTs) allocate funds and design packages of health interventions that more directly responded to evidence about the local 'burden of disease.' To generate the evidence, TEHIP supported local District Sentinel Surveillance (DSS) Systems, which used enumerators to regularly collect data from households in the districts, thus providing up-to-date vital statistics.

TEHIP also developed a series of computer-based planning tools to help DHMTs understand the relevance of that DSS-generated evidence to the health planning process. For example, the 'Burden of Disease Profile Tool' simplifies and communicates complex information on local burden of disease by transforming it into easy-to-read graphs, tables, and charts. Instead of presenting the burden of disease by specific disease categories, the profiles emphasize the proportional burden addressed by various essential health interventions.

The 'District Health Accounts Tool' graphically shows how individual spending commitments coalesce as an overall plan, whether they conform to Ministry requirements, where the funding is coming from, and how proportionally it is being spent. DMHTs used those tools to adjust their budgets so that less would be spent on treating marginal illnesses that had previously consumed an amount of funding disproportionate to their impact on mortality. As a result, new investments could be made in areas like the treatment and prevention of malaria and, because malaria and childhood diseases were shown to contribute greatly to local mortality rates, the Integrated Management of Childhood Illnesses.

Parallel with the provision of these planning tools, TEHIP provided small amounts of top-up funds that DMHTs could apply to what they saw as major weaknesses in the district health systems. This led to the implementation of new initiatives, such as the Integrated Management Cascade that breaks the health system into tiers and local clusters. This 'cascading' organizational structure facilitates the supervision of health facilities and gives them easier access to drugs, lab tests, emergency consultations, and other services provided from higher levels. Funds were also applied to rehabilitating health facilities, with communities themselves providing labour and some of the materials.

The role of research

As these actions suggest, research was not a discrete or self-contained element of TEHIP's work, but part of a combined, interlocking 'research and development' agenda that used research data as raw material, contributing to the creation of concrete and timely improvements within the health system. In this respect, TEHIP was unique among IDRC-supported projects: it was one of the very few projects to have the funding and mandate to move its research findings forward into the development stage. In the field, this clear link between research and development set TEHIP apart from typical research projects, giving TEHIP a higher level of credibility among busy health workers who might otherwise have seen the arrival of researchers from the capital as a fruitless distraction, or a drain on their time.

Employees, struggling to keep an overstretched health system functioning, knew that 'the goal of TEHIP's approach was not just to produce some papers for *The Lancet*', remarks TEHIP project manager Graham Reid. 'It was actually working with a living system, in context, working with people, and trying to influence a health system that was already in the process of being changed.'

Stephanie Neilson of IDRC's Evaluation Unit, who interviewed a wide variety of workers within the Tanzanian health system, agrees that the practical orientation of the research encouraged a 'buy-in' to the project's goals and methods by participants, ranging from ministry and district planners, to village health workers, to individuals within communities. 'The way it was often articulated to us,' she says, 'is that this wasn't the kind of abstract, theoretical research where people come in, try to prove something, and then walk away. They were trying to do something that would be valuable and useful to people on the ground.'

'What people in Tanzania's health sector really identify with TEHIP are the planning tools—particularly the burden of disease and resource allocation tools,' she says.

> They are things that give people a greater capacity to go about their work. In the communities, people really associate TEHIP with the rehabilitation of health facilities. That whole exercise gave people the resources, skills, and tools to maintain their own health facilities, and it told people in the communities that the goal of TEHIP was to actually improve the system.

In fact, the research and development functions of TEHIP were so closely intertwined that it was often difficult to ascertain where one left off and the other began. Staff were organized in an integrated team structure, for example, where the researchers and the development specialists were highly aware of and highly dependent upon each other's work. Forming a kind of continuous 'feedback loop', the development side depended upon a steady stream of research to determine whether the tools and strategies were working, how they could be improved, and what new interventions might be needed at the next phase of work. Researchers crafted their agendas around the practical requirements of developing and implementing those new tools and strategies. The research component was divided into three modules examining:

1. Health systems—how planning took place and how the health system operated;
2. Health-seeking behaviour—how, when, and why community members sought health care, and what their experience was; and
3. Health outcomes—what level of health and burden of disease existed.

Ongoing work in these three areas of inquiry allowed researchers to submit new innovations to continual evaluation: were new developments changing the way planners plan? Were they improving the public's experience of the health care system? Were they improving health outcomes and reducing mortality? And where should we go from here?

Multiple layers of influence

To assess whether TEHIP succeeded in influencing public policy in Tanzania, Terry Smutylo and Stephanie Neilson looked at a number of possible types of policy influence. Evaluators considered whether TEHIP had helped expand Tanzania's policy capacities (for example, by increasing the ability of Tanzanian health officials to use research), whether it had broadened the range of debate around research and policy issues, and whether it had an impact on the actual policies that were adopted by the government.

Stephanie Neilson remarks that while all those forms of influence are important, an area where TEHIP had, perhaps, its most profound impact was in broadening the debate and altering the dominant thinking on the use of research in policy formation. 'It was said to us by many people, on numerous occasions, that the idea of planning based on evidence has influenced the way the health sector operates,' she says. 'Not only that, but it has crossed boundaries, seeping into other areas like education.'

Dr Gabriel Upunda, Tanzania's Chief Medical Officer, agrees that there has been a shift in perspectives and practice across the entire decision-making structure. 'We have learnt the use of data in making decisions', he declares.

> Fortunately, the outlook of our National Institute for Medical Research is now oriented in the same way. This means that, whenever there is a decision to be made, there is evidence on which to base that decision. I can go to the politicians and tell them 'you have this to decide, and here is the information that we have from a scientific point of view'.

One obvious reason why decision makers appear to have embraced the use of research in policymaking is that the introduction of evidence-based planning has been associated with a dramatic improvement in health outcomes in the demonstration districts. In the four years following the introduction of evidence-based planning (and with financial top-ups amounting to only US $1 per capita per year) child mortality rates have fallen by 46 per cent in Rufiji, and 43 per cent in Morogoro. In the same period, Rufiji's mortality rate for adults between 20 and 50 fell by 18 per cent. These results make a powerful case that using research to make health spending more proportional to the prevailing burden of disease can have a significant, positive impact on health outcomes. This dramatic demonstration was arguably the most critical factor in promoting a new 'culture of planning' within the Tanzanian health system.

Capacity and content

The evaluation team also found that TEHIP significantly influenced workers' capacity to use research and policy content. A great deal of health planners' increased capacity to use research in support of policymaking was attributed to the provision of the planning tools. The tools provided a critical link between research and planning by expressing data in a simple form that DHMTs could use in their daily work (for instance, through charts that translated mortality figures into 'intervention-addressable shares' of Burden of Disease). 'It wasn't until TEHIP came here that we used the information [generated by household surveillance],' said one district team member. Another interviewee told the IDRC evaluation team that 'before, the Ministry talked about information, but they didn't see how they could use it, didn't see how they could display it. Now they do.'

The ongoing impact of TEHIP is also reflected in recent changes in Tanzanian health policy. By helping to facilitate the presentation of relevant mortality information, for instance, TEHIP helped move malaria higher up on the agendas of both the districts and the Ministry of Health, which intensified its national anti-malaria campaigns by increasing the promotion of insecticide-treated bed nets. It also switched to more effective anti-malarial drugs. The lasting impact of TEHIP can also be seen in the Ministry's endorsement of strategies, such as the Integrated Management Cascade, and its creation of a 'basket' of funds—modelled after the TEHIP top-up that funded innovations such as the management cascade, and the facility renovations. The Ministry now provides these funds to Tanzania's other districts by pooling its health sector contributions from international donors.

Expanding future influence

The loudest note of caution was sounded by interviewees who feared that TEHIP would be swallowed by the 'project trap'—that the influence of TEHIP would cease after the project had wound down. They also feared that the Ministry would not adequately promote the use of the tools and strategies throughout the country. TEHIP has developed an 'exit strategy' involving the Zonal Training Centres operated by the MoH that will train trainers on the use of the tools. They will, in turn, be sent to other districts.

Clearly, TEHIP has created linkages between research and policy formation in a number of different ways. The real test of its influence, however, will be whether TEHIP's approach and its specific innovations (such as the planning tools, which are portable and adaptable to other national contexts) will move beyond the demonstration districts to bring improvements to health systems in the rest of Tanzania and, indeed, to other countries facing similar circumstances.

Basic Data

Time Period: 1996–2004

Objective: To test the feasibility and measure the impact of an evidence-based approach to local health planning in two districts in Tanzania.

Research Outputs: 1. Developed 10 tools to collect, organize, and present data on mortality and disease.
2. Analyzed data for policy options.
3. Research on governance and organizational design.

Networks and Innovation

13

Patience Brings Rewards: The Lessons of the Asian Fisheries Social Science Research Network

This brief is based on a case study by Robert Pomeroy.

Sometimes it takes years of effort to achieve a positive result. In Southeast Asia, IDRC embraced a long and patient commitment to building capacity for social science research in the fisheries industry. This strategy has succeeded: it has trained a whole generation of scientists whose impact on policymaking will be enduring.

Since the early 1980s, serious problems have troubled Southeast Asia's fisheries sector. Although both fishing and fish farming are time-honoured occupations in the region and they provide people with the cheapest and most popular forms of animal protein, most fishing households are mired in poverty. In spite of loans and subsidies, and other government programmes designed to aid the fisheries, and in spite of advances such as motorized boats, better gear, and improvements in aquaculture techniques, most small-scale producers have remained desperately poor.

In the so-called capture or harvest fisheries, many factors have contributed to keeping incomes low. The common property nature of the resource has meant that there is no individual incentive to limit the catch ('If I don't take the fish, somebody else will'); inevitably this has led to overfishing. Meanwhile, traditional forms of regulating access to fishing grounds have broken down with the arrival of highly mobile vessels. Moreover, fuel and other inputs have become more costly. Population growth, combined with a lack of alternative jobs in rural areas, has pushed many more people into an already crowded business. Finally, there has been little state support for a marketing infrastructure that would welcome the small-scale operator.

Meanwhile, in aquaculture—a husbandry activity where productivity can be improved through better technology and increases in inputs—a few large and successful enterprises have competed with many smaller and marginally profitable enterprises. The advantages of large size and corporate know-how have meant that much of the growth in aquacultural production has come from a relatively small number of farms.

Not only has each fisheries sector had its special problems, but they have competed with one another for territorial resources such as mangrove swamps and shallow water lagoons, for a share of the consumer food budget, and for government and private investment.

The quest for information

Both overfishing and the environmental degradation of coastal resources have concerned the region's governments. Issues of food security, rural development, employment, foreign earnings, tourism, and the environment have all put fisheries and coastal resource management high on policy agendas.

Unfortunately, in the early 1980s, much of the scientific research being undertaken on these issues was biological in nature, even while people were beginning to recognize that the real solutions were social, economic, political, and institutional in nature. Too little of the right kind of information was available because too few social scientists were conducting fisheries research in the region. Economists in particular had scant professional interest in these subjects. Consequently, no programme of economic and policy research was being carried out either by government fisheries agencies, research centres, or universities.

Meanwhile, policymakers increasingly demanded better social science information. These demands were being met by a growing dependence on countries outside the region for this type of education, consultation, and research. Clearly, Southeast Asia needed its own capacity to undertake social science fisheries research.

So it was that in 1983, under the coordination of the International Centre for Living Aquatic Resources Management (ICLARM) in the Philippines—and with funding support from the IDRC, among others—the Asian Fisheries Social Science Research Network (AFSSRN) or the Network was launched. The Network's mandate was to overcome the lack of social science research capacity in Southeast Asia through a combination of formal and informal training, scholarships, research activities, information exchange, seminars, workshops, and staff exchanges.

During the period of IDRC funding, which lasted until 1996, the Network went through four phases. Its membership grew, and the emphasis of its work shifted from straightforward capacity building to the provision of social science research for policy purposes. All the while, its activities were closely coordinated by ICLARM.

In 2001, IDRC launched a long-term evaluation of the policy influence of the research it has supported. This ambitious exercise aims to improve the design of specific projects and programmes where public policy may be an objective, and so to give better focus to IDRC's overall strategic plan.

Part of the evaluation process reviews a series of rich case studies. IDRC engaged Dr Robert Pomeroy to assess the policy influence of AFSSRN. He carried out this study mainly by interviewing members and associates of the Network.

History of the network

Dr Pomeroy outlined the development of AFSSRN and the gradual shift in its mandate.

Initial capacity building, 1983-86

The charter members of AFSSRN were universities in Malaysia, Thailand, and the Philippines. The Network's initial focus was economics, and its broad objective was to build long-term social science research capacity in Southeast Asian institutions in fisheries and aquaculture.
It had three specific goals:

1. To help institutions strengthen their capacity to carry out research. Its methods were direct funding and technical support for projects, the training of researchers, and the planning of large research programmes.
2. To build enduring research capacity by fostering training in fisheries economics. The affiliated institutions offered graduate and undergraduate courses in such areas as fisheries management, and the economics of aquaculture.
3. To encourage stronger professional links and working relationships among these institutions and policymaking bodies.

Expansion and consolidation, 1985-88

Six new institutions from Indonesia, Thailand, and the Philippines joined AFSSRN. The Network continued where it had left off in the opening phase, funding research projects, hosting workshops and courses, and encouraging links among researchers and policymakers. By now, however, the emphasis had shifted slightly towards policy issues. Most of the Network's research projects during this period dealt with the economics of aquaculture, marketing, and small-scale fisheries management. Since many of the fish resources of Network member countries were already exhausted or threatened, research on the economic and social consequences of fisheries management, particularly in villages and households, was regarded as crucial for finding policy solutions.

As it happened, although the stated objective was to provide information for the design of better fisheries policies, little actual research on policy analysis was carried out. It was felt that such an analysis would be premature because the basic applied research and social science skills of Network members were not yet fully developed.

Review of progress, 1988-94

By now, AFSSRN comprised 14 teams with 80 researchers in Indonesia, Malaysia, Thailand, and the Philippines. The general objective was to develop social science research capacity as a partner to the 'hard' sciences in aquatic systems management.

This phase also concentrated on the publication of research findings. It also introduced a national networking programme to connect AFSSRN members and other national fisheries organizations. And it put greater emphasis on generating results useful for formulating development policies and management strategies. A shortage of research in the capture fisheries led to the creation of a research and training programme in 1990—funded by IDRC—joining the efforts of AFSSRN and Canada's Simon Fraser University.

A review of AFSSRN's entire history, carried out during this period, concluded that the Network had succeeded in its goal of pulling together economists and other social scientists to promote research and training in the social science aspects of fisheries and aquaculture.

The review also found that the Network had improved members' research skills, supported their research endeavours, helped them connect with other researchers in the region, and expanded the pool of trained researchers. The review further concluded that although the actual impact of Network activities on fisheries policy and management had been modest, AFSSRN had helped members develop their capacity to address these issues.

Emphasis on policy, 1995–96

In this phase AFSSRN extended its membership to Vietnam.

Much of the Network's focus continued as before, but policy-relevant social science research became a central goal. Members had achieved the necessary skills base and so could concentrate more on research related to decision making.

While this shift was taking place, it was recognized that members needed other new skills if their emphasis was now to focus on developing management-related policies and programmes. Networking, education, and training were therefore accorded higher priority.

AFSSRN made an extra effort to publish its research reports, over 50 of which had been generated since 1983. It developed a publications series and distributed the reports in the region, in particular to policymakers.

1997 and beyond

After the IDRC funding ended, members were concerned that the activities of AFSSRN would cease. With support from ICLARM, the Network became part of the Asian Fisheries Society.

The Network continues today. Its members meet at regional meetings, and there is an AFSSRN news section in ICLARM's quarterly publication *NAGA*.

Influencing public policy

Until its final phase, the Network was not designed explicitly to have an influence on public policy. Instead, its early objective was to build national research capacity to address important social science issues in the management of fishery resources in the region. As it turned out, however, its networking, training and education, research support, and information dissemination activities did influence policy.

AFSSRN played a large role in helping to expand policy capacities in the region, in particular by developing new talent for undertaking issues-based research and analysis. In other words, the Network helped improve the institutional framework surrounding policymaking.

AFSSRN also helped broaden policy horizons. It introduced new ideas to the agenda, and nourished dialogues among researchers and decision makers. In other words, the Network helped improve the intellectual framework surrounding policymaking.

The Network achieved its policy influence in a number of overlapping stages:

1. Before the Network was launched, fisheries social scientists in the region had a low skills base and almost no capacity to undertake policy analysis. The Network first provided training and education in the basics of social science research. This foundation exposed members to new concepts and methods, and helped them advance their careers.
2. Research projects supported by the Network helped members gain more experience in using the new concepts and methods. The small grants provided by the Network for research projects often produced important results with policy implications.
3. As Network members gained more confidence, the level of research improved, and many of the projects produced policy recommendations that were used by both public and private sectors.
4. Network involvement advanced the careers of members. Many early members have become senior officials in universities or government fisheries departments, where they now direct public policy. In all cases they attribute their advancement, in part, to membership in the Network.
5. The collegial relationships that have been developed through networking have linked researchers and policymakers. These connections have been critically important in influencing policy in all Network member countries.
6. Network members have published research results in all the important peer-reviewed scientific journals. These articles serve as the foundation for developing new policies on fisheries and aquaculture not just in the region, but worldwide.
7. Having achieved this skills base, scientific maturity, career advancement, self-confidence, and partnership with policymakers, Network members became better able to conduct policy analysis, and began to influence policy.
8. In a region that at one time was obliged to import its social science expertise, Network members began to act as consultants and started advising others on projects, including policy projects, throughout Asia and around the world.

Dr Pomeroy's study concluded by underscoring two important points. First, IDRC's capacity building networks in Asia, such as AFSSRN, have had wide and lasting impacts. The lives of many people have been improved as a result of these efforts. Second, these networks have succeeded in part because IDRC has had the patience to support them, sometimes for very long periods of time, until their objectives were met.

Before the AFSSRN it was difficult to find economists working on fisheries issues in Thailand. We did not have good economic information on which to make decisions. We relied on biological information, but that only gave part of the information that we needed to make good policy. Now, in part as a result of the AFSSRN, we make more informed policy. (Prayot Supavivat, Department of Fisheries, Thailand)

Originally I would just do research for research's sake. My audience was not the policymaker. Now, being in government, I better understand the need for good research to inform my decision-making and I better understand why the AFSSRN was pushing, through training, the need for us to do policy-relevant research. I request our researchers, both in government and in academe, to do research which I can use to support or not support decisions. (Victor Nikijuluw, Ministry of Marine Affairs and Fisheries, Indonesia)

Basic Data	
Time Period:	1983–96
Objectives:	To improve the capacities to manage the fishery, and to indirectly influence policy and management regimes. Increase supply of social researchers on fisheries and strengthen institutions.
Research Outputs:	Over 50 research reports were produced over the life of the project and a special publication series was developed.

Promoting Traditional Knowledge: Indian NGO Influences Policy at the State, National, and International Levels

This brief is based on a case study by Leanne Burton.

The Society for Research and Initiatives for Sustainable Technologies and Institutions (SRISTI) has documented and disseminated more than 10,000 grass-roots innovations and traditional practices in India's agricultural sector. By enabling farmers to share their knowledge, SRISTI has deepened awareness of labour-saving techniques, and other innovations. At the same time, by introducing new ideas to politicians and bureaucrats, encouraging networking, and educating researchers, it has had an impact on policy at the state, national, and international levels.

Faced with rapid population growth, food shortages, and widespread poverty, many developing countries embarked on a 'Green Revolution' in the 1960s by producing high-yield crop varieties, increasing irrigation, and expanding use of chemical fertilizers and pesticides. In India, the Green Revolution led to expansion of farmland, double-cropping, intensive irrigation, and hybrid seeds. In so doing, it swept aside much of the focus on traditional seeds and crop varieties, herbal pesticides, and organic farming.

While the changes helped India produce enough food to feed its people, they created new challenges. The new agricultural policies mainly benefited large commercial producers, which could afford to buy fertilizer and hold out for best prices, and which had better access to subsidized credit and irrigation. Traditional agriculture, and the farmers who practiced it, were largely left behind.

By 1989, an informal group of academics, farmers, scientists, and others known as the Honey Bee Network emerged. Just as a bee moves among flowers collecting and distributing pollen—doing good without causing harm—members of the Honey Bee Network moved among local innovators to document and disseminate their knowledge in local languages, ensuring that the originator received some benefits.

At its heart, the Honey Bee Network sought to improve the socioeconomic conditions of knowledge-rich but resource-poor farmers and other rural dwellers. The Network believed it was crucial to acknowledge and, if possible, reward innovators for their creativity. Moreover, it believed that formal and informal sciences were complementary: traditional knowledge could expand the frontiers of science, which in turn, could enhance or build upon local creativity.

By the early 1990s, the Network needed to consolidate and institutionalize its work, a desire that led to the founding of SRISTI in 1993.

IDRC's partnership with SRISTI

Strengthening grass-roots capacity and innovation

IDRC provided core support for SRISTI's first phase (1993–96) through the auspices of the Indian Institute of Management Ahmedabad (IIMA), enabling the new non-governmental organization (NGO) to evolve from a volunteer-based network of researchers and activists into a more structured and permanent organization. Phase I had four objectives designed to strengthen the capacity of grass-roots innovators: protect intellectual property rights, experiment to add value to innovators' knowledge, evolve entrepreneurial ability to generate returns from this knowledge, and enrich the cultural and institutional basis for dealing with nature.

By the end of Phase I, SRISTI was recognized for its innovative leadership. More than 1,000 groups had become members, including many farmers. SRISTI had documented and disseminated more than 5,000 innovative practices in six Indian languages through such tools as the Honey Bee Newsletter.

Expanding to the national level

Phase II (1997–2000) built on SRISTI's early work, emphasizing value-added stages of innovation, as well as material and non-material incentives for innovators. It expanded the organization's scope beyond farmers to include natural resource management, rural production, and cottage industries. It also sought to pay more attention to women's knowledge.

'By the end of Phase II, SRISTI had documented an additional 8,000 local innovations and had validated or improved several of them, including herbal pesticides, and veterinary and human plant-based medicines,' says Leanne Burton, who evaluated the public policy influence of SRISTI's work. 'SRISTI developed and tested various reward and compensation schemes, and had struck a royalty-sharing agreement with a private company interested in three veterinary drugs.'

During Phase II, SRISTI also worked with the Government of Gujarat to scale up grass-roots innovations by establishing the Gujarat Innovation Augmentation Network (GIAN). At the same time, to graduate its activities from the state level to the national level, SRISTI collaborated with the national government to set up the National Innovation Foundation (NIF).

Women, wisdom, and well-being

At the end of Phase II, an IDRC consultant evaluated the project, which helped identify its limitations and gaps. As a result, in its current phase (2000–present), SRISTI's overarching theme is 'Women, wisdom, and well-being: local knowledge and value addition of biodiverse resources of women in India'.

The organization has challenged its members to develop innovative solutions to reduce the drudgery associated with women's work. To that end, it has worked with the Self-Employed Women's Association (SEWA) to distribute several labour-saving technologies, including a modified water pulley developed by a local farmer. In addition, as planned in Phase II, SRISTI is working with women's NGOs like SEWA, to launch state-wide searches for female innovators.

In its 2002 interim report to IDRC, SRISTI noted that it had documented several hundred traditional practices and innovations in Gujarat; supported further thesis work on women's knowledge; documented women's knowledge of vegetative crops, less well-known uncultivated foods, medicinal plants, livestock management, and human health; and organized women-only village meetings, among other activities.

Assessing policy influence

Research can influence public policy in several key ways: by expanding policy capacities, broadening policy horizons, or affecting policy regimes.

Expanding policy capacities

SRISTI has expanded policy capacities by improving the knowledge of key actors, developing innovative ideas, improving capacity to communicate ideas, and developing new talent for research and analysis.

By documenting and disseminating more than 10,000 grass-roots innovations and traditional practices, SRISTI has improved and expanded the knowledge of diverse public. While its primary audience has been farmers, other innovators, students, and children, it has used media to spread its ideas both nationally and internationally. It has also invited different actors, for example, politicians, academics, NGOs, to collaborate.

'It is impossible to know how much of this information is being absorbed by the various actors', says Burton. 'However, there is evidence of some filtering through. SRISTI has put forward an agenda, with information to support it, and it is this framing of information that makes it useful and useable for policymakers.'

With respect to innovative ideas, SRISTI continues to develop original concepts, as well as to test and expand them. For example, it has proposed ethical guidelines for accessing and exploring biodiversity, as well as a 'prior informed consent form' to help innovators protect intellectual property.

Creative communication has been an integral part of SRISTI's strategy. The Honey Bee Newsletter combines technical and cultural information with the human appeal of personal stories, humour, and challenges. Beyond the newsletter, it has compiled databases on CD-ROM, and produced videos and posters in local languages. For illiterate villagers, it has produced interactive, picture-based computer kiosks. 'SRISTI has learned the power of a story, and will often use these to impress upon more remote audiences the human face of its work,' says Burton.

SRISTI has developed new talent for research and analysis by establishing the Sadhbav Sristi Sanshodhan Laboratory; this collaboration with the SADHBAV Foundation brings added value to local knowledge and green technologies. In addition, it set up an in-house herbal lab to conduct experiments with herbal pesticides.

SRISTI's success in expanding policy capacities has been often attributed to its storehouse of relevant research, and empirical evidence. 'Groundwork has been key to the influence of policymakers—documentation, providing evidence of the creative thinking happening at the grass-roots level, and scientifically validating this knowledge,' affirms V. Sherry Chand, a professor with the IIMA.

Broadening policy horizons

'SRISTI works simultaneously at all levels of government,' says Dr Sudershan Iyengar, director and professor at the Gujarat Institute of Development Research and a SRISTI board member. He adds:

> It has been able to identify issues requiring central government attention, those possible to address at lower levels, and has then pursued both courses simultaneously. By ensuring that there is a national element to its work, SRISTI makes the point that what is possible in one state is possible in all states of India.

At the state level, SRISTI has developed an effective relationship with the Government of Gujarat. In 1997, the organization invited government representatives to its International Conference on Creativity and Innovation at the grass-roots. Follow-up meetings with government led to the creation of the Gujarat Innovation Augmentation Network (GIAN, a registered trust with a 12 member board, including several state officials).

GIAN helps local entrepreneurs to access funding by acting as a go-between for innovators and government/business institutions. Among GIAN's achievements: it has signed agreements with several national entrepreneurship schemes; pursued collaborations with educational, research, and training institutions, and NGOs; and mobilized resources (financial, technical, administrative) for more than a dozen innovations at various stages of the development and marketing process. At least another three GIANs are planned for various parts of the country.

At the national level, in response to appeals from SRISTI, the Department of Science and Technology established the National Innovation Foundation (NIF). It is closely linked with SRISTI and GIAN, and enhances the work of these two organizations. NIF acts as a national register of grass-roots innovation and traditional knowledge, and helps to develop and market innovations, linking innovators with formal science and technology.

At both the national and international levels, SRISTI has contributed to the debate about intellectual property rights (IPR) for biological resources. It has organized or taken part in various workshops and consultations on topics such as the Convention on Biological Diversity, and worked with Indian stakeholders to help the national Ministry of Environment and Forests to develop a new policy for accessing and conserving biological resources. With respect to Trade-Related Aspects of Intellectual Property Rights (TRIPS), it co-organized a consultation in 1998 with the World Intellectual Property Organization and farmers on IPR protection.

SRISTI's renewed commitment to gender-based projects has had an impact on partners such as SEWA. 'I have worked with rural women for a long time, but I am now beginning to appreciate how women do things differently and why,' says SEWA's Reema Nanavaty. 'Previously, SEWA's focus was on women's access to resources; now we are also considering how women use these resources differently and why. There is more critical analysis.'

Another component of broadening policy horizons has been establishing networks between formal and informal science communities. NIF now has a Memorandum of Understanding with the Indian Council of Agricultural Research and the Indian Council of Scientific Research. In addition, grass-roots innovators have taken part in the Indian Science Congress.

Affecting policy regimes

SRISTI, along with GIAN and NIF, has affected policy in India, but successes have resulted from the influence of its president, Anil Gupta, rather than specific lobbying. Professor Gupta's involvement with both SRISTI and NIF has helped the two organizations enjoy a close relationship. Following NIF's invitation to a pre-budget meeting to share ideas on how to support innovation, for example, Professor Gupta provided the draft text for the Minister's 2002 budget speech, which announced the creation of a venture capital fund for grass-roots innovators.

'SRISTI's policy impact has been at the level of ideas,' suggests Sherry Chand. Several key officials at both state and national levels have expressed support for SRISTI's work, and acknowledged its impact on them personally. At the state level, the Ministry of Agriculture in Gujarat follows SRISTI's practice of rewarding innovators. At the national level, in addition to influencing the budgetary process, Professor Gupta helped draft India's biodiversity bill. At the global level, the International Crops Research Institute for the Semi-Arid Tropics (ICRISAT) now conducts research on several herbal pesticides that SRISTI helped identify.

Conclusions

'SRISTI has seen—and continues to see—policy influence as a means to an end,' says Burton. 'The organization's primary goal is to protect and value indigenous knowledge, and over time it has realized that sustainable and widespread progress on this front requires policy support.'

For Burton, SRISTI has had intermediate policy influence in two fundamental ways. First, by working with partners and through its own experience, SRISTI has increased its capacity to conduct research, analyze information, and communicate with a variety of actors. Second, it has enriched the policy arena for others by introducing new ideas, encouraging networking, and educating researchers who have then taken up new positions in related areas.

'Both the state and national governments have created space for SRISTI to pursue its policy work,' says Burton. 'This is uncommon in India, and is concrete evidence of—if not widespread impact at the policy level—some impact on the thinking of policy officials, and perhaps the beginnings of a more meaningful government response.'

Basic Data	
Time Period:	1993–2002
Objectives:	To protect natural resources by documenting local innovations based on indigenous knowledge, the protection of property rights, and recognition and dissemination of innovations.
Research Outputs:	1. Creation of databases including over 13,000 documented local innovations disseminated in six local languages.
	2. A network of over 1,000 local groups supported by newsletters and other means.
	3. Royalty sharing agreements with a private company on three veterinary medicines.
	4. Validation of several plant-based medicines.

Information and Communication Technologies for Development

14

Bringing It to the Senegalese People: A Participatory Approach has Helped Research Influence Public Policies

This brief is based on a case study by Khamathe Sene and Ramata Thioune.

In the small Senegalese town of Kouthiaba, dozens of pastoralists have turned out on a Sunday morning for the weekly market. All are trying to attract buyers to their livestock. They are also busy swapping information on pastures, diseases, and other essential matters. Some of these pastoralists now have new information and communication technologies at their disposal to obtain this information—the first time in Africa that these technologies (ICTs) have been used for such purposes. The main objective is to demonstrate—mainly to decision makers—that these modern tools can really help to improve pastoralists' living and working conditions.

These days, some pastoralists track their herds using cellphones and Global Positioning Systems (GPSs). In three trial zones, herders have been taught to read and prepare geographic maps by working with GPS devices linked to satellites.

Several of these herders have also been equipped with cellphones to speed up the information exchange, and to provide them with an 'early warning system' for impending disasters. Also, some have received training in accessing information on the Web. A site, built in July 2003 and nicknamed 'cyber shepherd', offers maps showing which grazing areas are occupied and which have green vegetation, together with an estimate of the number of animals that can be pastured there without risk to the environment and its resources. It also provides information on ways to treat animal diseases.

This is the first time in Africa that this combination of ICTs has been used for tracking livestock migrations. The main objective is to demonstrate—mainly to decision makers—that these modern tools can really help to improve pastoralists' living and working conditions.

The pilot project is supported by the IDRC through its Acacia Programme Initiative: Communities and the Information Society in Africa.

Risks and influence

IDRC was one of the only international agencies prepared to allocate funding for the establishment of ICTs on the African continent in the 1990s. Over the years, through Acacia, IDRC has invested more than $40 million in research, demonstration, and evaluation projects on key ICT issues. These include how ICTs can be used to reduce poverty, policies to bridge the digital divide, and the development of local content and knowledge (www.idrc.ca/acacia).

There is an expectation in many IDRC programmes and projects that the supported research will influence public policy at the national and local levels. In 2001, IDRC's Evaluation Unit carried out a strategic evaluation to observe whether and how the research IDRC supports influences public policy and decision making. The Acacia programme was selected as a focus and case studies were prepared on the Acacia experience in Senegal, Mozambique, South Africa, and Uganda. Khamathe Sene and Ramata Thioune carried out the Senegalese study.

The Senegalese experience

The Acacia programme began in Senegal in 1997, but the beginnings of what might be called a national policy for ICTs was apparent as early as 1985. At that time, the National Telecommunications Company (SONATEL) was established, reflecting the determination of the Senegalese government to give priority to development of the telecommunications sector.

It was not until 1996, however, that the government issued its first statement on a telecommunications development policy. In its Ninth Economic and Social Development Plan, published in 1997, the government set forth a strategy for strengthening access to information and promoting social communication. The Plan declared that 'information and communication technologies can no longer be regarded as a luxury for the elite, but must be seen as an absolute necessity for development.'

The strategy, however, was still no more than a vision for the future. As the Sene and Thioune study points out, there was no official national strategy for introducing and using ICTs to resolve the country's economic and social development problems.

The study suggests that since 1997 the national and international context has changed considerably, with growing awareness of the role of ICTs in development, and increasing efforts to introduce ICTs into key development sectors. A minister of communications, a computer expert by training, was appointed; he had set up the parliamentary network on ICTs with help from Acacia in 1999. The Senegalese president suggested that the costs of telephone service should be reduced and his ICT counsellor announced that the mobile telephone market would be opened to an independent operator. In 2000, the prime minister declared the government's intention to use ICTs to communicate more closely with citizens, and he announced that the implementation of the administrative information and communication system would be accelerated.

That same year, the main features of a national policy for democratizing access to ICTs was announced. In 2002, the Telecommunications Regulation Agency was created as an independent regulatory body responsible for ensuring fair and healthy competition for the benefit of consumers, telecommunications operators, and the Senegalese economy in general, and for accelerating the development of communications. The country now has some of Africa's most highly developed telecommunications infrastructure.

Today Senegal's 30 administrative subdivisions are connected to the central network through a digital transmission link, and all rural administrative centres have access to telephones. The network for data transmission, launched in 1988, gave enterprises access to databanks, and allowed them to connect to foreign networks. The country has 14 Internet service providers, 12 of them based in Dakar.

As the Sene and Thioune study points out, ICTs are accorded an important place in the New Partnership for Africa's Development (NEPAD), reflecting the vision of development championed by the Senegalese government that is responsible, among other things, for the ICT aspects of NEPAD. But the study adds:

> ... despite the favourable policy indicators and the fairly coherent view of the role of ICTs in development, Senegal does not yet have a coherent and integrated ICT policy. The emphasis is still on a sectoral approach. Moreover, implementation of these sectoral policies themselves appears to have stalled, although the education sector seems to be making progress in integrating ICTs into the education system and the Ten-Year Education and Training Plan assigns an important place to the technologies.

ACACIA's role in Senegal

Preparation of the Senegal Acacia Strategy (SAS) began in 1996 under the aegis of IDRC, and at the instigation of Alioune Camara, IDRC programme officer in Dakar. Various national and local institutions representing government and civil society, researchers, and development players were involved. The Senegal initiative was approved by IDRC in 1997. The SAS objective was to encourage the establishment of an independent framework for concerted action in the ICT field—a framework that would provide the political authorities with a solid basis for their ICT policy.

The study notes: 'In Senegal, Acacia sought to encourage a national strategy for adopting and integrating ICTs in support of development.' The SAS thus became part of the institutional framework for decentralization and empowerment of development players, in a context where decisions regarding the introduction of ICTs were haphazard and uncoordinated.

From the beginning, policies were the key topic of debate: regulation, incentives, access issues, as well as the role of the private sector.

> At the programming level, the Acacia initiative is participatory, and it has a two-pronged strategy. First of all, it seeks to influence policies by supporting the introduction of a regulatory body and an independent framework for coordinating ICT activities. On the other hand, as a research programme, Acacia seeks to develop scientific arguments that policymakers can use for integrating ICTs more thoroughly into the country's economic and social fabric.

As the study points out, the SAS was essentially based on a series of experimental projects. Several were undertaken in the main priority fields of education, health, governance, national resource management, employment, and entrepreneurship.

The Youth cyberspace experiment

One such project was the youth cyberspace experiment in secondary schools in Senegal. Aware that little attention was being paid to problems of the environment and reproductive health in the country's school system, a Senegalese NGO, (GEEP), had initiated 'family life education clubs' in several schools. Scattered throughout the country, they faced major communications problems.

In their report, Sene and Thioune state that, from the outset, the intent of the Acacia project was to influence education policy by introducing ICTs in the schools. Another aim was to change the attitude of the school community towards innovation. According to the project leader, 'teachers involved in the project now know that ICTs can revolutionize information, and that knowledge is not limited to textbooks.'

The study points out that the Ministry of National Education officials are increasingly interested in the problems of introducing ICTs in schools, thanks in part to their awareness of the project. The Ministry has noted that the project provides an innovative model for integrating ICTs into the daily work of teachers. There is also increasing evidence of greater quality in teaching and of better academic performance, thanks to the introduction of ICTs.

The study adds: 'It is because the project team belongs to the school system, and is highly familiar with it, and because of its openness to innovation and its strategy of developing a diversified partnership, that it has been able to achieve these results and to exert a surprising degree of influence on national education policy.'

Supporting gender equality and decentralization

Another project has used ICTs to support gender equality in Senegal by giving women the means to exert pressure on the authorities to amend the Family Code to replace the notion of parental authority to that of joint parental responsibility. The study points out that, thanks to the project, the ground has been laid for a national debate on the issue. A law has been drafted and, if adopted, should help to correct gender inequality.

ICTs have also been used to inform and sensitize local officials and the government about the role and impact of ICTs in Senegal's commitment to decentralization. Local governments are taking increasing responsibility, and several policy areas such as education, health, and governance have been transferred to them.

Many obstacles hinder this transfer of power, however, not the least of which is the fact that most laws and regulations are in the official language (French), while most local officials are illiterate even in their local language. One aim of the project is to summarize the major laws and regulations governing decentralization, translate this into local languages, and post it online.

Findings

Thanks to its participatory approach, Acacia has been able to exert influence of various kinds, directly or indirectly, on public policies in Senegal, the study suggests. These include the development of a new approach to ICT policy with an integrated and organized vision:

the establishment of the Telecommunications Regulation Agency is one illustration. Acacia encouraged this to achieve greater social equity in democratizing access to ICTs.

Acacia has had secondary or indirect influence on strengthening the capacities of policy makers and development players, providing a reliable database of experience in the use of ICTs to create conditions for partnership, and encouraging opportunities for interchange and learning.

In some cases, Acacia succeeded in bringing about changes in the way sectoral policies and programmes were introduced. The project on youth cyberspace sought to help the education ministry authorities prepare a programme for introducing ICTs into the schools. As a result of the public awareness raised by the project for using ICTs in support of gender equality, the Senegalese government has introduced legislation to modify the Family Code to achieve greater gender equity. Decentralization has been enhanced by using ICTs to provide access to information on decentralization policy, and to increase the effectiveness of local governments. And in the health field, the Senegalese government is currently supporting projects based essentially on experience with an Acacia project on telemedicine.

Acacia, says the study, has also made a significant contribution to raising awareness about the importance of ICTs for development. 'Many players have seized upon these technologies for use in the service of human development and have worked together to strengthen their ability to make progress on socioeconomic issues … and in politics (participation by individual candidates in municipal and rural elections).' It adds: 'ICTs have broadened the outlook of members of these organizations through the international exchange of experience, and have offered them greater possibilities to bring their projects to a successful conclusion with support from abroad.'

By involving national researchers in certain studies, Acacia has also helped to strengthen national research capacities on the issue of ICTs and development. The gender dimension was not a prime concern of Acacia in Senegal, but the SAS tried to correct this focus by supporting projects specifically devoted to women, and by commissioning a study on how to integrate the gender dimension into projects.

The study does suggest, however, that the SAS could have left a greater mark on policies if it had transformed itself into an independent national body that would have attracted other donors.

Basic Data	
Time Period:	1997–2002
Objectives:	To foster a national strategy and coordinated framework for ICTs through a series of demonstration projects, and through regulation and research projects.
Research Outputs:	1. A study of tele-services for the Government of Senegal.
	2. Representation on bodies developing local and national ICT policies and strategies, and hosting fora on ICT policy and implementation.
	3. Involving the government, private sector and the public (these are included here as output because of the strong action orientation of Acacia and its intent to leave the major research to a special component of Acacia, the Evaluation and Learning System).

Mozambique Enters the Information Age: New Technologies become Tools of Community Development

This brief is based on a case study by Zenda Ofir.

A decade ago, Mozambique was on the periphery of the global information society. But today, ask anyone in the town of Manhiça where the telecentre is, and they can easily point the way: along the main street, past the general store, down the alleyway next to the evangelical church.

The telecentre, one of the growing number in Mozambique, provides phone and photocopying services, and computer access and training. Even market vendors see the relevance of being 'on line'. The women want information to support employment and keep their families healthy. And the community recently put the final touches to a CD-ROM about malaria in the local language, Changana and in Portuguese.

IDRC was one of the only international agencies prepared to allocate funding towards the establishment of ICTs on the African continent in the 1990s. It also took the brave step of supporting a variety of high-risk projects in Mozambique. It invested in pilot projects, supported champions and events that would create an awareness of ICTs among key decision makers, and funded development of ICT policy for Mozambique.

Several developments converged to bring about a focus on ICTs in Mozambique: the country's stability after decades of war; the government's committed search for areas for national development; its exposure to influential global and regional ICT events; its recognition of the need for a national framework to prevent fragmented developments; and the tireless efforts of ICT champions to create an awareness of the importance of ICTs. These opened a 'policy window' in the ICT field in Mozambique.

The focus on ICTs began in Mozambique in 1995. Several donor organizations were interested in promoting ICT as a development tool in Africa, and that year the First African Regional Symposium on Telematics for Development, co-sponsored by IDRC, was held in Ethiopia. It brought together specialists from 39 African countries, among them influential Mozambicans. One of them, Dr Venàncio Massingue, chaired the Scientific Committee. Then director of the Center for Informatics at the University Eduardo Mondlane (CIUEM) and now the university's Vice-Rector, he has championed ICT use in Mozambique (see Box 14.1).

A high-risk arena

IDRC's Acacia Initiative emerged a year later at the Information Society and Development Conference, held in South Africa, to help sub-Saharan communities use information and communication technologies. Dr Massingue saw the potential and, with IDRC support, organized an international symposium on informatics and development in Mozambique. 'This meeting started the process of consultation between IDRC officials—who were already interested in bringing Mozambique into the proposed Acacia programme—and key Mozambican figures,' says Dr Zenda Ofir, who evaluated how the Acacia Mozambique projects influenced policy in the country, one of the number of studies undertaken by IDRC's Evaluation Unit.

'The discussions led to Mozambique becoming one of the priority countries for implementation of Acacia.'

The Acacia project would play a pioneering role by entering this high-risk arena at a time when few were prepared to do so. 'The Acacia timing was impeccable,' says Dr Ofir. 'Its timely involvement contributed greatly to the significant IDRC influence in this field in Mozambique.'

One theme at the international symposium focused on how to develop a national information policy. Dr Massingue had invited most of the Mozambican Cabinet, and afterwards the prime minister asked him to prepare a policy. 'I suggested that what would be better would be some sort of task force led by the prime minister or president,' Dr Massingue recalls. 'He accepted that and took on the job.'

Breaking new ground

Acacia, approved by IDRC in 1997, was one of the first major donor-supported initiatives in Africa to focus on breaking new ground in understanding the role ICTs could play in community development, especially among poor, disadvantaged communities. At the time, precedents in Africa did not exist, notes Dr Ofir in her report, and the focus was to be on lessons learned from project experiences.

Issues such as affordability, sustainability, and the easy use of technologies were priorities for study. The need for an enabling policy environment, and thus sound ICT polices in the participating countries, was also considered important. Activities were focused in four countries—Mozambique, Senegal, South Africa, and Uganda. 'At the time there was still considerable scepticism about the development potential of ICTs for Africa,' notes Dr Ofir's report. 'Donor agencies and governments were not keen to invest in ICTs and even interest from the private sector was limited [...] The IDRC was one of the only agencies prepared to invest in the support of demonstration and policy projects in what was at the time perceived as a high risk area for African development.'

In Mozambique, the use of ICTs was being hindered by the lack of a coordinated effort to promote the technologies on a national basis. Imported equipment, connectivity, and Internet access were expensive. The telecommunications infrastructure in rural areas was inadequate. The government feared that efforts to address these problems could become haphazard and fragmented. Policy frameworks were needed. There were four key projects in Acacia's initial phase: setting up the Mozambique Acacia Advisory Committee Secretariat; formulating an information and communication policy; establishing two pilot telecentres; and introducing ICTs to secondary schools and teacher training colleges.

University Eduardo Mondlane (UEM) took the lead in promoting ICTs for development in Mozambique. It organized seminars and worked hard to convince a variety of stakeholders, such as government, academic institutions, and the private sector, to participate.

Energizing the process

The first project Mozambique submitted to Acacia was the creation of the Mozambique Acacia Advisory Committee Secretariat. 'We needed something to serve as a reference point, a body to energize the process,' Dr Massingue recalls.

To demonstrate the value of ICTs, two pilot projects were initiated. One was telecentres: 'We wanted something people could see,' says Dr Massingue. 'For example, they could go to a remote area and see people using technology. This way they would know this is not the fantasy of politicians and academicians!' He adds: 'Rural communities in Mozambique have problems with communications, with getting information. By putting telecentres in place, people in these communities can obtain information quickly. Telecentres can facilitate access to education.'

No one knew what a telecentre would look like, so IDRC was asked to support a feasibility study. Two pilot sites were identified. To date, photocopying services and the public telephone have proven to be the most popular features. Much less used are email and Internet services. Connecting to the server means a long distance phone call and the high cost is prohibitive for most users. Computer training, however, is one of the most sought after services, and is something people will pay for.

Dr Ofir's report notes: 'There are increasing numbers of telecentres and similar forms of community access ... and so the opportunity is emerging to support networking and shared learning among these to further promote viability.'

With 42 per cent of the population 14 years old or younger, the second pilot project targeted youth. SchoolNet Mozambique was born, with education ministry representatives on the team. The aim was to introduce ICTs to schools and other educational institutions. Dr Ofir's report notes that when the pilot projects started to show results, people in various communities began clamouring for their expansion.

In 2000, a national ICTs policy was approved, the first in Africa. In 2002, the National ICT Policy Implementation Strategy provided the framework and opportunity for development partners. Mozambique was subsequently selected as one of the first three countries to participate in the Global Digital Opportunities Initiative of the UNDP and the Markle Foundation. The work of Dr Massingue had come full circle: research had informed policy to shape development. Dr Ofir notes:

> ... Massingue is widely acknowledged as a visionary in ICTs, who has contributed greatly to the development of this field in Mozambique ... The close links between Massingue and the government would prove to be a key factor in the support by the government of ICT as a national, crosscutting priority for development. Massingue stimulated the interest of government in ICTs at the highest level.

Findings

Of the four Acacia programmes studied by IDRC's Evaluation Unit to determine policy influence—Mozambique, Senegal, South Africa, and Uganda—the greatest policy influence occurred in Mozambique. This, notes a synthesis report, was because of some important differences between Mozambique and the other countries: the limited number of policy role players in Mozambique; the influential position and advocacy of its national Acacia Advisory Committee and Secretariat; the small circle of well-networked ICT champions; and exceptional government commitment.

Certain factors supported Acacia's role in influencing policy. For a start, there was the Mozambican government's central planning approach and focus on development priorities, and its open-minded approach to new ideas for development. The small ICT community in Mozambique, with its very well-networked group of key decision makers, allowed fast and easy transfer of ideas and information. And then there was the keen interest of the President and the Prime Minister in ICT promotion.

Other factors included the commitment to Acacia by various energetic and visionary ICT champions, especially during its initial stages; the early demonstration to the government and rural communities of the practical benefits of ICTs, generating enthusiasm for these technologies; the search by policymakers for action research results and studies of immediate value to inform the policy process; the lack of a significant body of knowledge related to ICTs for development in Africa; and the government's commitment to public consultation. The report notes:

> The IDRC was one of the first organizations to recognize and address ICTs as a priority area for development in Africa. It chose to focus its actions on community access and services—a difficult arena about which little was known in Africa and in the rest of the developing world. Its pioneering focus increased its risks as funder. Outcomes were uncertain and little was known that could direct strategies and approaches. The early emphasis on feasibility and background research studies, as well as the establishment of pilot projects, laid the groundwork for an integrated, multi-pronged approach to the Acacia strategies in each country. The approaches

Box 14.1: Key Lessons from Mozambique's ICT Champion

Dr Venâncio Massingue bridges the worlds of academia and politics. He has used his knowledge of both these worlds to help bring Mozambique into the 'information age.'

Born in 'one of those little round houses' that dot the Mozambican countryside, he took every opportunity open to him and eventually saved enough to study electricity at technical school. He went on to engineering studies at the UEM, but this interest was cut short when he was introduced to computers. It was during his time at Holland's Delft University, however, that he began to formulate some ideas about how ICTs might help shape his country's development path.

In 1992, he developed a model that became UEM's new Centre for Informatics. 'We brought the Internet to Mozambique and set up a computer maintenance centre at the university,' he recalls. He went on to lead Mozambique into the computer age. In spite of being appointed UEM's Vice-Rector in 1997, Dr Massingue has remained actively involved in the ICT arena.

He cites some key lessons learned from the Mozambican experience.

The main message, he says, is to be critical of the way things are done. Second, you have to identify or create or contribute to the creation of champions at all levels. Third, it is important to listen to what people say is relevant to them. 'Sometimes donors have their own priorities and ways of doing things,' he points out. 'New ideas can disturb these, but it is important that they find ways of accommodating new ideas because very small ideas can become very big.'

Fourth, is the need to create a critical mass of knowledge.' It is very important that you have people who can carry out research, who can do technical work, and who utilize technology correctly,' he says.

Fifth, it is important to maintain an element of research 'because research brings knowledge and knowledge can influence policies.' He adds: 'Policies, when well implemented, can bring the desired development. So it is very important that in all programmes, a research programme be always present.'

Basic Data	
Time Period:	1997–2003
Objectives:	1. To support national efforts to strengthen linkages to the global economy. 2. To support rural access to ICTs. 3. To share learning about ICT policies in the region.
Research Outputs:	Use of pilot projects as a form of action research, short-term studies and input into draft national policy papers, but not rigorous academic research.

and components which characterized Acacia strategies were similar in each of the case study countries and worked together to provide significant policy influence potential.

The case study points out that the Mozambican demonstration projects provided monitoring data that was systematically analyzed to draw out lessons. The research also had a direct effect on the ICT policy. One comment suggested that 'the issue the studies raised were not new, but they had more powerful impact due to the fact that there was now documented evidence of the impact factors, such as the high cost of connectivity.' The working groups took note of the positive and negative lessons from this and other demonstration projects, and found them to be good starting points for implementing ICTs in rural areas and in the field of education. 'Another important feature was Acacia's influence on the policy process,' states the case study. It adds, 'The consultative process used for ICT policy formulation caught the attention of the Minister of Higher Education, Science and Technology. She believes it accelerated the reform process of the telecommunications sector.'

ICTs Come to the Rainbow Nation: Information Technology as Tools for Development in South Africa

This brief is based on a case study by Zenda Ofir.

Sizwe Ngcobo was a 16-year-old, Zulu-speaking, special-needs student attending a school for the mentally disabled in South Africa when he first saw a computer. A year later, he gained international recognition for artwork he contributed to a collaborative student-designed website. He earned a silver medal in an annual Internet competition co-sponsored by SchoolNet South Africa, a project initiated and supported by IDRC.

* SchoolNet SA is part of a broader SchoolNet Africa initiative, which involves projects in more than 20 countries. Through its Acacia Programme Initiative: Communities and the Information Society in Africa, IDRC provides core funding for the organization.*

South Africa is often described as the 'Rainbow Nation' because of the diversity of its people and landscapes. 'It is a term of hope, yet the country's divisive past will continue to affect it for many decades,' predicts Dr Zenda Ofir, who evaluated how Acacia South Africa projects have influenced policy in the country. The evaluation was part of a broad study launched by the IDRC's Evaluation Unit in 2001 to determine if and how IDRC-supported research has influenced public policy. 'The goal of racial harmony remains somewhat elusive. Many people are still learning to live with newfound freedoms. The protection of human rights remains a major concern in a society in the throes of transition and faced with serious problems of unemployment, poverty, crime, and HIV/AIDS.'

The country's income disparities are among the most extreme in the world, with 13 per cent of the population living in 'First World' conditions, and 53 per cent in the 'Third World' conditions. Of the 'Third Worlders', only 25 per cent have access to electricity and running water, only half have primary school education, and more than a third of the children suffer from chronic malnutrition. More than 20 per cent of the population is HIV positive.

Despite this, South Africa's economy remains dominant in Africa. Its infrastructure, both in size and sophistication, dwarfs that of other African nations. Modern financial and industrial sectors are supported by highly developed systems of telecommunications, road, rail, air, and electric power grids.

The transition to democracy

South Africa's transition from an authoritarian apartheid rule to democracy in the mid-1990s meant that new governance systems and policy frameworks had to be created. The policy environment had to reflect a new set of values—transparency, participation in decision-making processes, and commitment to the development of the majority of South Africans neglected and oppressed by the past regime, Dr Ofir notes. She adds:

> Nowhere was this need more urgent than in the communication and information arena: one of the most important priorities was the transformation of the public sector decision-making environment. With the implementation of the new government's Reconstruction and Development Plan, effective communication and information systems were necessary to support planning, implementation, monitoring, and evaluation activities. [...] The new Government of National Unity was faced with the need to balance the desperate needs of the poor majority with those of a modern economy competing in a highly competitive global arena.

This helped to open a policy window for ICTs policy renewal during the transition period.

IDRC's history in South Africa

IDRC was active in supporting South Africa's transition to democracy during the 1990s. Prior to this, it had been funding the activities of South African exiles in neighbouring countries and had worked with many of the emerging leaders, building a relationship of trust. Between 1988 and 1994, when the imminent demise of apartheid was becoming apparent, the Centre changed its approach by funding projects in South Africa.

As one of the first international agencies to establish an office in South Africa (in 1992) during the transition, and one of the first to focus on the use of ICTs for development, IDRC's priorities were in synergy with those of the new government, Dr Ofir points out. Common issues included information sector reform, policy research capacity building, and a focus on the previously disadvantaged.

ICTs and their use for development had been a key area on the agenda of the African National Congress (ANC) in its exile years. In 1994, the ANC election manifesto for South Africa's first democratic elections already contained statements about the importance of ICTs and their use for development.

After the 1994 elections, IDRC involvement continued with a new strategy that focused on four broad themes. One of these was access to information and information technologies. IDRC supported several policy reform processes, each resulting in government Green and White Papers, and new legislation passed by the South African Parliament.

The decision to develop a National Information and Communication Programme (NICP) for South Africa was taken by IDRC after two missions to the country. The NICP goal was to advise and assist the new government in 'conceptualizing, designing, and implementing information programmes, systems, and policies in support of its development goals.' It was to support a number of different initiatives and activities that would together constitute a national information and communications programme.

In line with the IDRC focus on support for policy processes rather than for influencing policy content, the NICP was established as a major initiative to support the new government's efforts at creating an enabling policy environment, according to Dr Ofir. 'This project is perceived as one of the IDRC's most successful contributions to the ICT policy arena in South Africa,' adds Dr Ofir.

> Mechanisms and activities that contributed to its policy influence included the appointment of knowledgeable and respected key IDRC advisers and staff who could provide technical expertise where required; the support of research studies that raised policy issues and informed policy process; the support and facilitation of, and participation in, policy formulation process; and the support and facilitation of meetings and forums where policymakers and representatives of various sectors could meet to discuss policy issues.

Acacia in South Africa

The idea of Acacia emerged at the 1996 Information Society and Development Conference held in South Africa. Acacia South Africa's goal was community empowerment. It was to aim for stronger community voices in political dialogue, increased capacity to solve community problems and reduce community tensions, extended access to basic services including education and health, and promotion of income-generating opportunities.

After 1997, most of IDRCs ICT-related projects were conducted under the Acacia programme. Key areas identified were the development of multipurpose telecentres to support the growth of community markets, and the extension of the telecentres to address specific development problems. Projects were also carried out in three other main areas: policy, education/schools, and gender.

The South African Acacia Advisory Committee (SAAAC) and its secretariat were launched in 1999 to assist Acacia in defining and reviewing its direction in South Africa. It would disseminate lessons learned in Acacia, and coordinate national ICT-related development activities. However, it decided not to pursue the issue of an overarching information society policy. Rather, it would review policy and relevant implementation activities.

Dr Ofir describes the South African ICT environment as complex. She observes: 'With the strong private, organized labour, and civil society sectors, many agendas have to be considered and balanced.' She adds:

> It is therefore now far more difficult than in the early years for one party to play a leading role on policy formulation activities in the ICT sectors. Many more platforms and umbrella organizations exist in the private and NGO sectors, for example. Alliances are formed and pressure on processes exerted from many different quarters. The relevant government departments are usually the drivers of policy processes and do not [now] make use of external agencies....

She notes that the Acacia Advisory Committee was set up to represent the key sectors and focus on community interests and universal service. If the Committee was to influence policy, it had to have very strong leadership, a clear vision of its possible role in policy initiatives, and a strategy to fulfil that role. Members also had to be well-positioned, vocal, and respected among policymakers for their policy expertise. According to Dr Ofir, 'The key informants were of the opinion that to a lesser or greater extent these elements were missing from the work of the Acacia Advisory Committee.' The Acacia Advisory Committee was thus not prominently placed in the ICT policy arena.

The Committee was also affected by the strategic review of the impact of Acacia and the IDRC Regional Office, which curtailed some Acacia activities. There was tension, observes Dr Ofir, between Committee members' belief in a more grass-roots focus and the Committee's promotion of a role in high-level advocacy and assistance with planning. She adds: 'The Committee had been constituted to be representative of relevant sectors of society; not all members were recognized as ICT (policy) experts and this contributed to the perception that the Acacia Advisory Committee "was just another committee linked to a donor initiative", rather than a pool of expertise available to government.'

Findings

Dr Ofir acknowledged that South Africa's transition, and later changes in policy approaches and processes meant that IDRC could have significant policy influence during the early 1990s, but far less during the latter part of the decade. 'With few exceptions, the key informants in this study were of the opinion that the most significant IDRC contribution in the policy arena in the field of information and telecommunications in South Africa came about through the organization's activities in the period before the existence of Acacia,' says Dr Ofir.

Two key factors influencing IDRC's high profile during the period were the long-standing relationship between the Centre and the Democratic Movement, and the close relationship between key IDRC officials and government decision makers. This period was also seen as exciting and significant in terms of both policy formulation processes and content development. The IDRC focus on the support of such initiatives provided scope for pioneering interventions that could set the tone for policy formulation processes during the crucial first years of the democratic government.

Ofir notes that over the past decade, IDRC has been a leading voice on gender and ICTs for development in Africa, promoting gender-sensitive approaches to policies and projects.

It has also supported a number of women's projects, mainly through Acacia. During the past decade, at least three of the key officials in IDRC's regional office in South Africa have been highly respected women who provide excellent role models in South Africa's male-dominated ICT field.

However, Ofir is critical of the SAAAC's apparent lack of attention to gender-focused and gender-sensitive projects. She suggests that IDRC could play an important role in creating awareness and in improving understanding of the gender dimensions of development policies and projects.

Dr Ofir also points to the need to develop a sustained base of policy research expertise in South Africa by providing, among other things, secure long-term financial support to research centres to conduct 'longitudinal, comparative long-term research studies in order to assess whether policy models have failed or succeeded, and the factors influencing these successes or failures.'

IDRC's emphasis was on process, and on building consensus within that process, rather than on influencing a particular outcome through a specific piece of research, she states. However, IDRC is credited for having promoted the concept of universal services in various ways during that critical policymaking period. 'This helped to bring about a strong focus on universal service in the Telecommunications White Paper published in 1996, the establishment of the Universal Service Agency, and national telecentre and Multipurpose Community Centre Programmes,' she says.

Box 14.2: Evaluating IDRC's Influence on ICT Policy

IDRC was one of the first organizations to recognize and address ICTs as a priority area for African development. It was also one of the only international agencies prepared to allocate funding towards establishing ICTs on the African continent in the 1990s. Acacia's first five-year phase, approved by IDRC in 1997, promoted ICTs for community development, especially among the poor and disadvantaged. The importance of policy frameworks linked to research was acknowledged, as well as the need for demonstration models that could inform public policy initiatives. Over the years, Acacia has invested more than CA $40 million in research, demonstration, and evaluation projects on key ICT issues (www.idrc.ca/acacia).

In 2001, IDRC undertook an evaluation of the public policy influence of some of the research it supported, including the Acacia Programme in Uganda, Senegal, Mozambique, and South Africa. In all four countries, political stability and a government committed to modernization, and searching for effective new development methods provided opportunities for policy influence.

All the governments were relatively new, with most having come to power after long periods of turmoil and instability. They were thus actively seeking solutions to the development needs of their people, using among others, donor support to achieve their objectives. Key government officials, including ministers, were aware—or being made aware—of the opportunities presented by ICTs.

The early emphasis on feasibility and background research studies, as well as the establishment of pilot projects, laid the groundwork for an integrated, multi-pronged approach to the Acacia strategies in each country. The approaches were similar and provided significant policy influence potential.

Basic Data

Time Period:	1995–2002
Objectives:	To support communities in the use of ICTs for problem solving and community engagement; to enhance ICT access by rural and disadvantaged communities.
Research Outputs:	As an action research initiative some of the outputs relate to processes, including representation on policy initiatives such as the Task Team of the Government Communications and Information Service, representation to the e-commerce policy processes.

In South Africa, with its strong focus on racial equality, care has to be taken to ensure that processes, policies, and outcomes are sensitive to issues of gender and that implementation reflects this clearly, Dr Ofir suggests.

The NTPP [National Telecommunications Policy Project] consultative process included representatives from labour, the disabled, and women's organizations. Even though the government representatives and various committees assisting in the drafting process of the Telecommunications White Paper were overwhelmingly male, the national focus on the previously disadvantaged ensured that the policy reflected this priority quite strongly. Although it is not an engendered policy, the redress of existing imbalances is a major theme of the document and is most strongly reflected in the establishment of the Universal Service Agency.

Bridging the Digital Divide: Information and Communications Technologies Take Hold in Uganda

This brief is based on a case study by Zenda Ofir.

In the last decade, Uganda faced a problem in its efforts to bridge the digital divide. It needed to find a way to interest women in using computers—especially women who have little or no reading ability. Acting on information collected from women living near the Nakaseke telecentre, the International Women's Tribune Centre (IWTC) responded with a simple programme that does not require a keyboard and speaks to the women in their own language. Support from IDRC's Acacia Programme Initiative enabled the IWTC to develop its graphic-voice interface CD-ROM, 'Ideas for Rural Women Earning Money'. Using browser software, the programme allows users to move the mouse across the screen and click on pictures or text and then hear the information in their own language, Luganda.

Acacia's first five-year phase, approved by the IDRC in 1997, was one of the first major donor-supported initiatives in Africa to promote ICTs for community development, especially among the poor and disadvantaged. The importance of policy frameworks linked to research was acknowledged, as well as the need for demonstration models that could inform public policy initiatives. Over the years, Acacia has invested more than CA $40 million in research, demonstration, and evaluation projects on key ICT issues (www.idrc.ca/acacia).

In 2001, IDRC undertook an evaluation of the public policy influence of some of the research it supported, including the Acacia Programme in Uganda, Senegal, Mozambique, and South Africa. In all four countries, political stability and a government committed to modernization and searching for effective new development methods provided opportunities for policy influence. Dr Zenda Ofir, who carried out the Uganda evaluation, describes IDRC's policy influence efforts there as 'a longer, slower, and more winding relay race' than in the other three countries because of 'its greater number of policy role players.'

The Ugandan context

Uganda is one of the poorest countries in the world. Most of its 22 million people live in rural areas, and 55 per cent live below the poverty line. In 1986, as the country emerged from two decades of turmoil and trauma under various destructive political regimes, the Ugandan government and the people were committed to developing and modernizing their country. Key government officials were exposed to the concept of the Information Society, and this was enhanced by the expertise of Ugandans abroad or returning from exile. They brought new ideas and methods into the country, including knowledge of ICTs.

The telecommunications sector was reformed and liberalized, donor organizations were encouraged to engage in the ICT arena, and a dynamic private sector wanted to use ICTs for business development. Local institutional and individual ICT champions from government, academic, private, and non-governmental sectors were advocates, and they raised awareness. This was supported by effective and accurate media information.

By 1994, various voices had started calling for a national policy that could help create an enabling environment for ICTs. In 1996, the Ugandan government embarked on extensive reform of the telecommunications sector. This included restructuring the formerly state-owned monopoly, creating an independent regulatory agency, privatizing and introducing competition in the industry, and licensing multiple operators. A year later, the Communications Act was passed, aimed at increasing telephone use, improving telecommunications facilities, and opening the market to a variety of new services. The Act also provided for a Rural Communications Development Fund to help provide services across the country.

Uganda was represented at various ICT conferences during the mid-1990s. At the First Global Knowledge Conference in Toronto in 1997, Ugandan President Yoweri Museveni, made a political commitment to ICTs and invited the international community to assist in applying ICTs and traditional knowledge systems to the development of his country. A year later, Uganda sent one of the largest delegations to the Global Connectivity for Africa Conference.

By 1998, a number of governments and international institutions had indicated their support for the development of ICTs in Uganda. With their funding of projects and studies, and partnerships with local organizations, they had the potential to exert an extensive influence over policymaking processes. They were also well accepted by the government and had access to the highest level of decision makers.

The cellphone revolution

Cellphones revolutionized Uganda's communications industry. The first network went live in early 1995. In the next six years the number of mobile subscribers grew from 3,500 to 276,000. 'Mobile communication thus filled the communications vacuum,' says Dr Ofir. 'It made it possible for users to make a call almost anywhere, at any time, at an affordable price. This had a profound effect on the economy; it increased productivity and simplified the lives of business people, farmers, public servants, and others. People were suddenly much more aware of the potential effect that ICT could have on their development.'

The number of private computer vendors and Internet service providers (ISPs) had also been growing rapidly. By the year 2000 there were already nine ISPs, but most provided access exclusively in Kampala. Public access to relevant technologies outside the capital remained scarce—mainly some Internet cafes and private or Acacia-managed telecentres.

Meanwhile, the private sector pressured the government to promote ICTs for business use. In an effort to jump-start the economy, the Uganda Investment Authority identified ICTs as a priority area for economic development. One of the recommendations presented to the government was that it should formulate a national ICT policy and create an implementing body.

In Uganda, many individuals and organizations from different sectors championed ICT development. Dr Ofir names the president himself as one of the first champions, along with Communications Minister John Nasasira who has been lauded by several people interviewed for IDRC's evaluation as the visionary in the government and the country during early efforts to promote ICTs. Key institutional champions, especially in those years, were the Uganda National Council for Science and Technology (UNCST) and Makerere University's Institute of Computer Science.

Dr Ofir states: 'Although ICT development in Uganda was built on a wave of local interest in the academic and private sectors, international and local development agencies also played an important role in stimulating an awareness of the information society and the potential role of the new technologies in development.' The early IDRC-supported studies and stakeholder workshops, together with other early ICT initiatives such as the establishment of telecentres, are credited by many as having been instrumental in mobilizing the interest of the Ugandan government.

Acacia in Uganda

The first Ugandan Acacia initiatives were launched in 1997. An action plan was drawn up covering four areas: policy, infrastructure and technology, human resources, and content. The initial Acacia activities were 'intended to sensitize decision makers, policy designers, and opinion leaders and enlist their support for the use and application of ICTs for rural community development.' In addition to establishing a Steering Committee (later the National Acacia Advisory Committee) and National Secretariat, the programme supported a number of projects over the next five years.

Dr Ofir points out that one way of influencing policymakers was to expose them to pilot projects. The oldest telecentre, Nakaseke, known for its level of community ownership, proved a popular choice. More recent Acacia supported projects focused on exploring the expansion of the role of telecentres by promoting local content and language, as well as the role of telecentres and ICTs in areas such as promotion of women's development, agriculture, education, health, and small business development. The project 'Ideas for Rural Women Earning Money' was launched at Nakaseke and has apparently had a great impact on women using the telecentre.

IDRC's main technical assistance was to support international ICT experts to help carry out policy studies, says Dr Ofir. Acacia chose to support two distinct types of research in Uganda. It commissioned studies to provide background information and answers to specific policy questions, such as those conducted to inform the Rural Communications Development Policy process, the telecentre baseline studies, and four studies initially commissioned in 1998 to examine the status of ICTs in Uganda. It also supported action research in the telecentre projects, usually in the form of monitoring and evaluation. In discussions with participants and from project reports, Dr Ofir determined that the telecentres contributed to the policy processes primarily by raising key policy issues and sensitizing decision makers to the use of multipurpose telecentres for rural development.

Findings

Dr Ofir points out that the timing of IDRC's entry into the ICT development arena in Uganda—when a policy window was opening—provided the Centre with an excellent opportunity to influence relevant policy initiatives. IDRC focused on demonstration projects, processes, and events that could provide lessons leading to policy influence. This enhanced its credibility among Ugandans as a supportive, sincere organization. Its early establishment and promotion of telecentres as a concept 'provided a crucible of information' from which ideas could be obtained and lessons learned—for example the critical need for good management, ownership, and sustainability mechanisms. It also focused government and public attention on the concept of universal, rural access to ICTs.

Acacia's funding of two ICT policy development processes enabled IDRC to have 'an immediate and quite significant policy influence in the ICT field,' Ofir concludes. And the integrated nature of Acacia, with funding allocated for community-based projects as well as projects related to policy implementation, enhanced the opportunities for policy influence.

The Idea takes hold

As awareness and support of ICTs grew in Uganda within the government, the private sector, and the development agencies, more organizations entered the ICT policy arena, Dr Ofir reveals. The government developed its own strong focus on relevant policy development.

Acacia continued to play a significant yet supportive role, primarily by funding the two key policy processes. Acacia projects helped women to understand the role ICTs could play in their development; helped to make people aware of the importance of local content and language within the ICT sector; and stimulated application in the agricultural, education, and health sectors. 'It is likely that these experiences, if well documented and systematically researched, will play an important role in future policy development activities,' adds Dr Ofir.

This implies that, at this time, IDRC was no longer a pioneer, but continued to make contributions recognized by others as important, albeit as part of a wave of ICT developments.

Lessons learned from the Acacia experience in Uganda point to a need to clearly define roles for partner organizations. Acacia's impact could have been further enhanced if the National Acacia Advisory Committee had better determined its role in relation to the UNCST/ Acacia Secretariat, and to IDRC. Early Evaluation and Learning System for Acacia (ELSA) contributions and results could also have strengthened the research components. Dr Ofir also remarks that more time could have been spent on the development of gender-sensitive strategies for the various Acacia activities.

Dr Ofir concludes: 'A study of the *intended* policy influence of the four Acacia projects indicates that all the *intended* policy influence activities were undertaken—and more—and that they provided good opportunities and mechanisms for policy influence.' However, there were many players in the ICT policy arena in Uganda and each of them had the potential to exert some measure of policy influence. The *extent* to which the IDRC policy influence activities had been effective therefore remains quite difficult to determine. Policy influence is notoriously difficult to trace; it is often impossible to claim that a particular policy decision has been taken because of a certain influence. In many cases the 'percolation of information and ideas' provides a context within which policy decisions are taken.

She adds: 'IDRC has made major contributions [...] through its research activities. There is a need for greater emphasis on systematic, long-term policy research and on the building of this capacity in the country.'

Basic Data

Time Period: 1999–2002

Objectives:
1. To demonstrate how access to ICTs helps communities solve their own problems.
2. To build a body of knowledge on improving access by rural people, the poor and the disadvantaged communities.
3. To strengthen rural access to ICTs.

Research Outputs:
1. Pre-inception studies on the relevance of Acacia action research for Uganda.
2. Surveys and research studies on telecentres as well as issues around rural access; studies on the development of relevant content.
3. Several studies (on capacity, policy, infrastructure and technology); leading to National Acacia Secretariat playing a representative role on the committees that drafted national ICT policy.

Nepal Struggles to Enter the Information Age: Creating a National IT Policy Brings Together Government and Private Sector

This brief is based on a case study by Leanne Burton.

The government of Nepal did just about everything right when it set out to develop a national policy that would begin the process of transforming the country into a 'knowledge-based society.' The widely approved policy was finalized in 2000, but circumstances and geography conspired to make implementing the policy recommendations a slow process.

Perched between Asia's two economic superpowers—China and India—the tiny landlocked country of Nepal is famous as the home of Mount Everest, and seven more of the world's highest peaks. With a population of less than 30 million, Nepal was never likely to challenge either China or India, the latter having declared in 1998 its goal of becoming 'an information technology superpower' within 10 years.

Nevertheless, India's remarkable emergence as a leader in the world of information technology (IT) did inspire the government of Nepal to begin to transform Nepal into a 'knowledge-based society'. The goal was not to attempt to compete with the Indian colossus but to use IT as a tool for social development. The government hoped that computers would help deliver services more efficiently in sectors such as health, education, and agriculture, particularly in isolated mountain regions.

It was an ambitious goal given the realities of Nepal, one of the poorest and least developed countries in the world. Fewer than half the population can read and write. With an average life expectancy of just 60 years, 40 per cent of the population is under the age of 15. While tourism has long been an important source of foreign exchange, agriculture remains the mainstay of the economy. Much of the agriculture, however, is at a subsistence level. One-third of the population lives below the poverty line. Most rural areas have no electricity or phone service.

Expanding policy capacities

Until 1996 the country did not even have a government department responsible for science and technology. When the Ministry of Science and Technology (MOST) was created, however, it signalled a modest step into the technological age. 'The goal of the Ministry is to create a conducive environment for the adequate development of science and technology and make necessary arrangements for its effective application in the task of national development,' according to a MOST document.

Slightly more ambitious, the government's five-year plan for 1997–2002 promised an information technology policy that would 'place Nepal on the global map of information technology within five years.' And in 1997 the government began licensing Internet service providers (ISPs)—Nepal was officially on the Internet.

It was not until 1999, however, that a newly elected majority government established a National Information Technology Development Working Committee with a sub-committee tasked with developing Nepal's first IT policy. The chairman of that sub-committee, Dr Ramesh

Ananda Vaidya of the National Planning Commission (NPC), turned to Canada's IDRC for assistance in developing both the policy and an implementation strategy. The Centre responded with a research and development grant through its Pan Asia Networking (PAN) programme.

IT policy is a relatively new policy area, particularly in developing countries, where financial constraints make it difficult to keep pace with the rapid pace of technological development. The $60,000 grant was to cover research expenses, consultancies, a workshop, and a final publication. The work was monitored by a former IDRC staffer, Shahid Akhtar, who was then working with the International Centre for Integrated Mountain Development (ICIMOD), which has its headquarters in Kathmandu, Nepal's capital.

Broadening policy horizons

'To ensure smooth implementation of policy, we adopted a participatory process in which the government, private sector and civil society share a common discussion forum during policy design,' said Dr Vaidya. Such broad participation in making national policy was almost unheard of in Nepal, but Dr Vaidya was insistent. 'We believed such a process based on the consensus of IT stakeholders would lead to "goal congruence" among them and thus facilitate successful development of the IT sector,' he says. As a result, Nepal's IT policy was developed almost entirely through the efforts of Nepali professionals, with foreign specialists involved only as peer reviewers of the research that served as the basis for designing the policy. The research itself was an indigenous effort.

The policy design process took a year. It involved consultations with members of Nepal's IT industry, the creation of an IT Strategy Formulation Steering Committee at the NPC, and the preparation of six strategy papers by groups of Nepali academics, IT professionals, and government officials. The Steering Committee included representatives of government, the private sector and academia, as well as two members from ICIMOD.

Affecting policy regimes

Sanjib Raj Bhandari, CEO of Mercantile Office Systems, Nepal's largest and oldest software house, played an active role in the preparation of the strategy paper on 'Software production and applications'. He was also one of the three representatives of the private sector appointed to the National Information Technology Development Council. 'At the top levels of government there was goodwill towards the participation of the private sector in the formulation of the IT policy,' he recalls. Mr Bhandari believes that the policy will help to prevent problems often faced by private sector companies when dealing with government officials who lack an understanding of the industry.

Shahid Akhtar, who was an active participant as one of the ICIMOD representatives on the Steering Committee, believes that the process adopted in Nepal permitted 'buy-in' to the resulting policy by literally hundreds of key individuals and groups from all walks of life, including the Nepal Internet Users Group and the Computer Association of Nepal. 'This "ownership" in turn helped to ensure follow-up and implementation of the policy,' he says.

He adds 'For instance, decisions taken on the establishment of a National Information Technology Council, the allocation of substantial financial resources for IT human resource development programmes, and the establishment of an IT venture capital fund and an IT park.'

Bhoop R. Pandey, Chairman of the Nepal Telecommunications Authority, played a key role in drafting the telecommunications policy which opened up the VSAT sector, thereby helping to spawn many new ISPs. (VSAT, or very small aperture satellite transmission, is a technology that provides greatly increased bandwidth at reduced cost.) He is also the senior official responsible for regulating many facets of the new IT policy. He does not think that it will be difficult to regulate the IT sector according to the new policy: 'If you design it yourself, you know what you want, it is easy to enforce,' he says, adding 'Our culture is very different. We have to develop our own system.'

Nepal's IT policy was approved in 2000. It includes a set of 15 general strategies. For example, that 'information technology shall be applied for rural development'. It also includes 17 policies to guide implementation, and sets out an action plan that covers everything from infrastructure and human resources development to the dissemination of IT, and the promotion of e-commerce.

The policy calls for the creation of a number of institutions to oversee implementation, including:

1. National IT Development Council, to be chaired by the Prime Minister.
2. National IT Council to review and revise the policy, track progress, and resolve problems.
3. National IT Coordination Committee to promote R&D and capacity building.
4. National IT Centre to implement and monitor the policy, regulate private sector activities, and assist the government with computer services.
5. An IT Park Development Committee to plan a central industrial location to encourage the growth of IT companies.

Finally there is a provision that the policy may be reviewed and amended every two years, or sooner if necessary.

Diverting resources

All of this was approved in 2000, and was hailed as 'a significant milestone in the development of the IT sector in Nepal.' That year also saw the beginning of political and social upheaval in Nepal that has seen the murder of members of the royal family, and a worsening Maoist insurgency. As a result, the government has been forced to divert a large portion of its resources to restoring law and order. Exports and the tourism sector have both suffered, further exacerbating the Government's precarious financial position. At the level of MOST, multiple changes in both political and bureaucratic staff have frustrated efforts by the private sector to build IT capacity within the Government.

With scarce resources tied up in security efforts, implementation of the IT policy slipped from the Government's priority list. The National IT Council (NITC) was set up two years after the policy was approved, but its resources are too limited to effectively oversee implementation. A further roadblock is the fact that the policy implicates several other government departments in its action plan—such as the education and telecommunications sectors—but fails to take into account other sector policies, and in some cases actually contradicts them. Progress is also curtailed by the fact that some of the necessary prerequisites, such as adequate communications infrastructure are lacking in many parts of the country, and some of the existing infrastructure is being destroyed by the Maoist rebels.

In summary, comprehensive implementation has been slowed by the political and social upheavals, and by a lack of inter-departmental coordination to resolve contradictory policies, and to plan realistically for basic requirements. MOST has also inadvertently slowed progress by not being clear about the division of responsibilities between itself and the private sector.

Pushing forward

Despite these barriers, the Government has shown its good intentions by pushing forward on several fronts:

1. An IT Bill based on the policy has been drafted and is awaiting Parliamentary approval.
2. MOST has a programme to provide IT training to 50,000 unemployed university graduates across the country. So far 10,000 students have enrolled in the programme, but there is concern that a government spending freeze may curtail the programme.
3. Three of Nepal's four universities offer computer science or computer engineering degrees at the undergraduate level, and the MOST expects roughly 5,000 graduates from these programmes over the next few years. Also the Ministry is planning to establish an Institute of Information Technology in Kathmandu and an Institute of Technology in Western Nepal, focusing on biotechnology as well as IT research.
4. Universal access is being pursued through a UNDP project to set up 15 rural telecentres across the country. The project is an experiment to develop a sustainable telecentre model. Resources permitting, MOST plans to establish 10 more centres, and to set itself up as the central hub through which all information will be transmitted.
5. An IT park is also planned, and to date land has been purchased and construction started on two buildings. The park will also house the proposed Institute of Information Technology.

Despite the many setbacks over the years since the process began, there is still considerable optimism among stakeholders, including the government. There is a sense of shared interest that has been fostered by the policy development process itself. In fact, the process may prove to be more important than the policy in the long run. Bhoop Pandey, of the Nepal Telecommunications Authority, notes that 'Policy is not constant, we need to revise and update it from time to time.' ICIMOD's Shahid Akhtar agrees: 'The IT policy is good, but policies come and go,' he says. 'Circumstances change and policies need to be dynamic and adapt to changing needs. What is more important is how countries reach these policies.'

Some Lessons

1. A participatory process that involves a range of stakeholders helps to bring 'buy in' when it comes to policy implementation.
2. It is important to ensure that any new policy is not in conflict with existing policies in other related fields.
3. Any policy that involves government and the private sector working together should clearly indicate the division of responsibilities.
4. Implementation of even the best designed policy can be derailed by social or political upheaval, or other unanticipated events.

Basic Data

Time Period: 1999

Objective: To foster a national ICT policy and strategy by means of a participatory process.

Research Output: Six Background studies on key issues in ICT governance.

The Multiple Case Approach: A Methodological Overview[1]

Introduction

The evaluation study described in this volume was first conceived and conducted for IDRC's own use—to explore, explain, and improve how IDRC's support for research can influence public policy in developing countries. That said, our investigation quickly attracted a much wider interest outside the Centre, from other research and development funders as well as from researchers themselves. To address that wider interest—and to outline the procedures that led to the observations and conclusions reported in these pages—this appendix presents the methodology behind our study and its findings.

The study was initiated with a deceptively simple purpose: to get a better understanding of how the research that IDRC supports has had an influence on public policy. The intent was to inform the agency, and the researchers it underwrites, on the factors that affect influence so that they could take these into account in their own work. The study relied heavily on a multiple-case method. Twenty-five case studies were commissioned. Of those, 22 were completed within 12 months and one additional case reached completion the following year; two were never completed. These studies covered a wide range of research fields in countries as varied as Ukraine, Tanzania, Vietnam, and Guatemala. The diversity of cases strengthened our confidence in any common findings that might emerge as the evaluation unfolded. But the inherent complexity called for a careful design to ensure some learning across some very dissimilar experiences.

The study has had a significant effect on the work of the Centre—a point addressed in Chapters 15 and 16. In the words of IDRC's President, it 'has changed the way we fund projects' (O'Neil 2006). The concepts it introduced and the findings from the cases, have affected how IDRC research projects are designed and how they are evaluated. It is also fair to say that the approach we employed has paid off in other practical ways. Carol Weiss, an

[1]This appendix is based on a chapter written for *Handbook of Case-centred Methods*, edited by David Byrne and Charles Ragin, 2008, Sage. Early in the study a preliminary methods paper was published in a special issue of the *International Social Science Journal*, on 'Tracking Impact', March 2004, Volume 179: 135–51.

important collaborator in our work, has noted that 'not many cross-case studies have been conducted with the same attention to comparability of theory, method, and data. This work will surely have much to tell researchers about methods to adopt, adapt, and avoid' (Weiss 2003: 7).

Before presenting the methodology itself, some prior questions of definitions, limitations, and methodological choices need to be reviewed.

Definitions

Kingdon considers public policymaking as a 'set of processes, including at least (1) the setting of an agenda, (2) the specification of alternatives from which a choice is to be made, (3) an authoritative choice among those specified alternatives ... and (4) the implementation of a decision' (1984: 3). Succinctly stated, this definition includes the idea of policy as a set of processes, activities or actions resulting in a decision. IDRC recognizes that, 'decision-making occurs at various levels and is carried out by a broad range of decision makers: from heads of families to programme directors in other donor agencies, to government policymakers (*Closing the Loop: Communication for Change at IDRC*, 2001: 1). While both 'policy' and 'policymakers/ decision makers' can be defined quite broadly, for our purposes 'policy' is defined as 'public policy'. So the central focus of the study is on issues surrounding policy processes as they relate to municipal, regional, and national levels of government. Although community and household decision makers will be taken into consideration as part of the process, they are not the central focus of this work.

It should be noted that not all IDRC projects or programmes have or are expected to have an influence on policy. Still, it is an area of increasing importance to many activities across the Centre, both regionally and programmatically. This is one reason why the study focused on the particulars of research that influences public policy.

Limitations

The study was limited in three respects. First, it is a study conducted only once thus far; this means any learning and change over time will not be captured unless some effort is made to repeat the exercise at a future date. Second, because the study was not planned before the implementation of the projects, the study had to rely, to a certain extent, on the memories of project participants—starting with the tracking down of participants and locating project documents, not all of which were easily available. As far as possible, data was triangulated through more than one source, but inevitably some selective memory creeps into a study of this type. Finally, we did not expect the study to provide an all-inclusive overview of the success of every IDRC supported research project in influencing public policy. Instead, we deliberately aimed to assemble a 'positive sample'—cases where researchers could make a credible claim to have influenced policy. The logic here was straightforward: With a relatively small sample, positive cases ordinarily could tell us more about how influence is achieved— and tell us more efficiently—than we could learn from speculating about why negative cases had failed to influence policy.

Some Methodological Choices in Understanding Influence

Evaluation of research in support of development faces several recurring challenges, all having to do with how support for development should be judged. In many cases, evaluation attempts to look at the final impact of a project. It looks not so much for an understanding of how the project succeeded, but only at whether it succeeded. Evaluation normally also tries to determine the direct effects of a research project. That is, it tries to establish cause and effect links between the project and the final impact. A third problem is that of time. Contributions to development are often carried out in a series of short projects, three to five years in duration. But development, and especially the policy-influence process, is usually measured across a much longer time frame. As a result, the issue of when to evaluate is problematic. Some projects can alter organizational decision processes, so that if we detect influence during a project, or too soon after its completion, we may be looking at transitory project effects, not sustained influence—something also referred to as the 'project trap' (Lusthaus et al. 2002). Finally, the social sciences struggle with the issue of whether there actually is a generalizable social science, with findings that can be applied through a general model, or whether social science is more case-bound and context-specific. Social scientists labour more or less continuously in the tensions and stresses between scientific generalization and the specificities characteristic of social science subject matter.

Impact or influence?

While it is generally understood that development[2] happens because of a range of factors coming together to create change, there is considerable pressure on development (and development research) projects, and the agencies that fund them, to demonstrate a significant positive impact on development. Even though it is also understood that development results occur when the local partners take ownership of the actions and make the project their own, projects and agencies (including multilateral and bilateral funding agencies, and NGOs) are routinely expected to demonstrate 'good performance'. As a result, the project and the donor tend to elevate their own position in identifying the sources of any development change that occurs. There is a tendency to focus on final outcomes and to ignore important information on how the project achieved anything. It is then almost impossible to identify the critical success factors, and the emergence of new relationships and patterns, because these have not been tracked. When this happens, it is extremely difficult to apply the experience in other settings. *Outcome Mapping* (Earl et al. 2001) makes the case that development research contributes to outcomes, which then work with other outcomes and events to create impacts in local contexts. The intent here was to identify the real level at which a project or programme makes a difference and to assess that influence—not the final development impacts which remain the responsibility of the local partners.

---

[2]By 'development', I refer specifically to our experience in international development and research in support of improving the lives and conditions of people living in so-called Third World countries.

Attribution

Closely related to the concept of impact is that of attribution. There is often a call to attribute a certain change to projects that were supported. Governments want to know how their resources are spent on development (whether within their own country or in the form of development assistance) and, through evaluation, seek to know what changes can be ascribed to their support. Iverson notes that, 'insofar as multiple and often unknown confounding variables are the norm, complex systems present a serious obstacle for attribution' (Iverson 2003: 36). It is highly unusual that a single research programme can result in a development impact, unless all the other conditions have already been met and facilitating factors are already aligned. Any evaluation of development research needs to guard against claiming credit for causing change when the claim (implicitly, at least) involves discrediting other causes, and exaggerating the contribution of the research as against these other factors.

As Flyvberg notes, 'Proof is hard to come by in social science because of the absence of "hard" theory, whereas learning is certainly possible' (Flyvberg 2001: 73). The focus here is on learning about, and from, the contributions made through IDRC supported research, in order to contribute more effectively to change in future projects.

Time

A persistent issue in evaluation is that of timing. When is an evaluation 'final'? Can you ever render an evaluative judgement that is permanent? What happens over time when good things turn bad and bad things turn good? How do you modify the findings of the evaluation and take this into account? This problem is exacerbated in the study of influence on public policy, a notoriously long-term affair. If we consider a successful development effort as one in which the local partner has taken ownership of the ideas or knowledge and is using them for development purposes, the external agent is further and further removed from impact as time passes and the results of research take hold. Over time, if the programme is successful, the external agent plays a smaller and smaller role—precisely when impact occurs. Paradoxically, if all goes well, project managers and funding agencies are asked to assess their contribution at a point when they are least involved with the change that their research has affected.

Approaches

The final evaluation challenge that informed the design of this study was the debate on research approaches in the social sciences. The debate here is not about qualitative versus quantitative research methods; both are used and useful. Rather, the question is whether, in the social sciences, general knowledge is more valuable than concrete, practical knowledge. Flyvberg notes that, 'context counts' in the social sciences (Flyvberg 2001: 38). He goes on to observe that the issue for the social sciences in understanding how people and societies function is that this means there is a context-dependent relationship linking the context, how people act and how they interpret what has happened. The rules are not the game, just as the map is not the territory. The game is far more complex and subtle than can be captured through a statement of the governing rules and systems. Here we are trying to find out why things happened, and how they happened, so that we can use this knowledge in support of future research activities.

Flyvberg and others before him (Yin 1994) argue that the approach best suited to understanding context and relationships is the case study method. Case studies are widely criticized in the social sciences, to the point that Yin addresses this very problem on the first page of his excellent text on case study design and methods. Case studies are often seen as explanatory and are used in teaching. In these situations they may contain evident and deliberate bias to generate discussion around a particular interpretation of events. However, case study as a research method must be concerned with the rigorous and fair presentation of data. Case studies are particularly useful in answering 'how' and 'why' questions, because they look to processes, relationships, and changes over time, whereas one might use a survey or other methods to answer the more static 'what' questions. Here our preoccupation is with the how and the why of research and policy influence, and a set of case studies that strive for fair representations of events was selected as the most appropriate method.

The Multiple-case Approach

The design and implementation of this evaluation study was preceded by an extensive exploration to identify who would use the findings of the evaluation, and to what purposes. These preliminary discussions shaped both the design and the process of analysis. Past experience in evaluation at IDRC (and I would say more generally) has demonstrated that, in many cases, donors and research managers have not worked this question through on their own, and often have a very vague idea of how they will use the results. As Patton (1997) notes in his seminal work on 'utilization-focused evaluation', the potential for use is greatly enhanced when the users go through the process of specifying the nature of their needs and interests in conducting the evaluation study. Active engagement with researchers, programme staff, and IDRC management throughout the study was a hallmark of its execution.

Work on the design of this study began in January 2001. A series of staff interviews and an initial literature review were carried out in the first months of the year. This was followed by the development of several background documents. It was determined at the beginning of the study that it would be very important to include older projects as well as some that had been supported over a relatively long period of time.

Early in the design stage, the Centre approached Dr Carol Weiss for her input to the study because of her exceptional expertise in this field. External expertise was matched with an internal implementation team ensuring both methodological rigour and internal relevance to IDRC. This engagement of experts is a common feature of IDRC evaluation studies. They are engaged not to conduct the full study but to inform a design and analysis that relies heavily on input from the Centre staff and management.

Due to the varied nature of the Centre's work (as illustrated in the cases presented in Section II) and the range of regions where we work (Africa, Asia, Latin America, Middle East, and North Africa), the study was made up of a number of sub-studies brought together to build a corporate picture of our programmes. A variety of methodologies was used.

Data were collected, discussed, and analyzed as far as possible in collaboration with the users—researchers, staff, and executives in IDRC. Several methods were used to ensure participation. Products of the study started to appear late in 2001 and continued throughout, till the presentation of the final report in 2007.

Intended users of the evaluation

In our original design there were two primary users for this study, although the audience broadened considerably as the evaluation progressed, which was demonstrated not least by the number of demands for the insights it generated. And in view of the importance we placed on using the findings effectively within the Centre, a clear focus on users was essential. We needed to know their needs as they understood them, so that we could design and carry out the evaluation to meet those needs.

The first users identified were IDRC programme staff, who have a formal mandate to develop research activities (projects or programmes) with the objective of supporting the production, dissemination and application of research results leading to policies and technologies that enhance the lives of people in developing countries. The study was intended to provide them with a rich review of Centre experience from which they could draw the most useful and relevant lessons for their purposes.

The second primary users were IDRC's managers, and through them the Centre as a whole. For the management group the evaluation addressed two corporate needs. First, it provided a picture of how we were doing already; and second, it provided input for the drafting then under way of the IDRC strategic programme framework for the years 2005 to 2010.

Continuous user involvement in design and in analysis was crucial, and the methodology reflected that priority throughout. Members of both user groups—programme staff who support projects and Centre managers who set directions—were involved in the identification of issues as well as preliminary identification of cases, and they remained involved until the study was completed. The range and level of their interest reaffirmed the clear relevance of the study and its issues within the Centre.

Key questions

The strategic evaluation was discussed with all levels of IDRC staff involved in project and programme delivery, including those in IDRC's regional offices.[3] These initial discussions with the Centre staff and preliminary reviews of the literature, as well as of Centre documents, pointed to three questions that the strategic evaluation could fruitfully address:

1. What constitutes public policy influence in IDRC's experience?
2. To what degrees and in what ways has IDRC supported research influenced public policy?
3. What factors and conditions have facilitated or inhibited the public policy influence potential of IDRC supported research projects?

---

[3]The Centre maintains regional offices in Singapore, New Delhi, Cairo, Nairobi, Dakar, and Montevideo.

Elements of the study

To deal with the diversity of interests and needs as well as the complexities of the research-policy linkages, this strategic evaluation applied a variety of methods. Exploratory case study research was combined with deductive theory building, continually adjusted to accommodate one another (Burns 1981). It was a hypothesis-generating approach rather than a hypothesis-testing approach, given the limited range of work that has been carried out in this field. Collaboration with the users extended beyond the strict confines of each study, to engage them in synthesis and hypothesis-generation with respect to the study's implications for the programmes and the Centre as a whole. In addition, partners of the Centre were brought into the discussions from time to time. This reflected the systems-thinking focus on relationships (Maruyama 1976) and on equifinality, or the achievement of the same ends through multiple different pathways (Katz and Kahn 1969).

Three critical mechanisms were put in place to support user involvement. First, a small IDRC advisory group was set up to work with the evaluation team throughout the study. The group represented key users in different parts of the Centre and advised on issues of design, research, and use (IDRC 2003e). Second, consultations were conducted with IDRC's head office, regional offices, and regional activities were carried out with their support. Key outputs of these consultations are reported in workshop reports (IDRC 2003a, IDRC 2003b, IDRC 2003c, IDRC 2003d, and IDRC 2003f). Third, the evaluation design team established a space within the Evaluation Unit's intranet site for the posting of documents and other information. The creation of the site was posted in Echonet, our internal newsletter. As materials became available they were posted to the site. Most project materials are also posted to the Evaluation Unit's public Internet site at http://www.idrc.ca/evaluation. While the study was expressly focused on learning for the Centre, the implementation of research and any subsequent policy influence are meant to be done by our partners as well, not just by IDRC. The study therefore sought to integrate the perspectives and the views of partners in the study. This was achieved both through interview processes in the study and through partner engagement in regional and Ottawa-based consultations on findings.

The study was divided into three main parts: background research, case studies, and analytical outputs, addressing each in turn.

Background research

Preliminary interviews with staff, along with a preliminary review of IDRC documentation, revealed several ways of thinking about the connections between research and policy. As experienced by IDRC programme staff, 'policy influence' in practice can include:

1. Dissemination of research results to policymakers, in appropriate formats.
2. The interaction between researchers and policymakers during the design of the research, dissemination, and/or the research process itself.
3. The building of relationships between researchers and decision makers that last beyond the research project.
4. Public dissemination and debate of the research results.

5. Use of the research results by groups in society to encourage or advocate change.
6. Strengthening organizations in terms of their capacity to carry out policy inquiry.
7. Strengthening key individuals within a generation of researchers who, in the future, will be in positions to implement or encourage policy change.

Some of these links are also mentioned in the literature as factors or mechanisms that facilitate the use of research in policymaking. Indeed, various mechanisms have been established in IDRC supported projects and programmes to encourage these practices. Among them are: inclusion of government policymakers as researchers or advisers to research teams, and specifying the establishment of researcher relationships with policymakers as a criterion for approving research support.

Also, six studies were undertaken to ensure we had a good history of the Centre's approaches and prior experience in this domain.

Literature review (Neilson 2001).   This review of the main bodies of work that address the issue of research influence assisted us in the definition of key questions and, on an ongoing basis, informed the questions used as well as the methodologies for data collection and analysis.

Framework paper (Lindquist 2001).   Evert Lindquist prepared a background paper on frameworks for examining policy influence. This document, which complements the literature review, was based on his knowledge as an expert in the field and on a series of consultations with the Centre staff. The paper provided a preliminary framework that was tested and modified through the document reviews, case studies, and consultations. The framework defines policy influence on a broad spectrum, from enhancing policy capacities (that is, strengthening the capacity of researchers to address policy questions), and broadening policy horizons (building understanding and awareness of the multiple factors and actors in the policy process), to modifying policy regimes with actual changes in policy.

Project completion report (PCR) review (Edwards 2001).   Project Completion Reports (PCRs) are completed by programme officers on IDRC projects with a value of over $150,000. These provide insights into the results and management of the projects. For this study, PCRs were combed for information related to policy influence identified by programme officers.

Programme review (Gillespie 2003a).   In order to develop a clear picture of the priority given to policy influence, a review of the programming documents was conducted, including programme objectives and a survey of project objectives for all programmes and projects at the Centre, to identify the nature of policy-related objectives in each case.

Evaluations review (Adamo 2002).   The Evaluation Unit maintains an inventory of evaluations conducted throughout the Centre. A review was conducted of the 80 evaluations submitted from July 1999 to March 2001, to identify those with a mandate to address policy influence.

Policy influence and IDRC: A history of intent (Gonsalves and Baranyi 2003).
Accepted wisdom at the Centre held that in the early days (1970s and 1980s), IDRC and its staff were primarily preoccupied with good research and that responsibility for use of that research rested elsewhere. This study tested that belief by exploring and recording the progression of thinking on the relevance of policy influence in IDRC's evolution through a document review (*inter alia*, Board minutes and annual reports), and interviews with senior staff. The focus on management decision processes complemented the focus on staff interests and needs, so that both informed the case studies. This evaluation confirmed an early IDRC orientation to 'supporting good research' but showed that there were always some programmes with an interest in and orientation towards policy implications of their research.

These background studies were widely shared and discussed with the Centre staff and management to inform the development of the study and relate the documents to the tacit understandings of how the Centre carries out its work.

Case studies: The research

The case studies are the heart of this evaluation. Three key issues are treated here:

1. Selection of a suitable set of cases.
2. Conduct of the studies by reviewers from the countries where the research took place.
3. Collective analysis involving programme staff and partners. This latter element was critical to the success of the evaluation study given the study's strong use orientation.

Case selection.   As noted above, 23 case studies were completed. The cases were identified through a consultative process with the Centre staff and interviews with former senior officers of the Centre. Criteria for selection were considered with a view to assembling a good cross-section of IDRC supported projects. These included range of subject; uniqueness; comparability; type of influence; type of organization doing the research; type of organization being influenced; duration of IDRC involvement with the partners; intentional vs. unintentional influence; and diversity of IDRC programming mechanisms. In recognition of the finding from the literature that policy influence often takes a very long time, the study deliberately sought out some research projects of long duration and some that had been launched more than 10 years before the start of the evaluation.

In all cases, the projects selected were the ones where there was a claim of influence that could be clearly identified and articulated by the staff member(s) proposing the case. The purpose of the study was not to measure the extent of influence in IDRC supported research generally, but to understand more about how influence happens. Therefore, a purposive selection was seen as appropriate. It is worth noting that not all the case studies were selected prior to the commencement of the case work. A subset of 16 cases was identified at the beginning of the study. As the research became well known throughout the Centre, staff came forward with further examples of presumptively influential projects they believed should be included. Nine additions were made based on a combination of merit, geographic spread, and subject area coverage. This process permitted us to bring in some excellent cases that would have been left out had we made the full selection from the initial sample.

Consultant selection.   Consultants were identified in each region to carry out the case studies. Criteria for selection of consultants included: (*a*) experience with qualitative methods; (*b*) experience in the policy domain; (*c*) knowledge of participatory learning approaches to evaluation; (*d*) capacity for social/gender analysis; (*e*) ability to work across sectors; (*f*) strong knowledge of the region of work; and (*g*) availability. Our preference was for consultants from the countries where the studies took place. This was not possible in all cases; where it was not, the staff of the Centre (primarily from the Evaluation Unit) were asked to carry out the studies, and in most cases this was possible. In all, 21 consultants were engaged to carry out the 25 studies undertaken. Of these, 12 (six female, six male) were from the South and nine (five male, four female) from the North; of the nine from the North, six were IDRC staff and three were external consultants.

Pre-testing and case study preparation.   Before full implementation of the case studies, two pre-studies were carried out. Based on the experience in these two cases, consultants for the first group of case studies were convened for an orientation session. The consultants met as a group with the Centre staff, including programme staff, IDRC management, and the evaluation team working under the direction of the Evaluation Unit. Carol Weiss in her capacity as methodological guide and mentor to the study also participated in briefing the consultants. While not all consultants were able to participate, the workshop was seen as invaluable to the successful completion of the studies. The common frame of reference and shared language that developed among the evaluators resulted in a commonality across the case studies. This greatly increased comparability among very different cases.

Case content.   It was important for the cases to present detailed stories of the policy influence process. The study was not intended to create a 'checklist' or single set of lessons on policy influence. Rather, the focus was on the development of rich case narratives that explored not only the particular research done but the changing context in which the work was carried out, along with the processes that were deployed to achieve influence. It was the interplay between the research project and these other factors that provided a menu of experiences for use by programme officers planning future work, and by IDRC management at the strategic level in considering the relationships, strategies, and types of research required to influence public policy. The case studies were developed based on a common semi-structured interview guide that provided significant comparative data. Based on our background research and the test case studies, the following were the common elements that guided the interviews and case development.

Perspectives of decision makers.   Interviews with decision makers were an important element of the investigation, although this has to be tempered in some contexts with the willingness of decision makers to give credit to others in the decisions that are taken. Further, as Weiss notes:

> Individuals in policy-making positions do not act alone or in isolation from everything going on around them. They are bound by the availability of resources, the constellation of interests affected, the line-up of supporters and opponents.[4]

The ability of any individual decision maker to extract the influence of a piece of research on any decision or line of thinking is weak in most cases.

What is often more interesting is the extent of their knowledge on whom to ask if they do want to know something, their level of confidence in the research they receive, and their abilities to use data and knowledge in the decision process.

Pertinence to issues of the day context. While research is frequently anticipatory and precedes policy demand, context matters greatly in the use of the findings for policy processes. An understanding of the history of the investigation, from its entry to the research agenda, to timing on policy influence, is an important factor in understanding policy influence. Issues become pertinent through a variety of routes: leadership; crisis; and advocacy being three of the most common. Understanding how issues have become pertinent is important to understanding where and how research plays a role—whether in influencing the decision makers, the advocates, or being available in a timely way to respond to crisis.

The relationships of researchers to relevant communities. The study investigated the capacities of the researchers to introduce their findings to decision makers and to other relevant communities—groups representing those affected, public interest groups, advocacy coalitions, NGOs, and so on. This was reflected *inter alia* in communication skills, trust in the quality of research by the other groups, and ability to relate the findings to issues with currency.

Research quality. In the IDRC case studies, we investigated whether and how there had been any influence on public policy from a set of research activities that were deemed to be of reasonably high quality by the IDRC Officers who knew these projects well. We did not independently investigate the quality of the research; nor did we encounter in the (high number of) interviews for the case studies any reference that would cause us to question the quality of the research.

The nature of influence. The study started from the perspective that there were three different types of influence possible:

1. Change in policy itself, or the decision not to change.
2. Strengthening policy capacities of researchers and/or policymakers.
3. Broadening policy horizons by opening up understanding of the range of factors coming into play in a policy decision outside the sometimes narrow scope of research or decision.

One could conceive of 'regime change' as a further category here; it is not one that emerged in our case studies.

---

[4]Carol Weiss, speech at IDRC, March 2003.

The evolution of the policy community.   There is no clear divide between the research and policy communities. Rather these two overlap significantly (and differentially in different countries); so to understand policy influence it is important to understand the evolution of the policy community in a given context. For example, in the development of the policies around the economics of fisheries in Southeast Asia, it was important to follow the careers of the first trained fisheries economists, many of whom became directors of influential research institutions and some of whom became decision makers in their countries; and all of whom maintained a close contact with each other through a network to exchange findings, results, outcomes of policy decisions, and so on.

Use of case material.   The approach in this study put considerable responsibility on the intended users of the findings to delve into the products of the study and engage in their analysis in some depth. The second dimension of this approach was that it also put more responsibility on the evaluation team to ensure appropriate and accessible dissemination of the various products.

The core findings around context and process have already been used within IDRC to interrogate research proposals for projects intended to influence policy. Moreover, the methodology and framework now form the foundation of project level evaluations in many IDRC programme areas. The core concepts demonstrated in the evaluation have since become central in IDRC programme team discussions in yearly work plans and project assessments.

Analytical outputs

In order to analyze the case material, a three-stage process was undertaken. First, a set of regional workshops was held to review the case studies and obtain responses from the Centre staff and the research partners. Then detailed reports of these workshops were analyzed to identify significant issues raised across the regions. Finally, the cases were analyzed again around those specified core issues.

Regional analysis workshops.   Using a variety of methods, the regional workshops were structured around:

1. Review of the cases themselves.
2. Review of the IDRC role and position in the research and policy influence process.
3. Discussion of the policy influence typology developed for the study and position of the cases within this typology.
4. Discussion of research project performance, based on an analysis of the cases in their contexts, motivations, and capacities.
5. Small-group discussions on identifying inhibitors and contributors to policy influence.

These workshops resulted in a substantial preliminary analysis of the findings and provided insights for the review team on key foci for the full cross-case analysis.

Upon completion of the case studies, and the development of a regional analysis, a cross-case analysis was undertaken.

Cross-case analysis.   In order to identify categories for cross-case analysis first, the Harvard–IDRC team analyzed detailed workshop reports from the preliminary analysis and found the key common issues cutting across the discussions. These issues formed the basis for the final analysis (Weiss et al. 2004). On a continuing basis, as the evaluation studies proceeded, findings were presented and discussed at a series of workshops with some of the Centre's regional offices, with partners, and with other organizations engaged in similar work, particularly the Overseas Development Institute in the United Kingdom. This iterative approach to the analysis reinforced its relevance to the Centre and strengthened the use of the data.

Some comments on the implementation of this design

Implementing a study with 25 distinct cases posed significant challenges. These challenges were compounded by the focus on the use of the study results. This meant the active engagement[5] of the key users in all phases of the study. Six core issues emerged from experience as central to the experience:

Selection of cases.   In order to make the study meaningful to the wide range of actors within the centre, it was essential that the cases represent their core interests in some way. Achieving that meant ensuring staff involvement in the selection of cases, ensuring coverage across the range of development problems around which we support research and the regions in which we operate. This required several iterations and a flexible design that permitted the initiation of some case work while case selection was still going on. As indicated earlier in the chapter a first set of 16 cases was identified. The centre-wide discussions of the study raised the level of interest in it and also raised additional cases from those staff who had not made suggestions in the first round of consultations. In addition to choosing cases that appeared to demonstrate some sort of policy influence (based on a set of questions asked of the proponents), we also had to ensure coverage. This balancing act meant that some potentially good cases were left out. Given that the case studies would investigate the policy influence, we had to make choices based on the assertions of our informants with limited real data about how events transpired in the case. The process of case selection benefited from its conduct while the major consultations and workshops were going in within the centre on the design of the study, development of a framework, and literature review. The engagement of staff in these other exercises enhanced the level of understanding of what we were trying to

---

[5]I use 'engagement' here rather than 'participation'. Participation has become overused and is often abused, tending to mean anything in which someone outside the core team has been consulted for their opinion. As noted by Eric Trist in the 'Preface' to his three volume set (Trist, editor, 1990), 'engagement (which reflects the French Existentialist usage) has been chosen as the best single word to represent the process by which social scientists endeavour actively to relate themselves in relevant and meaningful ways to society.' Engagement therefore implies a commitment to, and an active involvement with, the data and its analysis in a given social context.

achieve, and enhanced our understanding as the study team, of what the Centre staff needed to know more about in their support of research for policy influence.

Identification of evaluators.   We sought evaluators from the region of the case. We had a hunch that context played a key role and therefore felt it important that the evaluators, as far as possible, were steeped in the context and could interrogate it more deeply as a result. We were successful in identifying just over half of the evaluators from the South. In addition to location, we were looking for a specific skill set: experience in qualitative methods, experience in evaluation, strong knowledge of the region, ability to work across sectors, and strong interview skills.

Timing.   Due to the importance of comparability across cases, it was important that the studies be conducted more or less simultaneously. Therefore, availability of the consultants was a key factor. With sufficient lead-time we were able to secure the services of our first choices.

A second aspect of timing related to this study is that as an emergent design, there was considerable overlap between the main elements of the study. As the timeline (see Figure 15.1) indicates, the design of the study continued until the case studies were virtually complete and well into the analysis phase of the study. Use of the findings started well before the analysis was complete; and dissemination activities started during the design phase and continued well past completion of the analysis. This attention to timing and overlap in stages of the study was inevitable in a use-oriented study. This approach certainly contributed to the success of the study. The effort necessary to sustain the balance between responsiveness and focus on the study itself should not be underestimated.

Consistency.   Cases in such varied sectors and regions posed a particular problem in terms of comparability. In order to ensure some comparability we:

1. Developed a common, semi-structured interview guide that was used in all cases;
2. Brought the consultants together to review the guide and its purpose;
3. Created opportunities for the consultants to discuss their cases while they were conducting the research;
4. Requested copies of all data so we could review should we encounter significant problems of comparison in the cross case analysis; and
5. Engaged in ongoing dialogue with the case study authors.

Each of these elements played an important role in creating a set of cases that gave us sufficient comparability of data to carry out cross case analysis.

Analysis.   The design of this study is based on the approach that it emerges from the study itself. That is, each stage of the study was reviewed and determined based on the findings of the previous stage. This emergent design was very effective in terms of the engagement

Figure 15.1: Timeline

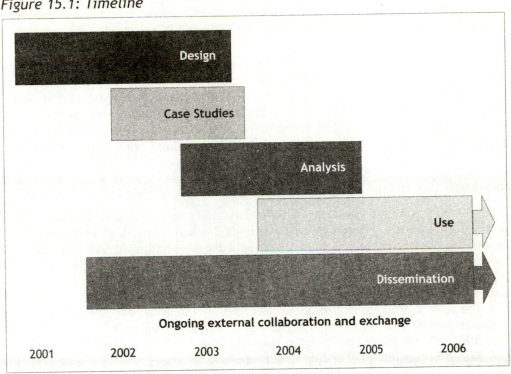

of our key partners in the study, notably IDRC programme staff and managers, and also IDRC partners. We maintained this engagement through the analysis by actively involving our partners in the determination of key issues for analysis. Our 23 cases totalled almost 3,000 pages of text which could be analyzed against a wide range of factors. In order to tease out what was most important to the Centre and its researchers we conducted a series of four workshops with subsets of the cases. A workshop in each region (Africa, Asia, and Latin America) brought together programme staff, managers, and researchers from that region to consider the findings of the cases from that region. A fourth workshop in Ottawa worked with a cross-section of cases from all regions. In all cases, we brought the evaluators to the workshops as well to highlight key findings from the cases. Each workshop was thoroughly documented, including a final workshop of the advisory committee (IDRC, Evaluation Unit 2003a; IDRC, Evaluation Unit 2003b; IDRC, Evaluation Unit 2003c; IDRC, Evaluation Unit 2003d; IDRC, Evaluation Unit 2003e). The reports of this preliminary analysis were themselves then analyzed to identify key cross cutting issues. This resulted in a remarkably consistent set of issues emerging from the regional workshops. These core issues guided the final analysis by the research team.

Engagement. As noted earlier in this chapter, engagement of our key partners was critical to the success of the study. Engagement was sustained through a constant focus on the issues and interests of the partners and through attempts to link the findings to their issues. As noted by

Patton in his description of utilization focused evaluation, 'evaluators should facilitate the evaluation process and design any evaluation with careful consideration of how everything that is done, **from beginning to end**, will affect use' (Patton 2002a; emphasis in the original).

Use.   Finally, while 23 case studies is a relatively small number, the depth of data collection in each case, the range of fields of research, and regions of undertaking gave a richness to the study that has permitted it to serve as a tool for the development of a common framework for the purposes of the Centre's work. It is serving now as a basis for the design of further evaluations of research projects that intend to influence policy. The findings of these studies should help inform and enrich the framework as it is applied to Centre-supported research.

Conclusions

As Carol Weiss has noted, these case studies have not concentrated just on the effect of research on individuals in policymaking positions. Instead, 'they have begun to take the policy-making *system* as their canvas' (2003: 5). This has significant implications for the evaluation of the influence of research on policy. It is no longer a matter of looking at how individuals are influenced but at how systems evolve, how they are influenced. Context matters. This brings us back to the points raised at the beginning of this methodological discussion: the complexities of attribution, impact, and time in evaluating the policy influence of a research project. Bringing context to bear will multiply the variables in attributing identifiable influence to a particular body of research. It increases the difficulties of claiming impact. And it brings into play changes over time in what the (positive or negative) effects of research might have been. Applying a use-oriented evaluation approach, which engages user–practitioners throughout the evaluation study, reduces the risk of irrelevance in the study and expands opportunities for users to take part in defining the areas of evaluation and modes of analysis. It is undeniable that involving users complicates life for the evaluation team, not only in extending the time required but in preserving methodological integrity. But these costs are amply repaid. Evaluation should never be done for its own sake. Engaging the users of evaluation from the start can dramatically increase the potential for relevance and influence—two of the most important goals in any evaluation.

Changing Practice: A Note on Using Evaluation for Organizational Change

16

Introduction

Evaluation studies succeed by affecting one of two categories of organizational use—and sometimes both at once. In the first category, evaluation findings are adopted to make changes in projects or programmes based on whatever the evaluation uncovers; not surprisingly, these are known as 'findings uses'. In the second category of success, changes occur in behaviours and attitudes in the organization itself, as a result of participation in the evaluation process. These 'process uses' (Patton 1997) of evaluation are often quite diverse, and can amount to significant and lasting changes in organizational culture and performance. Patton (2007) defines six process outcomes that are possible: (*a*) enhancing understanding of the programme; (*b*) reinforcing the programme intervention; (*c*) increasing commitment and facilitating learning; (*d*) programme and organizational development; (*e*) infusing evaluative thinking into an organization's culture; and (*f*) instrumentation effects (what gets measured gets done). IDRC has experienced some of these process uses as a result of our evaluation of research-for-policy, and it is an experience others might find useful.

Process use is defined simply as 'changes in attitudes, thinking and behaviour that result from participating in an evaluation' (Patton 2007). It signifies an interaction between organizational development and evaluation, and it reflects an evolution in the ways that evaluations have been undertaken and applied by organizations in both the public and private sectors. As soon as evaluation began to be understood not only as an accountability device, but as an institutional learning device, the utility of evaluation for organizational change and development began to emerge. The accountability origins of evaluation permitted organizations to show that what they were doing was good (or not), and that they were doing it well (or not). With the addition of the learning dimension, organizational change was more directly brought into the evaluation mandate. More than just demonstrating progress in an organization's work, evaluation now is about influencing that progress and defining its direction. This has been to some degree a natural maturation in evaluation practice. And it has had important implications.

1. It meant that we as evaluators needed to think more about engaging with stakeholders, getting alternative points of view.
2. It meant that we began to think more about how we evaluate.
3. It opened up the possibility that people need not be threatened by evaluation, that it could actually serve their own needs, that it need not be the sinister procedure used to reduce their funding or shut their programme—and that under the right conditions people could participate in designing and conducting the evaluation and using the findings.
4. It also meant that evaluators have to become more open and transparent about the purpose of evaluation; it best serves both learning and accountability objectives when those involved understand its purposes.

This process-use approach to evaluation is not without controversy, both in organizations and within the evaluation community. It blurs the conventional boundaries of evaluation and shifts evaluation's mission from the provision of data, information, and knowledge to a direct participation in the use of that knowledge. When process use is in play, evaluators themselves assume new accountability not only for the conduct of an evaluation, but for its use by the organization. Evaluation becomes a management function. And when an evaluation assesses worth, it inevitably raises potent and contentious questions of organizational norms and values. A little resistance to these process uses is understandable; there were bound to be those who argue that evaluation should keep to its customary confines of systematic assessment of programmatic ends and means, and not move into the business of helping people change.

Process Use in Practice

The evaluation described in this volume engaged IDRC staff and management from the start. It was, in short, designed and conducted with process-use objectives; it was intended to illuminate the dynamics of development research for influencing public policy, with the purpose of informing IDRC's organizational planning, programming, and performance. And that purpose has been achieved to a greater extent than we expected when the evaluation began to take shape in 2001.

This evaluation was also something of a procedural departure for IDRC. Although it built on our experience with several earlier studies, the study pioneered new ground both in methods and in organizational impact. To see the innovation in its design and execution, consider the conventional wisdom that has ordinarily governed evaluations. Traditionally, an evaluation was supposed to be:

1. Done quickly,
2. Closely focused and targeted,
3. Easily grasped, and
4. Presented in a concise report.

This study broke every single one of those rules, sometimes deliberately and sometimes accidentally. It took many detours over its six years of life. It is contained in some 4,000 pages of background studies, case studies, summary analyses, presentations, articles, and chapters in books as well as workshop reports. So the focus was broad and the output was expansive. Policy influence of research—the subject of the evaluation—is itself a moving target, not easily verified with certainty, and not easily condensed to a simple array of prescriptive advice. In place of simplicity, speed, and sharp subject focus, this study was characterized by multiple dimensions—watchful patience and continuous modification by an evaluation team collaborating closely with IDRC programme staff and management with the cooperation of friendly outsiders.

One rule the study did not break is about use. It was seen as centrally important in the Centre that we improve our understanding of research and policy influence in order to improve our support to projects that were attempting to affect policy for better development. We were also fortunate that IDRC overall understood the complexity of policy influence, and acknowledged the prevailing lack of practical knowledge about how to do research for policy influence. The agency and its principals wanted to learn. This provided the space for learning to happen.

In truth, questions of research and policy influence were circulating throughout IDRC long before we embarked on this study. It is hinted at in the IDRC Act of 1970 in which the first Object of the Centre is to, 'initiate, encourage, support and conduct research into the problems of the developing regions of the world and into the means for applying and adapting scientific, technical and other knowledge to the economic and social advancement of those regions ...' (Government of Canada 1970). The core issue had been identified in the Centre's 2000–2005 Strategic Plan (IDRC 2000), which declared that, 'IDRC will foster and support the production, dissemination, and application of research results leading to policies and technologies that enhance the lives of people in developing countries.'

We wanted to look at the policy angle more systematically, largely because little had been done on that front. So we started talking to people in our various programmes about the policy work they were doing. Extensive consultations were a necessary concomitant of the wide diversity of the Centre's programmes in environment and natural resource management, social and economic studies, information and communication technologies for development; and science and technology policy studies. Moreover, these programmes operate quite differently. They have very different agendas and fields of study and they work with different groups of researchers, from farmer field studies through to global financial researchers. As a result, the Centre housed many different views on the importance of policy influence in the research it supports; a few insisted, 'we don't work in the policy field' while others placed policy change as their main focus. We were also given many views of what constituted good research to influence policy—sometimes even offered a set of rules for what to do if one wants to influence policy with one's research. What quickly became clear was that there was no common and shared understanding in the Centre of what was meant by policy influence. And there was a relatively simplistic interpretation among many of how policy might be influenced by research. So we discovered early on that to evaluate the extent of policy influence would require us first to address three core questions in our discussions with IDRC staff and managers: What do we mean by policy influence? How has IDRC-supported research influenced public policy? And what factors facilitate or inhibit policy influence?

These core questions guided our study, along the lines described in Chapter 15. At the heart of our methodology was engagement with IDRC field staff, programme managers, and senior executives. It was this engagement—a more or less continuous dialogue punctuated by periodic workshops—that distinguished this evaluation as a process-use exercise. In the workshops, especially (and out of the detailed reports that flowed from them), we saw three crucial developments pertaining to process use. First, a number of staff members talked about insights that would help them almost immediately in their daily work. One programme officer, for example, at an early Montevideo workshop noted that the cases and discussion would affect how she reviewed project proposals she was reviewing that week, because she now had a new and clearer way to think about their policy influence components. Second, we were assembling a coherent picture of what people thought was important out of the many experiences and issues highlighted in the cases. And third, Centre staff talked across programme groups about what they were doing and how they were doing it. This was not a common occurrence at this stage in the Centre's history, so it fulfilled an important function in creating a Centre-wide perspective of policy-directed research. A number of programme staff singled out this innovation as an early benefit of the workshops.

The decision to involve expertise from the policy field was borne out through the involvement of Carol Weiss in the design and analysis of findings. Together with Carol Weiss and two of her Harvard graduate students, we analyzed the workshop reports to figure out what issues were most important to staff and partners of IDRC. This led us to findings in three clusters:

1. What we do (including how we allocate budgets and define our role as research supporters).
2. Where we do it (devising a typology of political contexts in which research is conducted).
3. How we work (including implications of cooperation in networks and partnerships, communication, the significance of time and timing, and gender in the policy process).

Weiss and her colleagues did the primary analysis based on these issues (Weiss et al. 2004). As Weiss notes in the foreword to this volume, the analysis they did was formative. Out of this analysis, we developed a series of presentations of various types for various audiences. We have held internal workshops, and addressed public audiences in Canada and around the world. All of these contributed to refining the issues and the presentations and, importantly, to the Centre adopting this analysis as its own. And all have contributed to the way the Centre talks about policy influence in our own programmes. We continue to maintain a website with the project materials, which have also been collated on a CD.

In summary, identifiable organizational changes in five separate categories can be attributed to process uses of this evaluation since 2001:

1. **Common language**
    (*a*) IDRC staff and managers recognize merits of the case studies and use these insights in their project design work.
    (*b*) Development of a common language in the Centre.

2. **Policy influence as a theme of Centre reporting**

    (a) Focus on policy influence in Centre discussions (as an example, during IDRC's in-house Annual Learning Forums).

    (b) Use of policy influence as a theme in Centre reporting (as in reports from directors of programme areas).

    (c) Change of orientation in Centre discussions—from 'we don't do policy influence' to 'how do we do this?'

3. **Use of findings for project review**

    Use of the evaluation findings in defining pre-approval project reviews and framing project discussions.

4. **Use of evaluation materials by project participants and the Centre as a whole**

    (a) Use of policy influence as a criterion of IDRC success.

    (b) Use of the evaluation materials by the projects involved.

    (c) Continuing use of the evaluation study materials in communications about the Centre.

    (d) Use of evaluation materials in exchanges with other agencies, sharing the Centre's knowledge in this domain.

5. **Uses outside IDRC**

    The primary emphasis here is on the internal process uses of the study. But we know of several external applications of the evaluation so far, including use of the materials by a professor at the Michigan State University for teaching, and as resource materials for African researchers in the area of food security and food policy. Such uses serve to strengthen IDRC's international partnerships and extend its reach in supporting development research.

Getting to Use

I have described a shift in the Centre on how it thinks about the relationship between the researches it supports and changes in public policy. IDRC has changed how it thinks about policy influence, how it discusses research-for-policy internally, and how it funds research that is meant to influence policy.

But why did this evaluation study result in such significant process use? Why did it contribute to considerable and lasting organizational change? Four main features of the study stand out as salient:

1. **We intended for process use to happen**

    This is not the case in every evaluation. Sometimes we are seeking simpler outcomes. So it is important again to be clear: Intentions have effect. Here we knew that the research-for-policy questions were significant and confused, and that they demanded answers.

2.   We asked the users!

And then we asked them again, and again, and stayed close to them throughout the study. But we did not only question. As we asked, we also gave. The value of the study emerged in these exchanges. If the users had not believed they were getting repaid for their participation, they would not have kept on giving. This sense of 'getting something back' operated from the very first workshops.

3.   Everyone wanted to know the evaluation story

Research-for-policy was a cross-Centre issue. This was not a study about a single programming decision or a single programme area; its implications touched everyone in the Centre. Among staff and management, participation in the study and uptake of its results happened frequently throughout the evaluation.

4.   We treated reality with respect, and did not over-simplify

We did not try to invent silver bullet solutions to any problem. From the beginning we recognized this is a complex topic and treated it as such. As Erich Jantsch says, 'reality is complex ... and greater complexity (which is not the same a greater complicatedness), therefore, means a more realistic attitude...' (Jantsch 1980: 267). That means evaluation should treat reality with deference, working to accommodate complexity and making no false claims to override it. A few other attributes, while maybe not essential, undoubtedly helped advance the process use of this evaluation.

5.   The timing was right

Good timing calls for alert attention, although it is perhaps something that can only be confirmed after some time has passed. In any event, the timing here was incrementally advantageous as early results encouraged fresh progress. Timing can start promisingly, but get out of sync with the rhythms of the issues or of the organization itself. It is wise to listen to those rhythms carefully, through the life of the evaluation, to maximize the chances of having good effects.

6.   Findings were evident and relevant to end-users

Relevance came up with increasing frequency as the evaluation progressed. Even in programme areas where managers claimed policy influence was not an issue, project staffers saw and welcomed relevance in the evaluation findings. Local researchers trying to affect policy were being stymied in the policy process—and were eager for guidance to overcome the blockages.

7.   External audiences were interested and interesting

Never underestimate the power of legitimation by respected peers to help you create change. We did not try to isolate our work from other studies. On the contrary, we brought in the efforts of others and emphasized their value.

8.   We had fun with the study

The evaluation team played with the data, and gathered people together socially as well as in the office to explore the findings. It was a pleasure to work on the project and that enjoyment was, in the view of many participants, a critical part of learning.

Should Anyone Else Care?

Just because we have learned something from this study does not mean it is of use to anyone else. But I think our evaluation and its effects illustrate what Patton (2002a) calls 'high quality lessons'. That is to say, these are lessons that others can care about.

So who should care about this study? Perhaps what is important here is the link between findings use and process use, the distinction drawn at the outset of this note. In terms of findings use—applying findings to future projects and programmes—the results are important beyond the 23 cases we analyzed and beyond IDRC. They are high quality lessons in that they:

1. Focus on an issue of concern to many researchers;
2. Provide several suggestive examples of how policy influence did or did not occur;
3. Present the evidence clearly, both in the cases and in the analysis;
4. Deal with many different types of research in developing countries;
5. Were developed with a solid methodology; and
6. Demonstrate consistency across regions and domains of research.

On the dimension of process use—the influence of the evaluation on organizational change—the same standards apply. As the issues addressed were timely and were treated in ways corresponding to the concerns, policies, and strategies of the organization, the potential for process use was significantly increased. This relationship between findings use and process use is critical. While it is conceivable that one could have process use without findings use and vice versa, both are dramatically strengthened when there is a synergy between them. If the issue is highly relevant and its evaluation treatment is broadly seen as appropriate, there will probably be more engagement from organization members, and likely to be more process use as a consequence.

I have touched only lightly on the literature here, and still less on theory, preferring to focus on the experience of this particular evaluation. But it is not unusual for theory to emerge from practice—not from a single case, but from multiple experiences that overlap and display consistent patterns. This is one such case that I know well. It confirms what some, including Preskill and Patton, have observed about using evaluation in organizational change. And I think it is indicative of a growth in evaluation that is emerging with increasing prominence and value in the field.

We came to these results through practice, not theory. But they have theoretical implications—and building stronger theory now might well help strengthen future practice. As Kurt Lewin is oft quoted as saying, 'There's nothing so practical as a good theory.'

Acronyms

AFSSRN	Asian Fisheries Social Science Research Network
AKI	Angelo King Institute of Economic and Business Studies
ANC	African National Congress
ARDA	Arsaal Rural Development Association
AUB	American University of Beirut
BARD	Bangladesh Academy of Rural Development
BBS	Bangladesh Bureau of Statistics
BIDS	Bangladesh Institute of Development Studies
CBMS	Community-Based (Poverty) Monitoring System
CCRE	Consultative Commission on Educational Reform
CGE	Computable General Equilibrium Model
CIDA	Canadian International Development Agency
CIS	Computerized Information System
CIUEM	Center for Informatics at the University of Eduardo Mondlane
CMS	Chronic Mountain Sickness
CNPRE	Standing National Commission on Educational Reform
COPMAGUA	Coordination Office of Mayan Organizations in Guatemala
CREA	Centre de Recherches en Économie Appliquée
DHMTs	District Health Management Teams
DSS	District Sentinel Surveillance systems
ECA	East and Central Africa
ECAPAPA	Eastern and Central Africa Programme for Agricultural Policy Analysis
ECLAC	Economic Commission for Latin America and the Caribbean
EHIP	Essential Health Intervention Project
ELSA	Early Evaluation and Learning System for Acacia
EMDU	Environmental Management Development in Ukraine
ESDU	Environment and Sustainable Development Unit
FLASCO	Latin American Faculty of Social Sciences
FRG	Guatemalan Republican Front
G-24	Group of 24
G-24 TSS	Group of 24 Technical Support Service
GDP	Gross Domestic Product
GEF	Global Environment Facility

GIAN	Gujarat Innovation Augmentation Network
GIS	Geographic Information System
GPS	Global Positioning System
GTZ	Deutsche Gesellschaft fuer Technische Zusammenarbeit (German Agency for Technical Cooperation)
HES	Household Expenditure Survey
HIPC	Highly Indebted Poor Countries
HIV/AIDS	Human Immunodeficiency Syndrome/Acquired Immune Deficiency Syndrome
ICARDA	International Centre for Agricultural Research in Dry Areas
ICBA	International Centre for Biosaline Agriculture
ICIMOD	International Centre for Integrated Mountain Development
ICLARM	International Centre for Living Aquatic Resources Management
ICRISAT	International Crops Research Institute for Semi-Arid Tropics
ICT	Information and Communication Technology
IDB	Inter-American Development Bank
IDRC	International Development Research Centre
IIMA	Indian Institute of Management Ahmedabad
IMF	International Monetary Fund
INWARDAM	Inter-Islamic Network on Water Resources Development and Management
IPR	Intellectual Property Rights
ISP	Internet Service Provider
IT	Information Technology
IWT II	Second International Water Tribunal
IWTC	International Women's Tribune Centre
LAC	Latin America and the Caribbean
LARI	Lebanese Agricultural Research Institute
LATN	Latin American Trade Network
MENA	Middle East and North Africa
MIMAP	Micro Impacts of Macroeconomic and Adjustment Policies
MoH	Ministry of Health
MPCE	Multi-sector Permanent Commission on the Environment
NEPAD	New Partnership for Africa's Development
NGO	Non-governmental Organization
NIF	National Innovation Foundation
NITC	National Information Technology Council
NPC	National Planning Commission
OCEEI	Office for Central and Eastern Europe Initiatives
ODI	Overseas Development Institute
PAN	National Advancement Party
PCR	Project Completion Report
PIDS	Philippine Institute for Development Studies
PMS	Poverty Monitoring System

PRSP	Poverty Reduction Strategy Paper
RAPID	Research and Policy in Development (a programme of ODI)
REMPAI	Resource Management and Policy Analysis Institute
SAS	Senegal Acacia Strategy
SEGEPLAN	Presidential Office for Planning and Programming (Guatemala)
SEWA	Self Employed Women's Association
SONATEL	National Telecommunications Company of Senegal
SONEDE	National Society for Water Exploitation and Distribution
SPCC	Southern Peru Copper Corporation
SRISTI	Society for Research and Initiatives for Sustainable Technologies and Institutions
TEHIP	Tanzania Essential Health Interventions Project
TG	Technical Group
TRIPS	Trade Related Intellectual Property Rights
TSS	Technical Support Service
UEM	University Eduardo Mondlane
UMC	Ukraine Management Committee
UNCTAD	United Nations Conference on Trade and Development
UNDP	United Nations Development Programme
VEEM	Vietnam Economic and Environmental Management programme
VISED	Vietnam Sustainable Economic Development programme
VSAT	Very Small Aperture Satellite Transmission
WDM	Water Demand Management
WDMF	Water Demand Management Forum
WDR '93	World Development Report 1993
WTO	World Trade Organization

References

Ackello-Ogutu, Chris. 2003. 'ECAPAPA Case Study'. Available online at http://www.idrc.ca/evaluation/ev-41432-201-1-DO_TOPIC.html

Adamo, Abra. 2002. *Strategic Evaluation of Policy Influence: What Evaluation Reports Tell Us about Public Policy Influence by IDRC-supported Projects*. Ottawa: Evaluation Unit, IDRC.

———. 2003. *The Influence on Public Policy through IDRC-supported Research: Synthesis of Document Reviews*. Ottawa: Evaluation Unit, IDRC.

Argueta, Bienvendo. 2002. 'Financing Education Reforms in Guatemala'. Available online at http://www.idrc.ca/evaluation/ev-41434-201-1-DO_TOPIC.html

Arregui, A., F. Leon-Velarde, and M. Valcarcel. 1990. *Salud y Mineria, El Riesgo del Mal de Montana Cronico enre Mineros de Cerro de Pasco*. Lima: ADEC-ATC/Mosca Azul and 'La Altura, el Mal de Montana Cronico en la Salud del Trabajador Minero', May 1992. Lima: ADEC-ATC, Asociacion Laboral para el Desarrollo. Available at the ADEC-ATC Library in Lima.

Ayuk, Elias T. and Mohammed Ali Marouani. 2007. *The Policy Paradox in Africa: Strengthening Links between Economic Research and Policy Making*. Trenton, NJ and Ottawa: Africa World Press and IDRC.

Brooks, David. 2002. 'Case Study of Sustainable Improvement of Marginal Land in Arsaal, Lebanon'. Available online at http://www.idrc.ca/evaluation/ev-31683-201-1-DO_TOPIC.html

Burns, Thomas F. 1981. 'Planning Networks and Network Agents: An Approach to Adaptive Community Governance'. Unpublished doctoral dissertation. University of Pennsylvania.

Burton, Leanne. 2004a. 'Society for Research and Initiatives for Sustainabile Technologies and Institutions (SRISTI): A Case Study.' Available online at http://www.idrc.ca/evaluation/ev-54202-201-1-DO_TOPIC.html

———. 2004b. 'The Development of Nepal's IT Policy: A Case Study'. Available online at http://www.idrc.ca/evaluation/ev-54195-201-1-DO_TOPIC.html

Caplan, N. 1979. 'The Two-communities Theory and Knowledge Utilization', *American Behavioral Scientist*, 22(2): 459–70.

Carden, Fred. 2004. 'Issues in Assessing the Policy Influence of Research', *International Social Science Journal*, 179 (March): 135–51.

———. 2005. *Capacities, Contexts, and Conditions: The Influence of IDRC-supported Research on Policy Processes*. Ottawa: IDRC Evaluation Highlight #5. IDRC.

———. 2007. 'Context Matters: The Influence of IDRC-supported Research on Policy Processes', in Elias T. Ayuk and Mohammed Ali Marouani (eds), *The Policy Paradox in Africa: Strengthening Links between Economic Research and Policy Making*, pp. 93–116. Trenton, NJ and Ottawa: Africa World Press and IDRC.

Carden, Fred. 2008. 'Using Comparative Data: A Systems Approach to a Multiple Case Study', in David Byrne and Charles Ragin (eds), *Handbook of Case-Centred Methods*. London: Sage Publications.

Carden, Fred and Stephanie Neilson. 2005. 'Confluence and Influence: Building Policy Capacities in Research Networks', in Diane Stone and Simon Maxwell (eds), *The Challenge of Transnational Knowledge Networks: Bridging Research and Policy in a Globalizing World*, pp. 139–55. London: Routledge.

Carden, Fred, Stephanie Neilson, Terry Smutylo, Denise Deby, Sarah Earl, and Molly den Heyer. 2001. *IDRC-supported Research in the Public Policy Process: A Strategic Evaluation of the Influence of Research on Public Policy*. Ottawa: Evaluation Unit, IDRC.

Court, Julius, Ingie Hovland, and John Young (eds). 2005. *Bridging Research and Policy in Development: Evidence and the Change Process*. Warwickshire: ITDG.

Cullen, M.J. 1975. *The Statistical Movement in Early Victorian Britain: The Foundations of Empirical Social Research*. New York: Harper and Row.

Earl, Sarah, Fred Carden, and Terry Smutylo. 2001. *Outcome Mapping: Building Learning and Reflection into Development Programs*. Ottawa: IDRC.

Edwards, Kimberley. 2001. *PCRs and Policy Influence: What Project Completion Reports have to Say about Public Policy Influence by Centre-supported Research*. Ottawa: Evaluation Unit, IDRC.

Evaluation Unit. 2007. Annual Report on Corporate Performance for 2006. *Section 10, Analysis across Performance Areas*, IDRC, Ottawa.

Feinstein, Osvaldo and Robert Picciotto (eds). 2000. *Evaluation and Poverty Reduction: Proceedings from a World Bank Conference*. Washington, DC: World Bank.

Flyvberg, Bent. 2001. *Making Social Science Matter: Why Social Inquiry Fails and How It Can Succeed Again*. Cambridge: Cambridge University Press.

Gillespie, Bryon. 2003a. *Intent to Influence Policy in IDRC Programs and Projects*. Ottawa: Evaluation Unit, IDRC.

———. 2003b. 'Water Demand Management in Syria: The Case of Brackish Water'. Available online at http://www.idrc.ca/evaluation/ev-66376-201-1-DO_TOPIC.html

Gonsalves, Tahira and Stephen Baranyi. 2003. *A History of IDRC Intent*. Ottawa: Evaluation Unit, IDRC.

Government of Canada. 1970. *International Development Research Centre Act*. Ottawa: Government of Canada.

Hagi-Bishow, M. and R.B. Bonnell. 2000. 'Assessment of LEACHM-C Model for Semi-arid Saline Irrigation', *ICID Journal*, 49: 29–42.

Hamadeh, Shadi, Mona Haidar, and Rami Zurayk. 2006. *Research for Development in the Dry Arab Region: The Cactus Flower*. Penang, Malaysia: Southbound and Ottawa: IDRC.

International Development Research Centre. 2000. *IDRC Program Directions, 2000–2005*. Ottawa: IDRC.

———. 2001. *Closing the Loop: Communication for Change at IDRC*. Ottawa: IDRC.

International Development Research Centre, Evaluation Unit. 2003a. *Cases, Concepts and Connections: Report of a Workshop, Ottawa, March 2003*. Ottawa: Evaluation Unit, IDRC.

———. 2003b. *The Influence of Research on Public Policy: Report of a Workshop, Johannesburg, November 2002*. Ottawa: Evaluation Unit, IDRC.

———. 2003c. *The Influence of Research on Public Policy: Report of a Workshop, Montevideo, December 2002*. Ottawa: Evaluation Unit, IDRC.

———. 2003d. *The Influence of Research on Public Policy: Report of a Workshop, Bangkok, January 2003*. Ottawa: Evaluation Unit, IDRC.

International Development Research Centre, Evaluation Unit. 2003e. *The Influence of Research on Policy: Advisory Committee Retreat, February 20–21*. Ottawa: Evaluation Unit, IDRC.

———. 2003f. *Seminar on Evaluating Policy Influence in Ukraine: Report of a Workshop, Ottawa, March 26, 2003*. Ottawa: Evaluation Unit, IDRC.

Iverson, Alex. 2003. *Attribution and Aid Evaluation in International Development: A Literature Review*. Ottawa: Evaluation Unit, IDRC.

Jantsch, Erich. 1980. *The Self-Organizing Universe*. NY: Pergamon.

Katz, D. and R.L. Kahn. 1969. 'Common Characteristics of Open Systems', in F.E. Emery (ed.), *Systems Thinking*, pp. 86–104. Harmondsworth: Penguin Modern Management Readings.

Kingdon, John. 1984. *Agendas, Alternatives and Public Policies*. Boston Toronto: Little Brown & Company.

Krastev, Ivan. 2000. 'Post Communist Thinktanks: Making and Faking Influence', in Diane Stone (ed.), *Banking on Knowledge*. London and NY: Routledge.

Leon-Velarde, F. and A. Arregui. 1994. *Desadaptacion a la Vida en las Grandes Alturas*. Lima: Instituto Frances de Estudios Andinos y Universidad Peruana Cayetano Heredia.

Lindquist, Evert A. 2001. *Discerning Policy Influence: Framework for Strategic Evaluation of IDRC-supported Research*. Ottawa: Evaluation Unit, IDRC. Available online at http://www.idrc.ca/en/ev-12177-201-1-DO_TOPIC.html

Livny, Eric, Archana Mehendale, and Alf Vanags. 2006. 'Bridging the Research Policy Gaps in Developing and Transition Countries: Analytical Lessons and Proposals for Action. Global Development Network'. Available online at http://www.gdnet.org/middle.php?oid=1283

Loayza, Fernando Careaga. 2003. 'The Cases of High Altitude and Mining, and the Impact of Copper Mining on Resources in Southern Peru'. Available online at http://www.idrc.ca/evaluation/ev-66333-201-1-DO_TOPIC.html

Lusthaus, Charles, Marie-Hélène Adrien, Gary Anderson, Fred Carden, and George Plinio Montalván. 2002. *Organizational Assessment*. Washington and Ottawa: IDB & IDRC.

Lyzogub, Iryna. 2002. 'Environmental Management Development in Ukraine'. Available online at http://www.idrc.ca/evaluation/ev-31684-201-1-DO_TOPIC.html

Macadar, Luis. 2003. *The Influence of Research on Public Policy: The Latin American Trade Network*. Ottawa: Evaluation Unit, IDRC.

Maruyama, M. 1976. 'Toward Cultural Symbiosis', in Erich Jantsch and Conrad Waddington (eds), *Evolution and Consciousness: Human Systems in Transition*, pp. 198–213. Addison Wesley: Reading, MA.

Neilson, Stephanie. 2001. *Knowledge Utilization and Public Policy Processes: A Literature Review*. Ottawa: Evaluation Unit, IDRC. Available online at http://www.idrc.ca/en/ev-12186-201-1-DO_TOPIC.html

Neilson, Stephanie and Terry Smutylo. 2004. 'The TEHIP "Spark": Planning and Managing Health Resources at the District Level'. Available online at http://www.idrc.ca/evaluation/ev-58698-201-1-DO_TOPIC.html

Ofir, Zenda. 2003a. 'Acacia: The Case of Mozamabique'. Available online at http://www.idrc.ca/evaluation/ev-104039-201-1-DO_TOPIC.html

———. 2003b. 'Acacia: The Case of South Africa'. Available online at http://www.idrc.ca/evaluation/ev-31663-201-1-DO_TOPIC.html

———. 2003c. 'Acacia: The Case of Uganda'. Available online at http://www.idrc.ca/evaluation/ev-31661-201-1-DO_TOPIC.html

O'Neil, Maureen. 2006. Interview with the author, March 2006.

Patton, Michael Quinn. 1997. *Utilization-Focused Evaluation: The New Century Text*. Third edition. Thousand Oaks, CA: Sage Publications.

———. 2002a. 'Utilization-Focused Evaluation Checklist'. Available online at http://www.wmich.edu/evalctr/checklists/ufe.pdf, downloaded on 1 February 2003.

———. 2002b. *Qualitative Research and Evaluation Methods*. Third edition. Thousand Oaks, CA: Sage Publications.

———. 2007. 'Process Use as Usefulism', *New Directions in Evaluation*, 116: 99–112.

Pomeroy, Robert. 2002. 'A Case Study of the Asian Fisheries Social Science Research Network'. Available online at http://www.idrc.ca/evaluation/ev-31677-201-1-DO_TOPIC.html

Reimers, Fernando and Noel McGinn. 1988. *Informed Dialogue: Using Research to Shape Education Policy around the World*. Westport, CT: Praeger.

Riggirozzi, María Pía. 2004. 'Bridging Research and Poverty: MIMAP Bangladesh'. Available online at http://www.idrc.ca/evaluation/ev-57584-201-1-DO_TOPIC.html

Riggirozzi, María Pía and Tracy Tuplin. 2004. 'The Influence of Research on Policy: MIMAP Philippines'. Available online at http://www.idrc.ca/evaluation/ev-57585-201-1-DO_TOPIC.html

Sabatier, Paul A. and Hank C. Jenkins-Smith. 1993. *Policy Change and Learning: An Advocacy Coalition Approach*. Boulder, CO: Westview Press.

Saumier, André. 2003. 'The Impact of Research on Public Policy: The Case of Vietnam'. Available online at http://www.idrc.ca/evaluation/ev-65386-201-1-DO_TOPIC.html

Sene, Khamate and Ramata Thioune. 2003. 'Acacia: The Case of Senegal'. Available online at http://www.idrc.ca/evaluation/ev-31406-201-1-DO_TOPIC.html

Shevchuk, V.Y., G.O. Bilyavsky, V.M. Navrotsky, and O.O. Mazurkevitch. 2005. *Preserving the Dnipro River: Harmony, History, and Rehabilitation*. Oakville, ON Canada & Ottawa: Mosaic Press/IDRC.

Smutylo, Terry. 2001. *Crouching Impact, Hidden Attribution: Overcoming Threats to Learning in Development Programs*. Ottawa: Evaluation Unit, IDRC.

Stone, Diane and Simon Maxwell (eds). 2005. *The Challenge of Transnational Knowledge Networks: Bridging Research and Policy in a Globalizing World*. London: Routledge.

Surani, Eman. 2003. 'Greywater Reuse: Jordan'. Available online at http://www.idrc.ca/evaluation/ev-31682-201-1-DO_TOPIC.html

Toulemonde, Jacques and Lise Rochaix. 1994. 'Rational Decision-making through Project Appraisal: A Presentation of French Attempts', *International Review of Administrative Sciences*, 60: 37–53.

Trist, Eric (General editor). Trist, Beulah (Assistant editor). 1990. 1993. 1997. *The Social Engagement of Social Science: A Tavistock Anthology*. Philadelphia: University of Pennsylvania Press. *Volume I: The Socio-Psychological Perspective*, Trist, E. and Murray, H., eds; *Volume II: The Socio-Technical Systems Perspecive*, Trist, E. and Murray, H., eds.; *Volume III: The Socio-Ecological Systems Perspective*, Trist, E., Emery, F., and Murray, H., eds.

Tuplin, Tracy. 2004a. 'The Influence of Research on Policy: The Case of MIMAP Senegal'. Available online at http://www.idrc.ca/evaluation/ev-57583-201-1-DO_TOPIC.html

———. 2004b. 'The Case of Water Demand Management in Tunisia'. Available online at http://www.idrc.ca/evaluation/ev-66377-201-1-DO_TOPIC.html

Tussie, Diana, M.P. Riggirozzi, and T. Tuplin. 2003. *A Study of Policy Influence: The G-24 Technical Support Service*. Ottawa: Evaluation Unit, IDRC.

Vibe, Maja de, Ingie Hovland, and John Young. 2002. 'Bridging Research and Policy: An Annotated Bibliography', ODI Working Paper 174, Overseas Development Institute, London. Available online at http://www.odi.org.uk/rapid/Publications/RAPID_WP_174.htm

Wagner, Peter, C.H. Weiss, B. Wittrock, and H. Wollmann (eds). 1991. *Social Sciences and Modern States: National Experiences and Theoretical Crossroads*. Cambridge: Cambridge University Press.

Weiss, Carol H. 1967. 'Utilization of Evaluation: Toward Comparative Study,' In House of Representatives, *The Use of Social Research in Federal Domestic Programs*, part III, pp. 426–32, April. Washington, DC: Government Printing Office.

———. 1977a. *Using Social Research in Public Policy Making*. Lexington, MA: Lexington Books, DC Heath and Co.

———. 1977b. 'Research for Policy's Sake: The Enlightenment Function of Social Research', *Policy Analysis*, 3(4): 531–45.

———. 1982. 'Knowledge Utilization in Decision Making: Reflections on the Terms of the Discussion', *Research in Sociology of Education and Socialization*, 3: 21.

———. 2003. *Studying Research Utilization*. A speech at IDRC, 24 March. Ottawa: IDRC Evaluation Unit.

Weiss, Carol H., Svetlana Karuskina-Drivdale, and Shahram Paksima. 2004. *IDRC-supported Research and Its Influence on Public Policy: Results from a Cross-case analysis*. Ottawa: Evaluation Unit, IDRC.

Yin, R.K. 1994. 'Case Study Research: Design and Methods,' *Applied Social Science Methods Series*, second edition, Volume 5. Thousand Oaks: Sage Publications.

Yin, R.K., C. H. Weiss, O.M. Cheung, and J. Capper. 1988. *Preliminary Study of the Utilization of A.I.D.'s Evaluation Reports*. Washington, DC: Cosmos Corporation.

Annotated Bibliography

Interest in the challenges of using research in public policy is growing dramatically. A growing number of research centres, as well as advocacy and think-tank organizations are carrying out research and publishing in this area. As a result, any attempt at a comprehensive bibliography is outdated before it is completed. It is nevertheless worth noting that the body of work on the links between research and policy produced by Carol Weiss has been signally important to directions and thinking in this field. Her first report addressing the question was produced in 1967, and she has continued active engagement with issues around the use of knowledge in policy since that time, with at least 70 articles and monographs to her credit on this subject. She has also produced several books on the use of research in the policy process, the first being published in 1977.

Here, we will not attempt to be comprehensive but rather present references and web links that have been particularly useful in our work. Each field of study has a rich and growing set of reference materials and so this list should be considered nothing more than a starting point. We will cover three bodies of material: first, the literature reviews that informed and guided this study; second, the publications of the study, both the grey literature and articles and chapters in other publications that also serve as useful starting points; and third, we note several websites—with the caveat that these are only a few and only a starting point.

Reviews that Informed Our Study

The IDRC study commissioned two reviews (Neilson 2001) and (Lindquist 2001) that informed the design of our work. The third study included here (Vibe et al. 2002) was carried out as part of the work of the Overseas Development Institute in this same research area.

Neilson, Stephanie. 2001. *Knowledge Utilization and Public Policy Processes: A Literature Review*. Ottawa: Evaluation Unit, IDRC. Available online at http://www.idrc.ca/en/ev-12186-201-1-DO_TOPIC. html
Completed in the design phase of this study, this wide ranging literature review covers the key material on the research to policy field and pays particular attention to the evolution of the field in developing countries where it notes limited literature until this study.

Lindquist, Evert A. 2001. *Discerning Policy Influence: Framework for a Strategic Evaluation of IDRC-supported Research*. Ottawa: Evaluation Unit, IDRC. Available online at http://www.idrc.ca/en/ev-12177-201-1-DO_TOPIC.html

Completed in the design phase of this study, this paper provides the core elements of the framework that guided the 25 case studies completed over the course of the study. It builds the framework both through an extensive review of existing frameworks and consultations with IDRC staff.

Vibe, Maja de, Ingie Hovland, and John Young. 2002. 'Bridging Research and Policy: An Annotated Bibliography', ODI Working Paper 174, Overseas Development Institute, London. Available online at http://www.odi.org.uk/rapid/Publications/RAPID_WP_174.htm
In addition to much of the core material covered in other literature reviews, this study brings in literature from other fields such as communications, social psychology, and media studies.

IDRC Study Materials

Here, we will highlight some of the publications that have been particularly relevant in the completion of this study.

All papers, reports, and presentations developed in the course of this study can be found on the IDRC website at http://www.idrc.ca/en/ev-26606-201-1-DO_TOPIC.html. The site includes the design documents and background reviews of IDRC documents as well as the various presentations and workshop reports and analyses that were used in the study. All the case studies, both in their long form and as executive summaries are also made available on the site.

In addition to the project materials, several papers have been published elsewhere:

Carden, Fred. 2004. 'Issues in Assessing the Policy Influence of Research', *International Social Science Journal*, 179: 135–51.
This paper reviews the methodology of the study and discusses some of the challenges in implementation.

Carden, Fred and Stephanie Neilson. 2005. 'Confluence and Influence: Building Policy Capacities in Research Networks', in Diane Stone and Simon Maxwell (eds), *Global Knowledge Networks and International Development*, pp. 139–55. Abington, OXON: Routledge.
This chapter looks at three of the case studies in particular all of which are networks. The volume as a whole, provides a coherent examination of how, why, and to what extent research informs policy in the field of international development. Drawn from think tanks, academia and development agencies, the contributors provide case histories of how research has informed local, national, and global policy. They investigate how development agencies have promoted the development potential of research, and outline various methods and techniques of policy entrepreneurship. The book provides an authoritative overview of the concepts and theories associated with the complex link between research and development. It also illustrates the complexity with case studies of projects bridging research and policymaking from all over the world.

Carden, Fred. 2007. 'Context Matters: The Influence of IDRC-supported Research on Policy Processes', in Elias T. Ayuk and Mohamed Ali Marouani (eds), *The Policy Paradox in Africa: Strengthening Links between Economic Research and Policymaking*, pp. 93–116. Trenton, NJ and Ottawa: Africa World Press and IDRC.
This paper is based on a presentation at a conference in Dakar, Senegal, on issues in strengthening economics research in Africa. It outlines the core findings of the case work, especially as they relate to the context and opportunities for influence that are affected by the context within which research is carried out.

In addition, this volume presents reflections by those active in the policy process in various countries in Africa, as well as frameworks for thinking about policy process and policy influence. More information on the work of this group can be found at http://www.idrc.ca/sisera/.

Carden, Fred. 2009. 'Using Comparative Data: A Systems Approach to a Multiple Case Study', in David
    Byrne and Charles Ragin (eds), *The Sage Handbook of Case-Based Methods*. London: Sage Publications.
This chapter discusses the multiple case method used in this study as part of a publication that explores the use of case-centred methods. This is a useful publication for anyone interested in pursuing a case study approach to research as it explores the development of the case method in a range of fields, provides a wide range of examples, and a final section explores approaches to the taxonomy of cases for purposes of measurement and analysis.

Websites

Below are noted several websites that are useful starting points for those who want to follow current discussions in this domain. The descriptions are based on text from these sites.

As noted above, many organizations and researchers are conducting related work and publishing it on the web. In every field there are some excellent think tanks and advocacy organizations that focus some of their work on thinking about how they influence policy. This bibliography will not attempt to do justice to the wide range of these. Rather, the focus here is on the subset of work that is looking especially at the influence of research to policy in the development field—as the Neilson review cited above notes, most literature to date has focused on policy influence in the North—Europe and North America; the question here is how that influence plays in the South—Africa, Asia, Latin America.

www.idrc.ca
The IDRC (Canada) is a Canadian Crown corporation that works in close collaboration with researchers from the developing world in their search for the means to build healthier, more equitable, and more prosperous societies. In addition to the materials for this study found at www.idrc.ca/evaluation (see IDRC study materials above), a significant proportion of the Centre's work is focused on research that can influence policy. Many of the programme web pages will contain useful and relevant studies and links.

www.odi.org.uk
The Overseas Development Institute (ODI) is Britain's leading independent think tank on international development and humanitarian issues. Their mission is to inspire and inform policy and practice which lead to the reduction of poverty, the alleviation of suffering, and the achievement of sustainable livelihoods in developing countries. From their own website, 'We do this by locking together high quality applied research, practical policy advice, and policy-focused dissemination and debate. We work with partners in the public and private sectors, in both developing and developed countries. ODI's work centres on its research and policy groups and programmes.'

Most ODI programmes have an element of policy influence to them but one programme in particular is focused on how to ensure findings are used in influencing the policy process, the RAPID programme—research and policy in development.

http://www.odi.org.uk/RAPID/index.html
Better utilization of research and evidence in development policy and practice can help save lives, reduce poverty, and improve the quality of life. For example, the results of household disease surveys in rural Tanzania informed a process of health service reforms which contributed to over 40 per cent reductions in infant mortality between 2000 and 2003 in two districts. On the other hand the HIV/ AIDS crisis has deepened in some countries because of the reluctance of governments to implement effective control programmes, despite clear evidence of what causes the disease and how to prevent it spreading. Donors spend around US $3 billion on development research annually, but there has been very limited systematic understanding of when, how, and why evidence informs policy. A better understanding of how research can contribute to pro-poor policies is urgently needed. In particular we need to know more about:

1. *how **policymakers can best use research**, for evidence-based policymaking;*
2. *how **researchers can best use their findings** in order to influence policy;*
3. *how to improve the **interaction between researchers and policymakers**.*

For example, a recent publication focuses on monitoring and evaluation of policy research:

Ingie Hovland. 2007. 'Making a Difference: M&E (Monitoring and Evaluation) of Policy Research', ODI Working Paper 281, ODI, London.
The paper is written with research programmes and institutions in mind, rather than individual researchers. It presents examples and approaches on how to do M&E (monitoring and evaluation) of policy research from the current experience of a range of research institutes, think tanks and funding bodies. The approaches have been divided into the following five key performance areas: (a) Strategy and direction; (b) management; (c) outputs; (d) uptake; and (e) outcomes and impacts. Research programmes or institutes may wish to focus on only one of these areas, or may combine approaches across the areas to form a more comprehensive M&E plan.

www.gdnet.org/
The Global Development Network (GDN) is a worldwide network of research and policy institutes working to provide a fresh and relevant perspective to the development challenges of our time. GDN strongly believes that policy-relevant research, if properly applied, can accelerate the pace of global development. What makes the GDN initiative different is that it aims to generate this research at the local level in developing and transition countries. Thus, it is in the generation of local knowledge that, GDN believes, lies a much needed alternative perspective on facilitating change. The GDN maintains an active and rich website; as well an annual conference is a core part of the functioning of the network. At any given time the GDN runs several major research projects. While many of the projects contain material relevant to this topic, one of the first projects that GDN initiated was focused specifically on the research to policy linkage, 'Bridging Research to Policy'. The research and report (Livny et al. 2006) can be found on the GDN site at http://www.gdnet.org/middle.php?oid=175.

Index

About the Author

Fred Carden is currently the Director of Evaluation at the International Development Research Centre in Ottawa, Canada. He holds a PhD from the Université de Montréal and a Master's degree in Environmental Studies from York University. In 2007–08, he was a Research Fellow in Sustainability Science at Harvard University's Center for International Development. He has written in the areas of evaluation, international cooperation, and environmental management.

His current work includes the development of use-oriented evaluation tools and methods and ongoing explorations into the influence of research on public policy. Recent co-publications include 'Outcome Mapping', 'Enhancing Organizational Performance', Organizational Assessment', and 'Evaluating Capacity Development'. He has taught and carried out research at York University, the Cooperative College of Tanzania, the Bandung Institute of Technology (Indonesia), and the University of Indonesia.